YALE AGRARIAN STUDIES SERIES
James C. Scott, series editor

The Agrarian Studies Series at Yale University Press seeks to publish outstanding and original interdisciplinary work on agriculture and rural society–for any period, in any location. Works of daring that question existing paradigms and fill abstract categories with the lived experience of rural people are especially encouraged.

–James C. Scott, *Series Editor*

For a complete list of titles in the Yale Agrarian Studies Series, visit yalebooks.com/agrarian.

Nine-Tenths of the Law

Enduring Dispossession
In Indonesia

CHRISTIAN LUND

Yale
UNIVERSITY PRESS

NEW HAVEN AND LONDON

Published with assistance from the foundation established in
memory of Amasa Stone Mather of the Class of 1907, Yale College.

Yale University Press books may be purchased in quantity for educational, business,
or promotional use. For information, please e-mail sales.press@yale.edu (U.S. office)
or sales@yaleup.co.uk (U.K. office).

Set in Electra LH type by Newgen North America, Austin, Texas.
Printed in the United States of America.

ISBN 978-0-300-25107-4 (alk. paper)
Library of Congress Control Number: 2020936439
A catalogue record for this book is available from the British Library.

This paper meets the requirements of ANSI/NISO Z39.48-1992
(Permanence of Paper).

10 9 8 7 6 5 4 3 2 1

CONTENTS

CONTENTS

In 2013, my friend Oji and I were talking to a group of villagers not far from Garut, in West Java. The land around had been the object of dispute and struggle for generations. It had been taken over from Javanese nobility and peasants by Dutch planters in the course of the nineteenth century. Later, when the Dutch fled during the Japanese occupation in 1942, the victors encouraged local peasants to take over the land. These smallholders continued to farm the land after Indonesian independence in 1945, and in the 1960s they were promised legal rights to it as part of government land reform. This legalization was offset by competing claims among smallholders and army groups, however. In 1965, land was confiscated by the military and handed over to a plantation company. The military had come to power through a coup, and the New Order was born in a veritable bloodbath. Hundreds of thousands of people, suspected of being communist, were incarcerated or killed throughout the country by the army and an assortment of paramilitary and civilian youth gangs, so-called *pemuda*. Many more were simply dispossessed of their land. Like many other places, the village we visited was seen by the military as a communist hotbed and was turned into a forced labor camp for the evicted villagers, who had to work without pay on the plantation. The village's status as labor camp was rescinded in 1979, but the villagers retained the stigma of former political prisoners from whom land rights were withheld. At the end of the New Order and the beginning of the democratic reform era—*reformasi*—in 1998, the villagers occupied parts of their old land anew, and after long negotiations between the Sundanese Peasant Movement (which they had joined) and the National Land Agency they received documents legalizing their possessions.

At every political rupture in Indonesia's modern history, political authorities have changed, and established property rights have been suspended as new ones have been claimed. These open moments of rupture have all been violent, and some have been extremely and systematically brutal, as acquired land rights have been erased. Yet alongside profound institutional uncertainty and well-founded anxiety, an equal desire has emerged to secure the possession as property beyond the vagaries of changing regimes. While the farmers and their ancestors in the village near Garut have occupied the land many times during the past century, occupations have always been accompanied by a desire for recognition and legalization.

Historically, Indonesia has been an agrarian society. Plantations and differentiated smallholdings—with landlords and a variety of smallholders and tenants—characterized the society at independence in 1945. Two decades into the new millennium, however, agriculture no longer dominates the economy. Services and industry overtook agriculture as economic sectors in the 1970s, and by 2010 the majority of Indonesians lived in urban areas. Moreover, the number of households engaged in agriculture has been declining with increasing speed. In 2010, around 61 million households eked out a living from farming, but by 2013 the number had dropped to some 26 million. This decline was, no doubt, partly due to new ways of enumerating "farming," but the exclusion of the smallest farming plots, of less than 0.1 hectare, from the national statistics was in itself a telling adjustment. Farming has become the mainstay for fewer and fewer people in Indonesia. All the same, the total agricultural area has increased, reflecting the steady increase in plantation agriculture. The overall movement is one in which smallholders are pushed or pulled off the land they farm and onto land in towns and cities. This produces conflicts at both ends of the process, and these conflicts are the subject of this book. Many rural people resist effective eviction from their farm land, while urbanized people struggle to secure a home in the city.

This "great transformation" may appear inevitable, reducing individual lives to specks of dust in the long run and the grand scheme of things. Yet the transformation affects millions of people, like the villagers near Garut whose immediate livelihoods and life-worlds depend on their access to space. Having a home, raising a family, working the land, aspiring and prospering, all happen in space. Moreover, the long run of this great transformation is made up of a lot of "meantime," and the political and legal dynamics of the meantime shape the outcomes for people in the long run. The meantime has human scale and deserves our attention as the horizon within which people's hopes and ingenuity meet with success or failure, all shaping and shading the long run. Speck by speck.

My interests have long focused on law and how land claims and citizen rights conjoin. Initially, I worked in Niger and later in Ghana, and even for societies so relatively close to one another the differences and variations were remarkable. However, if research results are always contextual and moored to time and place in social science, our questions travel more freely. I ask, who has what right, and how is it decided? In particular, I have been drawn to these questions in contexts where rights are not clear at all, where a multitude of rules is on offer, and where a similar number of institutions claim jurisdiction to adjudicate among them. These are simple empirical questions with complex answers, yet relevant in virtually any context. The answers will vary in time and space, but the questions can perform an incision into the mores and values of society, into the development of social classes and groups and their interests, and into dynamics of state formation. Questions of property and citizenship pry open central dynamics of any society.

Property and citizenship constitute a very dynamic field, and treating rights and authorities as a finished product gets in the way of understanding them. They are always in the making. Moreover, rights and public authority are mutually constitutive and contingent. When an institution authorizes, sanctions, or validates certain rights, the respect or observance of these rights simultaneously constitutes recognition of the authority of that particular institution. Authorization of rights claims works to authorize the authorizers, so to speak. The process perspective has implications for my empirical focus and consequently for the methodological choices.

Struggles over land form the focus of this book. People who want a place to farm, to build a house, and to make a living face competition from plantation companies, government authorities, national parks, forest authorities, urban developers, and others who equally have designs on the space. The book maps out the significant claimants in the cases of conflict and their fields of engagements with each other and with the ideas of land rights and law. Although violence is a big part of the conflicts, all actors also argue and legitimate their claims. Custom, established practice, need, and law are all mobilized to impress and convince the relevant public of the justice of the claims. It is striking, however, to what extent all actors try to make their claims look legal. I therefore examine a variety of legalization strategies of the different parties. Struggles have outcomes, and while it is a challenge to read long-term implications, we can at least see what appears to develop; how do claims form, who prevails, and whose prospects are blighted as an outcome of the conflict. My interests are not so much in the technicalities of legislation or the inner consistencies of law. Instead, I focus on law as a reference point and medium for social conflict, and on how law, as rules effectively sanctioned by public authorities, is mobilized or contested, and consolidated or modified. The focus throughout the book is therefore systematically on actors, their actions and arguments, and the institutional results. In this way, this book is an anthropology of postcolonial law.

The research was done in three different regions of Indonesia: West Java, North Sumatra, and Aceh, each home to the capitalist frontier in Indonesia of the seventeenth, nineteenth, and twenty-first centuries, respectively. West Java and North Sumatra have long experienced frontier convulsions as property regimes and social orders altered at the bidding of world commodity markets. More recently, Aceh has entered the vortex of the oil palm boom with wide-reaching consequences. Despite their obvious differences, the three areas share violent agrarian struggles and ingenious forms of legalization. Together, the three areas also demonstrate that capitalist frontiers are not appointed moments that pass, but extended moments—if moments at all. The regional history also demonstrates that anyone engaging in land politics is in it for the long haul.

ACKNOWLEDGMENTS

Of the many people to whom I owe thanks, first and foremost are Noer Fauzi Rachman (Oji) and Ari Nurman. I met Oji at Berkeley in 2009, and during many conversations he kindled my interest in Indonesia and its agrarian history of land occupations and evictions. Traveling with Oji through West Java, North Sumatra, and Aceh was the best induction I could have wished for. Through him, I met with activists and politicians, entrepreneurs and scholars, and, most of all, ordinary men and women who had thrown caution to the wind in occupying and reclaiming land from government and private companies. For obvious and sad reasons, my many field informants (except for people holding high public office or enjoying general notoriety or celebrity) must remain anonymous, but our conversations, interviews, meetings, and walks through plantations and smallholder plots braid together in a dense stream of impressions, information, and knowledge. It is true that the orderliness of one's method is easier to establish in hindsight and that what seems a detour to begin with often turns out to be significant later. I guess that is why we take notes even when something seems trite or irrelevant in the moment. Chapters 3 and 4 are reworked versions of two articles Oji and I wrote together. In addition to initial travels with Oji, I also conducted a series of larger and longer fieldwork projects. Ari Nurman accompanied me several times in the field in West Java, North Sumatra, and Aceh. These were always very pleasant journeys of discovery, even if we had a couple of close shaves in Langsa. Ari's own research in

Bandung gave us the opportunity to write together, and Chapter 6 is a re-worked version of our article.

In West Java, the research was conducted with the help of the Sajogyo Institute and RMI (*Rimbawan Muda Indonesia*, Indonesian Institute for Forest and Environment), and I owe great thanks to Dina Septi, Swanvri, Wahuiddin Noer, Didi Novrian, Dian Yanuardi, Ai Sumauri, Husni Tamrin Sidik, Yufik, Eko Cahyono, Mia Siscawati, Devi Anggraini, Mardha Tillah, and Nia Ramdhaniaty. In North Sumatra our research relied on HaRI (*Hutan Rakyat Institute*, South East Asia Institute for Forest and People Studies, Medan) and especially Wina Khairina, Saurlin Siagian, Erwin Sipahutar, Fachrizal Sinaga, Kartika Manurung, and Rianda Purba deserve credit for our results. In Aceh, the research owed much to LBH (*Lembaga Bantuan Hukum*, Legal Aid Institute, Banda Aceh), and especially Mustiqal Syahputra, Mirna Asnur, Aulianda Wafisa, Chandra Darusman, Muhajir Pemuling, Muhajir Abdulaziz, Rusli, and Zulfikar helped in the process. Despite the seriousness of our work, hospitality, generosity, and the lifted spirits that accompany doing something together remain my most indelible memories.

During the writing I have also incurred irrecoverable debts to people who have commented, questioned, and guided my thoughts. I wish to thank: Abdil Mughis Mudhoffir, Adriaan Bedner, Alice Kelly, Amanda Hammar, Anders Meinhard Hallund, Andrea Nightingale, Anja Nygren, Ann Cassiman, Annie Shattuck, Arthur Gill Green, Arun Agrawal, Ben Jones, Benedikt Korf, Bernardo Ribeiro de Almeida, Bert Suykens, Bruno Braak, Budi Agostono, Catherine Boone, Christian Cunningham Lentz, Christine Giulia Schenk, Dennis Rodgers, Derek Hall, Didier Péclard, Duncan McDuie-Ra, Edward Aspinall (who deserves special thanks for let-ting me use the phrase "Predatory Peace," from a piece he wrote in 2014, as the title of Chapter 5), Edy Ikhsan, Eric Hahonou, Erin Collins, Ewan Scott Robinson, Francesca Chiu, Freek Colombijn, Gamma Galudra, Gerry van Klinken, Giorgio Blundo, Gustaaf Reerink, Haslinda Qodariah, Henk Schulte Nordholt, Hilary Faxon, Ian Wilson, Ibang Lukmanurdin, Inge-Merete Hougaard, Iswan Kaputra, Iqra Anugrah, Jacob Rasmussen, Jacobo Grajales, Jakob Trane Ibsen, James Scott, Jan-Michiel Otto, Jason

Cons, Jens Friis Lund, Jeremy Campbell, Jesper Linell, Jesper Willaing Zeuthen, Jesse Ribot, John McCarthy, Jonathan Padwe, Jun Borras, Karen Lauterbach, Kasper Hoffmann, Keebet and Franz von Benda-Beckmann, Kevin Woods, Koen Vlassenroot, Kregg Hetherington, Laure d'Hondt, Laurens Bakker, Lee Wilson, Louise Fortmann, Mariève Pouilot, Markus Ritriyono, Maron Greenleaf, Mathieu Hilgers, Matthew Hull, Mattias Borg Rasmussen, Melanie Pichler, Michael Dwyer, Michael Eilenberg, Michael Watts, Mohamad Shohibuddin, Muriel Côte, Nancy Peluso, Nandini Sundar, Nia Ramdhaniaty, Nissa Wargadipura, Ole Mertz, Paul Stacey, Pauline Peters, Penelope Anthias, Péter Bori, Peter Vandergeest, Pierre Petit, Prathiwi Putri, Prof. Bas, Purabi Bose, Ramadhan Harahap, Ravinder Kaur, Rebakah Daro Minarchek, Reece Jones, Rony Emmenegger, Rune Bolding Bennike, Ruth Pinto, Santy Kouwagam, Seema Arora-Jonsson, Shrey Kapoor, Siddharth Sareen, Signe Marie Cold Ravnkilde, Soeryo Adiwibowo, Steffen Jensen, Stine Krøijer, Tania Li, Tanya Jakimow, Teo Ballvé, Thomas Sikor, Tim Raeymaekers, Tine Milton, Tirza van Bruggen, Titik Firawati, Tobias Hagmann, Tobias Udsholt, Tomas Martin, Tristam Moeliono, Veronica Gomez-Témesio, Ward Berenschot, Wendy Wolford, Willem van der Muur, Yance Arizona, and Youjin Chung. Special thanks go to Jean Thomson Black and Mike Kirkwood for helping me bring the manuscript to completion.

I have been fortunate to give presentations of my ongoing work along the way at Sajogyo Institute, Bogor Agricultural University, Universitas Gadjah Mada in Yogyakarta and University of North Sumatra, in Indonesia. I have also presented it at the Australian National University and the Universities of Amsterdam, Bergen, Cambridge, Columbia, Copenhagen, Cornell, East Anglia, Edinburgh, Ghent, Helsinki, Leiden, Lund, Oxford, Sorbonne, Zürich, the Swedish Agricultural University, and the Université Libre de Bruxelles.

I wish to thank four journals for letting me rework and reuse material from the following articles: "On Track: Spontaneous Privatization of Public Urban Land in Bandung, Indonesia" (co-authored with A. Nurman), *South East Asia Research* 24 (1), 2016; "Occupied! Property, Citizenship, and Land in Rural Java" (co-authored with N. F. Rachman), *Development and Change*

47 (6), 2016; "Predatory Peace: Dispossession at Aceh's Oil Palm Frontier," *Journal of Peasant Studies* 45 (2), 2018; and "Indirect Recognition: Frontiers and Territorialization Around Mount Halimun-Salak National Park, Indonesia" (co-authored with N. F. Rachman), *World Development* 101, 2018.

Finally, I have benefited from generous funding from the Danish Research Council and the European Research Council (ERC), with ERC Grant: State Formation Through the Local Production of Property and Citizenship (Ares [2015] 2785650-ERC-2014-AdG-662770-Local State). In addition, I have received precious support from the Indonesian Research Authorities (RISTEK), the Indonesian Embassy in Copenhagen, and my institutional home, the Department of Food and Resource Economics at the University of Copenhagen.

Outsiders, like myself, rarely recover fully from their initial bedazzlement by Indonesia. Nonetheless, I have tried to ensure that the reader with little or no knowledge of the country will be able to follow the arguments in the book. Most of what I write about here resonates with issues elsewhere as well. Property and law, land conflicts and violence, are not the preserve of Indonesia, although they come together here in a cocktail. My hope, equally, is that Indonesians and Indonesianists will be able to see something new and original in a context they know so well. Evidently, while I share whatever credit the book deserves with everyone above, mistakes and infelicities are mine alone.

AMAN	Aliansi Masyarakat Adat Nusantara, Alliance of Indigenous People of the Archipelago
AMANAT	Alliansi Masyarakat Nanggung Transformatif, The Transformative Alliance of the People of Nanggung
AMKA	Angkatan Muda Kereta Api, Train Youth Movement, a youth gang
AMPI	Angkatan Muda Pembaharuan Indonesia, The Force for the Renewal of Indonesia's Youth, a youth gang
AMS	Angkatan Muda Siliwangi, Siliwangi Youth, a youth gang
BAL	Basic Agrarian Law
Bitra	Bina Keterampilan Pedesaan Indonesia, The Activator for Rural Progress
BKM	Badan Keswadayaan Masyarakat, Community self-support unit
BPMP	Badan Perjuangan Masyarakat Pergulaan, Movement for the Struggle of the People of Pergulaan (Serikat Petani Serdang Bedagai)
BPRPI	Badan Perjuangan Rakyat Penungu Indonesia, Movement for the Rakyat Penungu People's Struggle, Indonesia
BKSP-M	Badan Kerja Sama Pemuda-Militer, Pemuda-Military Cooperation Board
BNI	Barisan Tani Indonesia, Peasant Front of Indonesia

BPN   Badan Pertanahan Nasional, National Land Agency
Brimob   Korps Brigade Mobil, The Mobile Brigade Corps, a special
             operations and paramilitary unit within the Indonesian
             National Police
BUDP   Bandung Urban Development Project
CCTV   Closed-circuit television
DKA   Djawatan Kereta Api, State Railway Company
DKARI   Djawatan Kereta Api-Repoeblik Indonesia, State Railway
             Company of the Republic of Indonesia
FKPPI   Forum Komunikasi Putra-Putri Indonesia, Indonesian Com-
             munication Forum for Sons and Daughters of Military
             Retirees, a youth gang mainly for the children of police
             and army officers
FOKRAT   Forum Keadilan Masyarakat Tani, Forum for Peasant
             Justice
FORKAB   Forum Komunikasi Anak Bangsa, Communication Forum for
             the Children of the Nation
FORMAS   Forum Masyarakat Sari Rejo, Peoples Forum for the residents
             of Sari Rejo
GAM   Gerakan Aceh Merdeka, Free Aceh Movement
GMKI   Gerakan Mahasiswa Kristen Indonesia, Protestant Students
             of Indonesia
GMNI   Gerakan Mahasiswa Nasional Indonesia, National Student
             Movement of Indonesia
Golkar   Golonkan Karya (literally, functional groups), the leading
             political party during the New Order
HGU   Hak Guna Usaha, Commercial Lease Rights
HMI   Himpunan Mahasiswa Islam, Islamic Students Association
HPH   Hak Pengusahaan Hutan, Forest Exploitation Rights
HSBC   Hong Kong and Shanghai Banking Corporation
IPB   Institut Pertanian Bogor, Agricultural University of Bogor
IPK   Ikatan Pemuda Karya, Association of Workers' Youth, a youth
             gang
JICA   Japanese International Cooperation Agency

KDTK   Kampung Dengan Tujuan Konservasi, kampung with conservation purpose

Komnas HAM   Komisi Nasional untuk Perlindungan Hak Asasi Manusia, National Human Rights Commission

KPA   Konsorsium Pembaruan Agraria, Consortium for Agrarian Reform

KRPT   Kartu Registrasi Pemakaian Tanah, Land Use Registration Card; sometimes also referred to as KTPPT

KTP   Kartu Tanda Penduduk, Indonesian ID card

KTPPT   Kartu Tanda Pendataran Pemakai Tanah, Land User Registration Certificate; sometimes also referred to as Kartu Tanda Pendaftaran Pendudukan Tanah, Land Occupation Registration Card) or KRPT (Kartu Registrasi Pemakaian Tanah, Land Use Registration Card)

KTPPTP   Kartu Tanda Pendataran Pemakai Tanah Perkebunan, extraordinary permits to farm in plantation areas

LBH   Lembaga Bantuan Hukum, Legal Aid Foundation

NGO   Non-governmental organization

NU   Nahdlatul Ulama, Indonesia's largest traditionalist Islamic organization

Ormas   Organisasi Kemasyarakatan, mass organizations

OKP   Organisasi Kemasyarakatan Pemuda, mass youth organizations

Pam Swakarsa   Swakarsa Public Security Force, a youth gang

PBB   Pajak Bumi dan Bangunan, tax for land and buildings

PETA   Pembela Tanah Air, Defenders of the Homeland

PKI   Partai Komunis Indonesia, Communist Party of Indonesia

PMKRI   Perhimpunan Mahasiswa Katolik Republik Indonesia, Catholic Students of Indonesia

PNI   Partai Nasionalis Indonesia, Nationalist Party of Indonesia

PNPM-MP   Program Nasional Pemberdayaan Masyarakat-Mandiri Perkotaan, national program for urban community empowerment

PNPM Perkotaan   Program Nasional Pemberdayaan Masyarakat-Perkotaan, National program for community empowerment-urban

PPK   Program Pengembangan Kecamatan, District development program

PRONA   Proyek Operasi Nasional Agraria, Government Land Title Legalization and Certification Program

PT LonSum   PT London-Sumatra, a multinational rubber plantation company

PTPN   Perseroan Terbatas Perkebunan Nusantara, The Archipelago Plantations Ltd.

RMI   Rimbawan Muda Indonesia, Indonesian Institute for Forest and Environment

RT   Rukun Tetangga, smaller neighborhood association

RW   Rukun Warga, greater neighborhood association

SABAKI   Kesatuan Adat Banten Kidul, Indigenous Unity for Banten Kidul

SKT   Surat Keterangan Tanah, Land Certificate, issued by the village head

SMP   Sekolah Menengah Pertama, middle school

SPI   Serikat Petani Indonesia, Indonesian Peasant Union

SPP   Serikat Petani Pasundan, Sundanese Peasant Union

SPPT-PBB   Surat Pemberitahuan Pajak Terutang-Pajak Bumi dan Bangunan, payable tax notification for land and buildings

SPSB   Serikat Petani Serdang Bedagai, Serdang Bedagai Peasant Union

SPSU   Serikat Petani Sumatera Utara, North Sumatran Peasant Union

STTS-PBB   Surat Tanda Terima Setoran-Pajak Bumi dan Bangunan, building and land tax payment receipt

SS   Staatspoorweg, Public Railway Company

VS   Verenigde Spoorweg Bedrijf, United Railway Service

WALHI   Wahana Lingkungan Hidup Indonesia, Indonesian Forum for the Environment

1619	Dutch East India Company (Verenigde Oost-Indische Compagnie, VOC) first established itself on Java
1799	VOC bankrupted; the company's debts and assets were taken over by the Dutch state and Indonesia became its colony
1824	Anglo-Dutch Treaty gave the Dutch a free hand to colonize Sumatra, except for Aceh
1860	*Max Havelaar* published
1865	Forest Law, established the basis for state-controlled scientific forestry, declaring three-fourths of the colony's territory as forest (one-fourth of the territory of Java), and making forests the domain of the state
1870	Agrarian Law, covering what land had not been categorized as forest by the Forestry Law, declaring that all lands to which there was no civil law ownership title were to be considered the domain of the state
1903	Aceh declared conquered
1909–12	Sarekat Islam (Islamic Union) established, the first mass-based organization to protest against Chinese traders, the Javanese elite, and Dutch colonialists
1910–25	A large number of political, professional, regional, and religious associations established

1912	Indisches Partij established, pioneering Indonesian nationalism (as opposed to religious, regional, or Marxist platforms)
1913	Indisches Partij banned and leaders exiled
1914	Indische Sociaal Democratische Vereeniging established
1920–25	Indische Sociaal Democratische Vereeniging turns increasingly Communist
1924	Partai Komunis Indonesia (Indonesian Communist Party) established from Indische Sociaal Democratische Vereeniging
1924	The Dutch administration and the Javanese elite encouraged the establishment of Sarekat Hijau (Green Union), gangs of thugs, policemen, and religious leaders attacking and intimidating Sarekat Islam and Partai Komunis Indonesia members, in Java
1926	Nahdlatul Ulama (The Rise of Religious Scholars) established as political party
1926–27	Communist uprising crushed, and Partai Komunis Indonesia banned
1927	Partai Nasional Indonesia (PNI) established by Sukarno among others
1930	Sukarno's nationalist speech "Indonesia Accuses" given in defense at his political trial; sentenced to four years in prison, he served one
1940	Germany invades the Netherlands
1942	Japan invades the Netherlands East Indies, and oversees the creation of Indonesian political organization (led by Sukarno and Hatta), and the creation of youth militias with two million members; these formed the core of the Indonesian armed forces at independence together with Indonesians from the Dutch colonial army
1945	Investigating Committee for Preparatory Work for Indonesian Independence established by Japanese with Indonesian nationalists (including Sukarno). 15 August, Japan

surrenders; 17 August, Sukarno and Hatta proclaim Indonesia's independence. Adoption of the Constitution of
Indonesia (Undang-Undang Dasar Republik Indonesia
1945, UUD '45). Beginning of the Indonesian Revolution. Partai Komunis Indonesia reemerges. Spontaneous
occupations of plantations.

1949 Constitution abrogated by the Federal Constitution of
1949, and the Provisional Constitution of 1950; Indonesian independence and sovereignty recognized by the
Netherlands

1949–65 Political struggle between Partai Nasional Indonesia and
Partai Komunis Indonesia

1954 Emergency Law no. 8 of 1954

1955 First national election

1957 State of war declared, beginning of Guided Democracy

1958 Nationalization of Dutch property, Government Decree
No. 23, of April 16, 1958; Law of the Republic of Indo-
nesia Number 1, 1958, on Liquidation of Private Lands
(Undang Undang Republik Indonesia Nomor 1, 1958,
Tentang Penghapusan Tanah Tanah Partikelir), and
Law of the Republic of Indonesia Number 89, 1958, on
Nationalization of Dutch Owned Companies (Undang-
Undang Republik Indonesia Nomor 89, 1958, Tentang
Nasionalisasi Perusahaan-Perusahaan Milik Belanda)

1959 Constitution of 1945 restored

1960 Basic Agrarian Law (Law no. 5, 1960)

1963 Aksi sepihak (unilateral action), Partai Komunis Indonesia
organized land occupations

1965 Miltary coup: the New Order, led by Suharto, assumes
power

1965–66 Anti-Communist pogrom largely organized and carried out
through the different youth gangs encouraged, armed,
and protected by the army; between one and two million
dead

1967	Forestry Law, Mining Law, Foreign Investment Law
1974 + 1979	Regional and Village Government Laws
1997	Financial crisis, krismon
1998	Reformasi, end of New Order; Habibie becomes president
1999	Abdurrahman Wahid becomes president; Decentralisation law
2001	Megawati Sukarnoputri becomes president
2003	Martial Law in Aceh
2004	Susilo Bambang Yudhoyono becomes president; Plantations Act no. 18 of 2004, criminalizing squatters in plantations; tsunami hits Aceh on December 26 (170,000 dead, 500,000 homeless)
2005	Peace Accord in Aceh
2009	Susilo Bambang Yudhoyono elected for a second term
2014	Joko Widodo becomes president

Sources: Anderson (1972), Aspinall (2005), Benda-Beckmann and Benda-Beckmann (2014), Breman (1983), E. Damanik (2016), Kurniawan (2018), McVey (1965), Pelzer (1978, 1982), Reid (1979), Ricklefs (1993), Stoler (1985a), Vickers (2005)

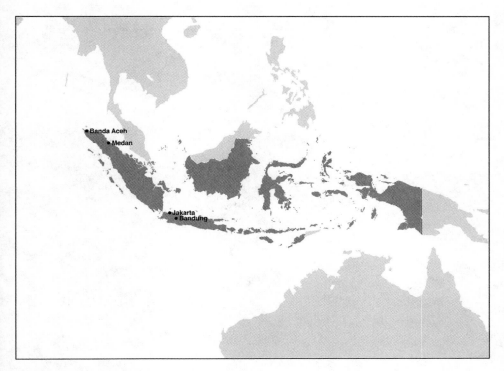

A map of Indonesia showing field sites on Sumatra and Java (Map by Liv Løvetand)

NINE-TENTHS OF THE LAW

CHAPTER ONE

Possession Is Nine-Tenths of the Law

In the early hours of November 17, 2016, six large diggers lined up outside the village of Mekar Jaya in Langkat, North Sumatra. It was the day of eviction. The plantation company had organized the diggers, and around 1,500 police officers and army personnel set about removing people from their gardens and fields. The inhabitants put up a fight. After two weeks of violent eviction and resistance, 554 hectares were cleared to make way for a plantation of oil palms. The farmers of the community had been granted the land in 1974 through a land reform, and they held individual documents signed by the then governor. In 1979, they were, nonetheless, evicted, but in 1998, in the euphoric moment of *reformasi*, they had taken their land back. Now they were kicked off again. This time, the plantation company claimed to have obtained a long-term lease. Although the company refused to produce any official document at the moment of eviction, government recognition was represented by the massive presence of soldiers and police. The company proceeded to expand its operations with the help of government force and claimed that its invasion was entirely legal. In March 2017, the diggers and police returned. This time, in a single day, they flattened the entire village, and buried the debris in a huge hole in the ground. The 221 families were left landless and homeless.

Possession and Recognition

For many people in Indonesia, rights remain a faint promise, and justice a mere rumor. Land conflicts and dispossession have placed unjust burdens on ordinary people for generations and under different regimes. Some people acquire land, but more seem to lose it when their lack of wealth, knowledge, language, connections, and organization leaves them vulnerable. What is outrageous about the event in Mekar Jaya is its utter banality. Such evictions are commonplace. They are frequent, they happen now, and people have endured them for generations. Villagers, peasant movements, indigenous people's organizations, and urban neighborhood groups are challenged by a combination of violence, political power, and paperwork. They struggle against companies and different branches of government—ministries, districts, and municipalities—aided by police and army forces, together with the private youth gangs that opportunistically affiliate with the powerful. In this unequal slew of dispossession and resistance, the many stakeholders in Indonesia struggle over what effectively becomes property. They are all law makers. This book investigates how.

The old aphorism that "possession is nine-tenths of the law" suggests that property rights ("the law") are not merely about legal rights, but, more importantly, about social relations and the political and physical capacity to hold things of value: land, in particular. Possession, control of benefit streams, and the ability to exclude others from what is yours generally require instruments that can often seem more important than rights on paper. Work on access (Ribot and Peluso 2003) and powers of exclusion (Hall, Hirsch, and Li 2011) advocate approaches to the understanding of resource benefits and control that are not centered around law. By focusing on the benefit stream, and the various ways access to it is obtained, Ribot and Peluso point out that formal legal rights are no guarantee of access to benefits. Access may well be sustained without legal rights. Indeed, access may be upheld in direct contravention of the rights of others. It requires force, mobilization in numbers, money, connections, and savvy to conjoin them. Similarly, the powers used to exclude others from resource access encompass much more than simple legislation. Hall, Hirsch, and Li demonstrate how economic clout, social

Eviction day at Mekar Jaya, North Sumatra (Photo: Serikat Petani Indonesia)

norms, and outright force, in addition to government regulation, make up the landscape of access and exclusion.

These are useful analytical reminders that law isn't everything. There can be little doubt that physical presence, force, and the threat of both, have been integral parts of how access to land has developed in Indonesia, and most other places on the planet. Moreover, it is tempting to downplay the role of law in struggles over resources, because it so often does not do what it claims to be doing. Law has often been the handmaiden of power and instrumental in plunder. Colonial dispossession of land has often been accompanied by a dispossession of political power and legal rights. Rule of

3

law has often been a claim to legitimize the unjust; law has codified and racialized hierarchies of profit; and we should definitely not equate "legal" with "just."[1] Finally, engaging with the law is a costly, tiring, and dispiriting affair that can lead to violence by the state.

However, broad perspectives on access and exclusion do not explain the importance people and companies attach to law, and the energies and efforts they invest in the legalization of their claims. If legality is not important, why does anyone even bother to use law? Why did the company in Langkat *claim* to have a legal lease on the land? And why did the farmers, however ineffectually, show their documents from 1974? My suggestion is that it is because the distinction between legal and illegal is important to people and governments alike. Moreover, it is a distinction that is constantly under construction and consequently subject to socio-political struggle.

Law is both a solvent and a solidifier. Legalization seeks to secure state power backing for a claim in order to solidify it as a right that forces competing claims to dissolve. When a claim becomes a right, in theory, the cost and responsibility of its protection and enforcement shifts from the landholder to the state and its institutions. This is attractive to companies and peasants alike. However, legalization holds a second attraction. Law *promises* some enduring predictability. This is especially attractive in situations of regime change when incoming authorities threaten to upset and undo established structures and maybe even usher in volatile and arbitrary politics. Consequently, the prospect of locking makeshift settlements into relatively tough and durable structures of recognition through legalization and reference to law incentivizes most landholders to legitimate and legalize possessions as property. Whether people try to cash in on tenuous opportunities when they arise, or seek to confirm established rights anew, legalization is key. It promises to take claims safely through times of changing political fortunes as *rights*.

Consequently, despite law's frequent betrayal of its promise of justice, it is often considered a hard currency in a fundamental consensus that legalized claims are law's bequests to all, and, just as importantly, that such rights may endure. Although different kinds of citizens have different modes of access to the law, and laws can change, the institutional paraphernalia of ritual and

4

documents undergird the idea of law's universality and permanency. More-over, while the powerful may control political structures and the means of force, and while they may write the laws and captain legal institutions, they often compete among themselves and rarely coalesce into a monolith exercising a fully accomplished hegemony. Hence, law and politics are not simply the weapons of the powerful, or government, however consolidated their cohorts are.[2] Most acts of politics and justice are accompanied by pub-lic justifications. They may be contrived, hypocritical, and false, and often are. Yet, policy or legal rulings are, by their public nature, sometimes also available to the people they dispossess, and they can become a means of claiming new possessions or reclaiming lost ones. Legal struggles are sel-dom equal, fair, or easy. But, as a language and an instrument, law is tacti-cally polyvalent, and offers not only the occasional victory against the odds, but the hope for more (Foucault 1978: 100–104, Thompson 1975: 258–69). Often, even in the face of systematic disappointments and the rarity of tri-umphs, the common human belief in legality is important.

Possession may be nine-tenths of the law, but the last tenth, recognition, still matters a great deal. Furthermore, recognition often takes the form of legalization, through efforts to make claims and decisions *appear* legal. And, crucially, this very plausibility of legality can have the effect of law. This book is therefore about how and why people and institutions work to make claims stick by legalizing them. It is about the relationship between legal recognition and possession. It is about how the last tenth of the law relates to the other nine.

Legalization of Land Claims

Law and property are central in this work. However, they are not simply "master concepts" for the analysis; they are the *objects* of our investigation. Thus, rather than being fixed and firm, these concepts are arenas of struggle over meaning and institutional significance. The process of becoming law and property is therefore critical. Let us start with law.

A rule's quality as law is not intrinsic to the rule itself, but something attributed to it in social and political interaction.[3] I therefore take law to be the rules and regulations whose creation, protection, or enforcement is attributed to the most powerful and credible political institutions in society. Obviously, this is, itself, conflictual, yet often people attribute this role of lawmaker to government and statutory institutions. Hence, statutory legislation by statutory institutions forms an important part of law, but law is more than that. Many other actors and institutions are, in fact, active in bringing about what become the *actual* rules and sanctions in society. In this wider perspective, statutory and other institutions engage with each other and operate with statutory and other norms to form what becomes law; the rules effectively sanctioned and justified by various authorities or communities *in the name of law* (Moore 1978). In fact, actors at all levels exert great efforts to persuade the relevant public of the justice and legality of their particular claims. It is in this sense that all are law makers. Such effective law and its embedded claims rarely correspond perfectly to actual statutory law. But *legitimation* of them through explicit reference to statutory law plays a particular role in the broad repertoire of legitimation of claims. When people attribute the qualities of "law" and "legal" to decisions, they are understood as legal and have that effect. Hence, successfully legitimizing claims by evoking law can amount to their legalization whether they actually conform to statutory texts or not.

I use the term "legalization" broadly to encompass processes whereby particular rules, claims, or administrative operations are legitimated through reference to law, regardless of whether a genuine correspondence between them and statutory law actually exists. The affinity between statutory law and legalization is often assumed and asserted, as both villagers and company representatives did in Mekar Jaya, but not necessarily juridically accurate. In this, I part from a narrower doctrinal view that insists on key characteristics of rules and procedures, or legalization's perfect match with statutory law (see Abbott et al. 2000, Ubink 2009). The point of legalization is to bestow upon a rule or claim an *air of legality*. Legalization of property is, therefore, the successful persuasion that a claim to land and other resources is legal. One may legalize illegal acts and claims and quash established rights, as long as the operation is sustained and justified with *reference* to the law.[4] Consequently, legalization is not merely a question of law categorizing acts; it is as much about acting on the perception of what is legal, fickle as that might be.

Legalization may be driven by a desire for justice, but more importantly, it establishes a link between the claim and the state as an idea and a set of institutions. Claims with reference to statutory law refer to the powers of the state, and legalized claims enjoy the backing of its apparatus.[5] Crucially, therefore, legalization evokes the hope and possibility—faint for some and more realistic for others—of backing by state power.

Legalization, in this broad sense, is done by parliaments, governments, administrative institutions, courts, and all their statutory extensions, but, as we shall see, the field is crowded by a much bigger cast of potential law makers. It is rare that any institution has a monopoly on rule making and enforcement. This is a bargaining process where the context—the issue at stake, the other actors, their political and other powers, and the relevant repertoires of legitimation—conditions the outcome. In a context of legal and institutional pluralism, where multiple legal and political systems co-exist and intersect, many groups and actors claim rights to the same land, and many institutions claim the authority to govern it. The field of land struggle in Indonesia is made up of some thousand-and-one institutions and actors with varying degrees of relative autonomy. In fact, this field is itself honeycombed with many localized subfields of land struggle. Indeed, the same fields also leave open conduits for critique and resistance, slender as they may seem.

Comprehending the socio-legal struggle over land as fields has a distinct advantage. A field is constituted not by its boundaries or organizations, but around a problem or an issue, such as land control. The field is therefore defined by the generation of rules and forms of compliance around the issue in question. This means that a field offers the analytical opportunity to refrain from privileging any particular institutional architecture or pre-determining its actors, their numbers, interests, or ideas. They all change over time and develop as a consequence of competition (Bourdieu 1985, 1994, Chauveau 2017, Moore 1978). Companies and developers, army and police, and other government institutions encounter people organized in movements and gangs, in NGOs and political parties. All these actors act opportunistically in a context of constraints. They produce, reproduce, and change different structures while they, themselves, also evolve. They are in the business of creating categorical distinctions between who is entitled and who is a thief, and what shall be "property and what shall be crime" (Thompson 1975: 259, Tilly 1998).

In the competition to create and undo orders, people deploy a broad range of resources. Capital and wealth as well as political organization, social contacts, language, specialized knowledge, and force are mobilized alongside ideology and law. The relative importance of different resources varies over time, and the ability to combine them effectively is vital. The combination and concentration of these resources allows certain actors to effectively legalize their property claims, while others fail or resort to forms of resistance where they produce more random representations and assertions of rights. Consequently, struggles over legality are not conducted by legal means alone, and possession, acquired in many different, frequently violent ways, is often laundered and legitimated as rightful property through the medium of law and legalization.

Similar to law, property is also not a master concept but an object of inquiry. Property is more than "private property." Rather, it is a legitimized claim to something of value sanctioned by some form of public authority (Sikor and Lund 2009). Struggles over property can therefore be seen as struggles for the *recognition* of a wide variety of rights to access resources in various ways. The ability to lodge a property claim often differs according to political identity. That is, attributes such as gender, race, and caste, as well as class, creed, and conviction, have different valences allowing for more or less punch in the property claim. Furthermore, membership of an organized political body—like the Indonesian nation, an indigenous community, or a peasant movement—may entail property rights (or the right to claim them), and claims to membership can therefore work as indirect property claims. Thus, when we talk of property claims they very often articulate with and through claims to citizenship in a broad sense (Bhandar 2018, Lund 2016). Both claims solicit and depend on recognition and relate to public authority in a particular way. Property and citizenship, on the one hand, and public authority, on the other, are mutually constitutive and contingent. When an institution authorizes, sanctions, or validates certain rights, the respect or observance of these rights simultaneously constitutes recognition of the authority of that particular institution. Consequently, authorization of property claims works to authorize the authorizers. The ability to entitle and disenfranchise specific groups of people with regard to property, to establish the conditions under which they hold that property, is, thereby, constitutive of public authority. Claims to rights prompt the exercise of authority. They invoke public authority and governing capacity in different institutions, be they statutory or not. And, conversely, the active allocation of property and citizenship is a way to acquire and exercise public authority (Lund 2016). As a consequence, struggles over property are as much about the scope and constitution of public authority as they are about access and rights to resources. As rights and public authority are co-produced, the erosion of one also means the dissipation of the other. Ruptures may break the social contract, and rights held under one regime may evaporate under the next. This challenges land holding in general and suggests that when people try to ostentatiously legalize their claims it is to see them unscathed through regime change.

No single institutional actor unilaterally authorizes and fixes claims to property and rights. In situations of institutional pluralism so characteristic of post-colonial societies, public authority is not exclusively or solidly vested in statutory institutions—and these, in any case, seldom demonstrate a coherent entity. Rather, institutions with the capacity to define and enforce collectively binding decisions concerning property and other rights are distributed throughout society in various ways. This governing capacity, I suggest, is what political institutions try to seize and concentrate—sometimes as hegemonic constellations. However, it is a constant struggle, and even for statutory institutions, struggling among themselves, it is an aspirational project rather than a constitutional given. Statutory institutions aim to do this, but in situations of deep societal rupture other institutional actors such as peasant movements, indigenous peoples' movements, or even violent gangs may also claim jurisdiction by effectively defining property and rights subjects.

Social and political ruptures are open moments when new relations of mutual recognition may emerge and form the bases of new social contracts. I use the word "contract" loosely, because such contracts are not exactly voluntary or necessarily consensual, often contentious, and always under renegotiation. Thus, they do not necessarily imply continuous or stable recognition of the legitimacy of the contractual terms. But social contracts require mutual visibility between actors and institutions. Actors must have a social, legal, fiscal, or cultural presence visible and acknowledged by an institution, and the institution must appear credible to provide the desired recognition of a claim. What actors have and who they are, therefore, are made up not of individual features but of relational, politically visible, attributes.

Visibility and Representation

Legalizing a claim—to successfully persuade the relevant public and authority of the legality of a claim and have it recognized as a right—is both relational and performative (Butler 1990, Rose 1994, Strathern 1999). People who believe they have rights, but who have no rightful means of exercising them, improvise and mimic legal arrangements. Most people learn about the law not by comprehensive study or through experts but through individual experiences of diagnostic events that reveal interests, arguments, and settlements of conflicts (Krier 1994, Moore 1987). Often people refer to the law with a rather minimal knowledge of actual formal legislation. Instead, they—and this includes government representatives—may refer to doctrines and precedents as they imagine or recollect them, adapting them to the actual circumstance (see Fortmann 1990, Kunz et al. 2016, Timmer 2010). In societies where the state claims legal hegemony, as is indeed the case in Indonesia, we should, Benton points out, expect people to "actively reference state law, however inaccurately or opportunistically" (2012: 29, see also Benton 2002, 2010, Benton and Staumann 2010, Peñalver and Katyal 2010). In the context of a violent and powerful state, many have pursued a strategy of defining claims that somehow align with (one of the many competing) statutory legal principles and to solicit (one of the many competing) government institutions for recognition. Actors shop for institutions to recognize their claims, and institutions of authority shop for controversies to settle and claims to grant (K. von Benda-Beckmann 1981, see also Agrawal 2005).

In such situations, both claimants and authorities look for mutual visibility. In the chapters that follow, there are many examples of how ordinary people attempt to become visible to the relevant authorities to which they would otherwise be invisible. Peasant and indigenous movements have tried to establish land registries and administrative procedures; they have made attempts to pay tax; and recruited important political figures to endorse their claims. Some have tried to fit into the "indigenous slot" and produce maps to document timeless presence. People who live on occupied plantation land, in national parks, or on state land in urban slums act in the anticipation of government by organizing their settlement in conformity with their ideas of formal government norms. Sometimes, actual conditions prohibit the observance of official norms and rules, and new practical norms develop. Thus parallel, practical, and indirect contracts of recognition emerge where authority and rights are functional and effective despite being only faintly connected to official norms and law. Ordinary people improvise, not to act in illegality, but, on the contrary, to access what they believe is legally theirs. In all its technical illegality, such counterfeit legalization does not undermine the ideas of the state, law, or rights. It underpins them.

Struggles for recognition rely on *representations*. Yet the peculiar thing is that representations of legality and of property may exist *before* what they represent. Sometimes, the echo precedes the cry, and property and legality come into actuality through their representations. The public manifestations, the deed, the rental contract, the tax receipt, even the fine, articulate what they represent and thereby conjure up legality and property. A receipt for payment of rent brings forth what it represents: tenants and landlords. A certificate of land rights produces what it represents: property.

Documents, therefore, constitute important reference points for state recognition and the representation of a right.[6] Legalization, by producing documents that have the appearance of genuine permits, deeds, lease agreements, and contracts, is pursued in varying forms by ordinary people who find proper legal and administrative avenues inaccessible. Such documents constitute a particular language of legal posturing letting people and other actors enter the orbit of certain governing institutions and establish a potential "contract" of mutual recognition. Lease contracts, tax receipts, residence permits, construction permits, receipts for payment of public utilities—authentic, doctored, or outright fabricated—together with court rulings, political announcements, road signs, and inaugurations attended by public officials, can all be mobilized as suggestive inferences of rights.

Paradoxes of Legality in Indonesia

The assumed legality of the state and of law itself is a paradox, and the pith and marrow of legalization in Indonesia. First, the representation of state and law makes government institutions *appear* as promising credible authorities to secure possession as property—even when the actions of these same government institutions are in violation of the law. Their statutory status helps to create the necessary *air* of legality and makes their legalization with reference to law and state work *regardless* of the formal legal nature of the claim. Even illegal acts committed and successfully enforced by a violent government apparatus confirm its power of enforcement. It recursively constitutes the proof of state power. The very capacity of enforcement ultimately makes the claim backed by statutory institutions appear legal. This, in turn, structurally favors government institutions and those connected to them. Often, they are simultaneously authorizing institutions *and* stakeholders with resource interests; they recognize property rights and enjoy them. The opportunities for rent seeking by state officials under such circumstances are gigantic, and the competition between institutions therefore endemic.

The second part of the paradox relates to law's claim to a singular universality in a context of legal and institutional pluralism. While law is always issued out of circumstances and context, modern law presents itself, Mitchell (2002: 77) argues, as an abstraction from the "actual circumstances and political struggles out of which [it] came." As law provides a schema of axiomatic principles, it can perform as if it has no genealogy but is its own origin. The naturalization, abstraction, and universalization of colonial and later government usurpation—or original dispossession—of land in Indonesia and the state's claim to ultimately control it, is a case in point.

Original dispossession "plays in political economy about the same part," Marx argues, "as original sin in theology" (1978: 667). Marx's analysis of England, where landlords and capitalists practiced theft of land "on a colossal scale" through enclosures, foreshadowed the global reach of this fundamental dynamic. He further remarks that all this dispossession "happened without the slightest observation of legal etiquette" (Marx 1978: 677). Here, Marx, no doubt, hints at two of the particularities of law and force. First, law appears deficient without the possibility of enforcement, so the two go together, yet, seemingly with law half a step ahead of its enforcement. Enforcement suggests the ultimately violent measures of exclusion of others and protection of *already* established rights. Law enforcement simply enforces the established law. However, as Marx shows, this in-built sequence in the concept, from established law or right to subsequent enforcement, is misleading. Just as often, we face forceful eviction and acquisition, and, only then, measures of legalization. Possession is often ahead of the law, so to speak. This way, legalization launders violent conquest, usurpation, and theft. With time, the subtler nuances of what begat what may fade from memory, and records may suppose that prevailing ownership or land control descends directly from an initial uneventful acquisition. Yet violence is inherent in law and property. The Lockean idea of creating property by simply mixing one's labor with nature has so often depended on the capacity to create "nature" out of others' property by denying their rights, their rules, and sometimes their own very existence (Locke 1994, Proudhon 1966, Rousseau 1977). Violence can hardly be said to be alien to law, since legalizing possessions as property means legalizing the violence that brought it about. The second element Marx was hinting at was the unflinching insistence on the rightful and lawful acquisition of land, on the one hand, and the complete disdain for the idea that any rights to the same land could have existed before. By editing out prior rights, acquisition could seemingly take place without compromising the ideal of law's universality.

In Indonesia, land acquisition took a different form, but "legal etiquette" was lacking nonetheless. Instead of legalizing after the fact, so to say, perfunctory legalization was established *long before* dispossession was actualized in most parts. Statutory land laws in Indonesia date back to co-lonial times.[7] By 1870, actual legislation concerning land and property had been passed for Java and Madura, and in the following years for Sumatra and the other so-called "outer islands." The Forestry Law of 1865 established the basis for state-controlled scientific forestry. The law declared three-quarters of the colony's territory as forest, and forests as state domain, with draconian measures of exclusion directed at the population (Bielefeld 2004, Djalins 2012, 2015, Gautama and Hornick 1974, Gellert and Andiko 2015, Peluso, 1992: 44–78). The Agrarian Law of 1870 covered whatever land had not been categorized as "forest" by the Forestry Law, and declared that all lands to which there was no civil law ownership title were to be considered the domain of the state. The sweeping legal declarations of the Forestry and Agrarian laws simply established the "state" as the owner of virtually the whole archipelago, disenfranchising all existing institutions and communi-ties. They ensured a veneer of general legality for all the subsequent specific appropriations when the time came. Theft was laundered in advance, and the actual appropriations would then look like simple technical operations of legal confirmation for each specific area in question. In the language of Benjamin (2004), the law-making violence was initially mostly a construc-tion on paper, but as these laws have eventually been actualized through evictions for government-decided land use, the law-preserving violence looked an awful lot like the law-making violence.

This furls back on the first paradox. By turning land into the property (or the *domain*) of the state, the law now recognized all other rights as weaker and inferior customary or temporary lease rights of third parties. Hereby, government gave itself the legal instruments of repeated—perpetual—primitive accumulation, or dispossession. The Forestry and Agrarian laws legitimated the colonial acquisition of land and legalized the dispossession of virtually the entire population. To paraphrase E. P. Thompson, the law became a superb instrument by which colonial rulers were able to impose new definitions of property, as in the extinction of indefinite agrarian use-rights and the furtherance of enclosure (Thompson 1975: 264). Conse-quently, successive governments in Indonesia have consistently, since colo-nization, operated *as if* all land ultimately belongs to the state. They have felt confident enough to override any current uses, however time-honored or customary, and backed by whatever legal document, by invoking *state interests*. As with the introductory example from Langkat, even genuine government documents acknowledging people's rightful presence have been brushed aside when stronger interests called for it.

Reiteration and predictability connect to universalization in modern law. The juridical field is described by Bourdieu as the "site of a competition for monopoly of the right to determine the law" (Bourdieu 1987: 817). It acquires a relative autonomy, Bourdieu suggests, through its proper procedures, hierarchies, norms, and language that *signal* universality and neutrality, although access to the field is characterized by neither.[8] A certain auto-authorization takes place through reiteration of rules and procedures. Credibility of rules and rights is established through citation of other, prior instances. Such repetition eventually promotes the *formal* authority of bureaucracy and law itself rather than the *substantive* legitimacy of the regime, rule, or right. Although auto-authorization resonates with the Indonesian context, Indonesian law is not self-referential in the substantive ways that Bourdieu suggests. Since independence, and especially since the authoritarian New Order in the mid-1960s, the state consolidated its power to allocate land at will and enforce its will as law. A range of pressures and tactics—limited public rights of consultation, highly discriminatory application of the law with excessive bureaucratic discretion, threats and violence by army, police, and hired gangs against landholders to make them accept low levels of compensation—have systematically favored government over citizens. Governments have even dismissed statutory law on the basis of the state's ultimate right to control land (Fitzpatrick 2008: 239–40, see also Bakker and Reerink 2015, Lindsey 2001).

In addition, the public and official memory is fragile in Indonesia. No publication of legal journals has taken place since the Japanese occupation in 1942 (Bedner 2016b). This could have facilitated a substantive reiteration, self-referencing, and thereby consolidation of jurisprudence. Obviously, such situations make it more than difficult to establish a systematic reiteration of reasoning and establish a substantial jurisprudence. Nonetheless, in the field of land conflicts, the near systematic judgments against smallholders throughout the New Order period built an ersatz jurisprudence based on the reiteration and virtual predictability of *outcomes* regardless of the situations, documentation, and evidence. Thus, despite the many examples of the impaired immunity from political bias characterizing the judiciary and the government administration and known to everyone else in Indonesia, law and bureaucratic procedure could be held aloft as a form of jurisprudence, namely the idea that any claim backed by the power of the state becomes legal.

Therefore, contrary to law's representation of itself as predictable, rule-bound, and neutral, it is pliable, context-bound, and biased in favor of government institutions. There is no right amount of "evidence," or any golden ratio that makes legalization work in all cases. Outcomes depend on the ability of claimants to amass a sufficient combination of suggestive props of legal rights and to frame the claim in accordance with prevailing values in order to convince the appropriate authority to acknowledge, recognize, and protect one's claim as a right (or, at least, to provide sufficient cover for the authorities to be able to claim to have acted in good faith). This is why both the company and the residents in Mekar Jaya in Langkat kept their mutually contradictory documents, one set granting smallholders cultivation rights and the other granting the company plantation rights. These were their respective appeals to legal backing for their claims and their attempt to consolidate their nine-tenths of possession into a durable right. Such appeals are made in a context of profound historical inequality. However, if people's efforts to claim land and rights through law were to be dismissed merely because they are not often successful, the outcomes of the struggles would be endowed with a quality of inevitability and foreclose detailed analysis. People's *perception* of the emancipatory potential of law as the last tenth of property is hardly inconsequential. At the very least, it reflects their experience and grasp of opportunities at the time.

One of the ironies is that smallholders, who often feel the sharp end of state power, try to legalize possession by mobilizing the paraphernalia of state, law, and government, whereas large players like companies, entrepreneurs, or government agencies themselves are sometimes more cavalier. As the law holds the potential to be an instrument of security as well as one of dispossession, it is possibly more crucial to smallholders, common folk, and ordinary people for the acquisition and protection of what they believe is theirs. Bigger players, like public and private companies, and entrepreneurs also depend on legalization. Yet they have often exhibited less urgency. Like ordinary people, they have made claims based on counterfeit and imitation, perhaps having these subsequently properly rectified by the National Land Agency, or a development plan. Yet often their claims, too, have simply drowned in a morass of doubt about the status of a particular piece of land. For example, the Ministry of Forestry was strong enough to control state forest land with uncertain legality during Suharto's authoritarian New Order. The ministry and the other politically connected actors could hold their possessions in technical illegality but with the certainty of political protection. Actual legalization and paperwork were possible afterthoughts. The Constitutional Court rulings only challenged the ministry's claim to jurisdiction in 2011, more than ten years into a democratic period. Hence, the mere fact that government possessed land gave it an air of legality. Nonetheless, the absence of credible legalization caught up even with a ministry, whose claim did not hold up in the aftermath of regime change.

Legalization in a Context of *Reformasi*

Indonesian land law remains a thicket of permissions and restrictions, competing rights and overlapping jurisdictions, and many land rights seem equivocal. Fundamental ambiguities of ownership and entitlement, wrapped in a byzantine web of legal and administrative rules and exceptions, have often made it virtually impossible to disentangle competing claims by rational procedures (Fitzpatrick 2006). Instead, the de facto control of land by companies and smallholders who settle for the first time, settle anew, or have lived there all along, often precipitates the legitimation and subsequent legalization of land claims. In this light, law is used, not merely to make just decisions, but equally to call whatever decision "just." That is, the overlapping jurisdictions and the ambiguities of law may, under the right circumstances, be stretched to cover actions and transactions that would otherwise be considered illegal and perhaps illegitimate. Such ambiguity may sometimes be cultivated by institutions that wish to claim or disown jurisdiction over a particular issue. For the rights subjects, this ambiguity is more of a liability. In essence, legislation has historically backed competing interests and has established overlapping jurisdictions for rival authorities to a degree where many contradicting claims can find justification within the law. The more ambiguous the legal legacy and the more competitive the institutional landscape — most post-colonial societies provide extreme examples — the more elastic the legalization (or denial) of the claim. What was considered lawful possession yesterday may be deemed squatting and illegal tomorrow as people are stripped of citizenship and the capacity to own, or as land is recategorized into zones of conservation, plantation, urban housing, infrastructure, and so on. It may ultimately make most sense to view Indonesian law as a repository of more or less congruous legal principles, which are invoked by claimants engaging with various public authorities, and whose enforcement largely depends on the political power of the particular authority at the given time.

Regimes have changed many times in Indonesia over the past century. Different political regimes have followed one another after dramatic ruptures of colonization, war, independence, and social revolution, "guided democracy" under Sukarno, authoritarianism and New Order under Suharto, and democratization after 1998. Each rupture has constituted an "open moment" when opportunities and risks multiplied, when the scope of outcomes widened, and when new structural scaffolding was erected. Thus, at every turn, property in land has been at stake, and law has been an important instrument to determine access to it. The centuries-long struggles over land in Indonesia have thereby, effectively, also been struggles over the categories of property, authority, rights, rights subjects, and law.

The most recent rupture in Indonesia occurred in the late 1990s as the Suharto regime spiralled into decline and finally imploded. The collapse of the New Order in 1998 opened a path for democratization and a series of decentralization reforms, which provided increased autonomy to local government. Known as *reformasi*, these reforms inspired different social organizations and political entrepreneurs, leading to the efflorescence of new political actors. *Reformasi* promised agrarian reform, restitution, and democratic politics, and propelled smallholder land occupations at a significant scale. All the same, old landholders and new powerful operators often frustrated their claims.

Peasant movements, indigenous movements, student movements, labor unions, political parties, different associations, vigilantes, youth and criminal gangs, all flourished with the demise of government repression so emblematic of the Suharto era (Bachriadi et al. 2013, Bakker and Moniaga 2010, Gilbert and Afrizal 2018, Juliawan 2011, Li 2000, Lucas and Warren 2003, Peluso et al. 2008, Schulte, Nordholt, and van Klinken 2007, Steinebach 2013). Some organizations were new, while others had longer histories, but all seized the new moment to lodge claims, assert political ideas, and exploit opportunities. Some claimed rights, some claimed authority, some claimed both. They all worked on the last tenth of the law: legalization. In the field of land and property, an open moment seemed to have occurred. As Rachman explains,

> Seizing the political opportunity that opened with the fall of Suharto in May 1998, agrarian movement activists and scholars launched a national campaign to change agrarian and natural resource management policies. Their demands resonated with reformist leaders in the highest state institution in Indonesian government structure, the People's Consultative Assembly. . . . Consequently, the campaign got a policy outcome: A People's Consultative Assembly Decree on Agrarian Reform and Natural Resource Management (TAP MPRRI No. IX/2001), which set principles and directions, and mandated the national parliament and the Indonesian president to implement agrarian reform and natural resource management policies, including the provision to redistribute land for rural poor. The work of the new head of the National Land Agency to develop the *Reforma Agraria* was an official follow up of the Decree. [Rachman 2011: 5]

The political atmosphere was very positive toward land reform in the first years after *reformasi*. A speech by President Abdurrahman Wahid epitomized the turn of the tide. It was inappropriate, he argued, to accuse people of stealing land, because "in fact, the plantations had stolen the people's land." Instead, he advocated, "some 40 per cent of plantation land should be distributed to cultivators who need it. Moreover, people could even hold shares in the plantation itself" (Fauzi and Bachriadi 2006: 19). In short, his statements encouraged people to take back what they believed to be their land.

While the political context changed with *reformasi*, the fundamental interests in society did not. As the redistributive element of the reform required land to distribute, the National Land Agency was quickly confronting the largest landholders in the country: the Ministry of Forestry and the Ministry of Agriculture. Both ministries refused to "release" close to 15 million hectares for land reform, just as they had done back in the early 1960s. *Reformasi* may have marked a new moment in politics, but it did not change the powers or interests of the ministries overnight. Despite intense public debate with new organized stakeholders, redistributive land reform gradually slid from the government's agenda, and by 2008, ten years after *reformasi*, the concern was no longer to transfer land to the landless, but rather how to register the property of landowners.

Reformasi held the promise of democratization, but its twin element, decentralization, held the potential for a renewed intensity of local politics. Thus, decentralization transferred significant powers in land matters to the district administration. Districts could henceforth determine what land was available for redistribution and who were eligible recipients. Districts were also to deal with "neglected land," where plantation leasehold on undeveloped land would revert to public ownership according to law. However, the transformation of smallholder land to large-scale plantations was accelerated, rather than curbed, when the power to allocate land was decentralized to districts in conjunction with requirements that they expand the revenue basis (Pichler 2015: 525). Coalitions of interest would form between local government, politicians, developers, and various entrepreneurs in violence, such as youth gangs, police, and army groups.[9] And just like smallholders and their movements, these new coalitions eyed an opportunity to acquire land in the social and political rupture of *reformasi*.

With *reformasi* the New Order regime disappeared. Nevertheless, some of its constituent elements remained, although they developed more mutual autonomy. With the "normalization" new political parties emerged and Suharto's political party, *Golkar* (*Golonkan Karya*, functional groups), no longer exercised an exclusive right to control the state and its institutions. With authoritarian rule on the wane, the armed forces became less directly involved in social and political life. This partly decoupled the youth gangs from the military, and henceforth, with their "camouflage uniforms of distinct colours and regalia, they represent[ed] private armies [and could] be mobilized on behalf of the rich, the powerful, and the ruthless" (Hadiz 2010: 138). Thus, *reformasi* did not undo the predatory nature of local politics, and the creation of access to "opportunities for private accumulation on the basis of control over public resources and institutions" remained central (Hadiz 2010: 172). There have been moments when opportunities have aligned and where common folk have prevailed, but as this book will show there are structural reasons why this outcome has been rare.

Method and the Chapters

The research method for this book has been consistently exploratory. A primary focus has been on a specific conflict over land, and the first step has been to identify and talk to the primary protagonists. I have subsequently moved outward in the attempt to talk to any- and everyone who would know about the specific case: public officials, politicians, civil servants, plantation officials, and entrepreneurs; journalists, academics, university alumni, students, and activists; as well as lawyers, notaries, school teachers, imams, community leaders, shopkeepers, police, and gangsters. All cases are of course individual and cannot simply be added up to produce a quantitative basis for analysis. However, by examining several cases, a certain resonance emerges among them and recurrent features begin to form a pattern (Becker 2014, 2017, Lund 2014, Moore 2005). And by asking the same generic question, "Who has what rights, and how are rights established?" both pattern and variation are accommodated. In this way I broadened the data collection and increased the number of studied cases through collective and team fieldwork, together with scholar-activists from different organizations in the areas studied.

For each of the chapters on West Java (3 and 4), North Sumatra (2 and 7), and Aceh (5), my scholar-activist collaborators and I first made a brief pilot study as a group of four to eight people. The study was designed to emphasize depth and variety in the data it assembled. We gathered as much written material about the place as we could, and we identified what looked like central actors; we talked to them and to many of the people they, in turn, identified. We tried not to limit the scope of the analysis in the field, but instead to remain open to events and actors that had not seemed important at first glance. More than once, this helped to connect outlier dots that had seemed to be scattered outside the emerging pattern. After each pilot study, we held a workshop to discuss findings and produce a simple research template on the basis of the most interesting aspects of this first case. Following this, between six and eight new field sites were investigated individually or in pairs by me and the local scholar-activists with whom I worked.[10] For each field site, we prepared a report of five to eight pages. Consequently, the cases presented in this book are selected from this larger number of cases researched in depth over one to three months in 2012, 2013, 2015, 2016, and 2017. We designed the research to be useful to me as well as the local researcher-activists, and we share ownership of it.

The chapters are individual texts, each focusing on a specific aspect of the main question, and can be read in random order or selectively. All chapters, therefore, have some historical background that is necessary to understand the patterns of the present. Combing through different aspects of Indonesia's history provides some counterbalance to the inevitable simplification that all books are. Reality is messy—that is a given. Analysis should provide clarity—that is a given as well. But it should not be at the expense of variation, contradiction, accident, and chance. By joining together cases spanning locations, rural, urban, Java, and Sumatra, I hope to provide sufficient polyphony and sufficient conceptual concentration to make my point.

Different political regimes have followed one another after dramatic ruptures in Indonesia. Yet, in contrast to these ruptures and the truncated political and legal underpinning of land claims, plantation agriculture as a form of production and agrarian structure has proved remarkably resilient. Chapter 2, "Ground Work," examines the *longue durée* reproduction of the material agrarian structure and the violently and radically changing political regimes. The contrast challenges the very idea that they are connected. In reality, though, they are. The chapter operates at two levels. First, on the large scale of time and space, it shows how the political contexts over time have supported and undermined various land claims at different junctures—from the first Dutch land acquisition in the 1860s through Japanese occupation, social revolution, "guided democracy," the "New Order," and *reformasi*. The chapter also shows how the patterns of claims and counterclaims, acquisitions and evictions, occupations and retreats, have emerged. Second, it provides a detailed analysis of a single, emblematic, enduring conflict.

Government institutions and local people in Indonesia have entrenched, resurrected, and reinvented space through their different territorial and property claims. From colonial times onward, government institutions have dissolved local political orders and territorialized and reordered spatial frontiers. Local resource users, on the other hand, have aligned with, or undermined, the spatial ordering. Chapter 3, "Indirect Recognition," analyzes government-citizen encounters in West Java and the dynamics of recognition in the fields of government territorialization, taxation, local organization, and identity politics. If direct claims to resources were impossible to pursue, people would instead lodge *indirect claims*. In everyday situations, indirect recognition can perform important legal and political work. After the authoritarian New Order regime, in particular, claims to citizenship worked as indirect property claims and as pragmatic proxies for formal property rights. The chapter examines how people struggle over the past, negotiating the constraints of social propriety for legitimation and indirect recognition of their claims.

Recent land occupations by peasant movements in Indonesia have done more than challenge the existing ownership of plantations and forests. They have restructured local property and authority relations by stimulating a strategic critique of public authority and governance practice within the peasant movement. However, legalization of land occupations has remained rudimentary, and possession has not been recognized as property by government institutions. Chapter 4, "Occupied," examines the land occupation history from West Java in detail and shows how claims to citizenship and property have been opposed, ignored, and denied by statutory institutions despite land-occupying farmers' attempts to become "visible" to and recognized by government institutions. As long as government institutions refused to see citizens, people solicited recognition from the peasant movement, which in turn experienced a sovereign moment.

The end of the civil war in Aceh brought peace, but it has been of a predatory nature. Peace held promise of land reform. As a moment of rupture, the peace revealed interests, powers, and dynamics, and it offered an opportunity for their reconfiguration. Yet old patterns of smallholder dispossession were entrenched as the former insurgency leadership aligned with the old elite of plantation companies. When unrest ceased, old agrarian conflicts between smallholders and planters resumed. Chapter 5, "Predatory Peace," shows how smallholders were denied recognition of independent rights and property on a violent oil palm frontier. As a result, large-scale plantation production expanded. Oil palm contract-farming schemes have thus effectively alienated smallholders from their land, and violence has precluded their organization.

Encroachment of state land and its gradual privatization by ordinary people sometimes gnaw at government property. While the modern history of land control in Indonesia is overwhelmingly one of colonial conquest, government enclosure, and expropriation of traditional property rights, underneath these great transformations countercurrents also flow. Through a series of small, innocuous, but surprisingly effective actions, people sometimes manage to undo government ownership. Chapter 6, "On Track," shows how settlers over a period of some thirty years managed to appropriate, formalize, and effectively privatize land belonging to the state-owned railway company in the city of Bandung by mixing tactics of civil disobedience and civic compliance. Disobedient occupation and subsequent obedient payment of taxes, documentation of residence, and "normalization" of the area reduced the company's ownership to thin formality, whereas new residents held all substantial elements of property in the land.

Construction of urban neighborhoods resembles a dance between actors looking for recognition and other actors who might be able to provide a semblance of it. Medan is the city of the plantation belt in North Sumatra. The city is expanding and has grown onto plantation land for almost one hundred years. Some of the land on which the city stands, is, in fact, still under lease for crop production. This expansion is little regulated and mostly a result of spontaneous settlements and land occupations. Neighborhoods are built on uncertain terms, and inhabitants, peasant movements, entrepreneurs, businessmen, gangsters, and elements of the armed forces all see opportunities in this development. Three neighborhoods dating from 1920, 2010, and the present are studied in Chapter 7, "Another Fine Mess," to map out the contentious patterns of legalization of urbanizing land. Inhabitants meticulously recorded settlement and gestures of recognition from government or significant personalities in order to justify their claims. Crafty entrepreneurs, in turn, built in political insurances when they constructed "new towns," and gangs and peasant movements tried to consolidate property by exercising force. This quest for legality was not conducted by legal means alone, but when the dance for recognition lasted long enough, the neighborhoods became established facts.

What is the connection between the nine-tenths of the law and the last tenth? How do government agencies and their auxiliaries in all their guises, companies, and ordinary people in movements and less cohesive groups consolidate possession as property through legitimation and legalization? On the basis of the previous chapters, Chapter 8, "The Last Tenth," discusses the structural contingency of change and endurance, and the respective powers to fix and undo property. While all the implicated actors are law makers, in principle, they are not equally in control of its direction. Undoing competing claims often requires the momentary capacity of violence and abrogation, whereas entrenching new ones requires an enduring capacity to perpetuate the recognition of claims. Whereas institutionalization is an achievement demanding stamina, its destruction only has to succeed once.

CHAPTER TWO

Ground Work

Legalization and Land Struggles in North Sumatra

In 2006, the inhabitants of a small village in North Sumatra filed a lawsuit in the District Court against the London-Sumatra plantation company (LonSum), the Indonesian National Police, the Armed Forces of Indonesia, the Ministry of the Interior, and the National Land Agency. The charge was that the company had unlawfully seized village land in 1974, thirty-two years earlier, and that the police, the army, the Ministry of Interior, and the National Land Agency had colluded in this operation of dispossession. A legal procedure was new terrain for the villagers who, since the late 1950s, had been engaged in land struggles against LonSum and government agencies. Villagers had obtained Land Use Registration Cards (*Kartu Registrasi Pemakaian Tanah*) in the late 1950s. Nonetheless, three significant evictions took place in 1959, 1971–74, and 1984, leaving the villagers practically landless. With the assistance of farmers' movements, NGOs, and legal aid lawyers, a civil case was launched demanding the return of the land, compensation for lost earnings, and damages from prolonged trauma: altogether some 5.5 billion Rupiah (approximately U.S.$600,000 at the time). In 2006, the District Court dismissed the Land Use Registration Cards as invalid and "communist" because they were issued in 1959 when the Indonesian Communist Party was influential. In the subsequent appeal in the

High Court and the Supreme Court of Cassation, the case was thrown out on a technicality: the possibility of filing a case like this expires after thirty years.

Ever since the first Dutch land acquisition linked the area to the world tobacco market in the 1860s, possession of land has been contentious in North Sumatra.[1] The defeat of smallholders by companies and government described above was just the latest in what seems an endless struggle. North Sumatra Province currently hosts 381 plantations with long-term leases, ranging in size from a few hundred to more than 10,000 hectares. Plantations cover a total of 895,000 hectares out of the province's total area of 7,200,000 hectares, concentrated in the districts on the east coastal plains. In Simalungung, Deli Serdang, Labuhan Batu, Lankat, and Asahan districts on the east coast, 337 plantations cover from 17 percent of the land in Lankat to 65 percent in Simalungung. In 2008, the regional office of the National Land Agency registered 699 ongoing conflicts between state- and privately owned plantation companies and the local populations (Khairina 2013: 125), but exact numbers are impossible to ascertain.[2]

Different political regimes have followed one another after dramatic ruptures of colonization, war, revolution, authoritarianism, and democratization. Yet, in contrast to these ruptures and the truncated political and legal underpinning of land claims, plantation agriculture as a form of production and agrarian structure has proved remarkably resilient, relentlessly excluding peasants from land holding. This contrast between a *longue durée* reproduction of the material agrarian structure and the violently and radically changing national political regimes challenges the very idea that they are connected. In reality, though, they are: here I investigate *how*.

The chapter therefore operates at two levels, contrasting regime changes with enduring agrarian inequality. Looking across various regions and times, it first shows how the political context has supported or undermined various outcomes. Despite the opportunities regime changes created for change in the agrarian structure, it has proved very resilient. To understand why, I subsequently conduct a deliberately detailed analysis of a single specific enduring conflict. The ability to dig in and institutionally consolidate an achieved advantage relies on the dynamic of capital, political power, populist politics, resource access, and force riveted in by law. The local case shows how legalization, in connection with the other nine-tenths of the law, allowed plantation agriculture to hold off smallholder challenges for decades. Some claims in this land struggle challenged the status quo, but proved to be ephemeral and short-lived. Other claims, however, reproduced effectively. They hardened and institutionalized, propped up by statutory law, regulation, force, and other practices. By tying the specific details of this case at a human scale to historical currents, the chapter shows how moments of rupture may be open to all, but not equally easy for all to seize. As a result, agrarian inequality and exclusion endured.

The Field of Agrarian Struggle in North Sumatra

Colonizing North Sumatra

The history of Indonesia and North Sumatra is characterized by a series of dramatic ruptures where rights and authorities have been suspended, reworked, or replaced.[3] As a part of the colonial division of tropical spoils, the Anglo-Dutch Treaty of 1824 gave the Dutch a free hand to colonize Sumatra except for Aceh, which was recognized in its own right. Actual territorial control was slow, however. War on Java and the mere size of Sumatra stretched the Dutch military forces. Only by 1865 had the different states and principalities on Sumatra south of Aceh conceded to Dutch sovereignty. From this point on, however, plantations were created, and between 1880 and 1930 the population of East Sumatra grew from 90,000 to 1.5 million (Pelzer 1978: 106). There were 22 tobacco plantations in 1872, but 148 in 1888 (E. Damanik 2016: 75–115, Pelzer 1978: 7–13, 52). The plantation belt represented an intense field of spatial transformation, massive profits, and conflict. The tobacco boom in the latter half of the nineteenth century made the main city, Medan, a place where European planters and adventurers, entrepreneurs, and hustlers sought their fortunes, earning the area the sobriquet *het land dollar*, the land of money. However, as Tan Malaka, a leading Indonesian intellectual of the first half of the twentieth century, added, it was also a "land of sweat, tears and death, a hell for the proletariat."[4]

Typically, the Dutch and other European planters obtained long-term concessions from local sultans and princes. "In the absence of any model, it is not surprising that concession contracts written during the first . . . years varied considerably. Some concessions were for 99 years, others for 70 or 75" (Pelzer 1978: 67).[5] Most importantly, however, a concession established the conceder as well as the concessionaire. While a plantation asserted the rights of the new landholder, it equally established those of the "owner" to concede, and there was, no doubt, a mutual interest between planters and princes to consider land as under the primordial authority of the indigenous nobility. On the "inside," so to speak, concessions constituted virtual feudal estates where the concessionaire assumed authority over the land, the villages, and anyone in them.[6]

From the turn of the twentieth century, a discussion arose in government circles about the legal nature of a concession, together with a concern that, increasingly, the indigenous population was facing a land shortage. A government Bureau of Conversion was established, tasked with sorting out how concessions were to be divided up between planters and smallholders. The tricky operation of hemming in the plantations and separating out the smallholders was by no means concluded when the Japanese invaded Sumatra in March 1942.

War and Revolution

During the Japanese occupation land control was profoundly reshuffled and the plantations became integrated into the war economy. Some plantations were run by their Indonesian staff without Dutch management. Food supply proved a critical problem and many rubber trees and other perennial crops were cleared, while tobacco cultivation—with its seven to eight years of fallow—was especially targeted for replacement by food production. Encouraged by the Japanese, former plantation workers developed individual smallholdings in the plantations. They became landholders for the first time (Pelzer 1978: 178). At the same time, the intrusive Japanese war economy eliminated the authority of the nobility in land matters (Reid 1979: 107). The Japanese occupational forces still depended on some continued cooperation with the local Indonesian elite and administration, but they focused on nurturing nationalist—anti-Western—political forces.

The Japanese promoted the creation of a multitude of youth organizations (*pemuda*). Some were armed volunteer auxiliaries under their command. In this way a large contingent of young Indonesians became familiar with the use of weapons and organized military tactics (Reid 1979: 117). At the time of Japanese surrender in August 1945, the Indonesian national or social revolution picked up pace. Anderson explains: "The central role of the *Angkatan Muda* (younger generation) in the outbreak of the Indonesian national revolution of 1945 was the most striking political fact of the period. For the returning Dutch and their British allies, as well as for the Eurasian and Chinese communities, the once innocent word *pemuda* (youth) rapidly acquired an aura of remorseless terrorism" (1972: 1). Thus, when the new nationalist leadership in Jakarta declared independence for Indonesia, the social and political, and, indeed, military, role of youth organizations is hard to exaggerate; they had become an important—albeit amorphous—part of the political dynamic of the country.[7]

The new Indonesian government tried to establish itself and appointed governors, including one for Sumatra. However, at the same time, Dutch and British troops had landed in Medan determined to retake the Dutch colony. In the last months of 1945, the entire political and institutional structure of rule and property was in the balance. In Medan, Dutch and British troops, as well as not-yet-disarmed Japanese troops, all operated in the city, together with a fast-increasing number of semi-militarized young men from a raft of different youth organizations and militias. They ranged from street gangs, nosing around for opportunities, to disciplined outfits maneuvering with confident ideological poise. Sometimes, they would be both. While all these claimants to authority had "order" as their declared priority, none of them could provide it. The new nationalist government in Jakarta had not been able to put together a wing of the national army in East Sumatra. This allowed the federation of youth organizations in Medan to seize the day and declare that they were "the republic's armed forces in East Sumatra." The youth gangs mobilized veterans from the Japanese auxiliary force, acquired non-decommissioned weapons from the defeated Japanese, and further attracted people "accustomed to violence in the semi-criminal Medan underworld" (Reid 1979: 162, see also Sato 1994, Stoler 1988).[8] Medan was in a situation of absolute uncertainty as different armed youth bands operated in the city's neighborhoods against the Europeans and each other. Meanwhile, the Sultans of Deli and Lankat, among others, were treading water, while secretly sending off pledges of loyalty to the Dutch. As Reid points out, the "dichotomy between the fighting bands and the conservative [traditional rulers] of East Sumatra grew steadily more acute. The *pemuda* held the power of physical force but were so disunited that any attempt to use it internally raised a spectre of anarchy. The [traditional rulers] maintained the fiction of governing but were steadily more isolated from its substance" (Reid 1979: 218). At the same time, the aspirant nationalist government, led by Sukarno from Jakarta, attempted to get a foothold in Medan. Yet, while the nationalist-appointed "governor" enjoyed a degree of recognition from the British and the Japanese, he did not control any youth gang but had only some moral influence because he embodied the idea of the "republic" that they held dear.

In the months that followed the Japanese surrender, an increasingly radical nationalist conception of the new republic was cultivated among young intellectuals around the Communist Party and the youth gangs, and ideas about nationalization of the economy flourished. During this mood, the different Indonesian movements turned against the old nobility, such as the *ulèëbalang, imeum, sibayak,* sultans, *rajas, datuks* and *raja urung.* Pressure was mounting against the traditional rulers, and on March 3, 1946, the terror of the "social revolution" engulfed North Sumatra. The coalition of some 140 youth gangs sought out all traditional leaders. The lives of some were spared, but many more were killed (McTurnan Kahin 2003: 180, Reid 1979: 230–38). The class of nobles—the traditional landlords—was thereby definitively taken out of the property-authority equation in East Sumatra. The following months degenerated into disorganization. De facto nationalization of plantations was widespread, and expropriation shaded into looting for private gain. The governor left North Sumatra, and outside of the British

Sector of Medan, government forces, the youth gangs, young war lords, the Communist Party, and more isolated militia outfits all wielded violence and exercised authority in the hope of its consolidation. While no institutional structure consolidated immediately in the field of land struggle, one thing was clear: the nobility had had its moment in history, and any future land-holder would be beholden to a different political institution.[9]

Political parties also began to form or re-emerge after being banned earlier in this period. Scores of political groups firmed up, especially the Nationalist Party (*Partai Nasionalis Indonesia*) and the Communist Party (*Partai Kommunis Indonesia*), along with different Islamic organizations. The challenge for all of them was how well they organized and consolidated their relations with the popular organizations in Indonesian society.[10] Different mass organizations equally developed in the years after independence, including labor unions, peasant unions, women's movements, associations of artists and intellectuals, a variety of alumni associations, as well as youth organizations or gangs, the *pemuda* (White 2016: 3).[11]

The 1950s saw great unrest and confusion, featuring land occupations, evictions, and loss of property rights. By the early 1950s, the Indonesian government was beginning to see the plantations not merely as an exploitative colonial artifact, but equally as a source of revenue. In 1951, the Ministry of the Interior decreed that half of the approximately 250,000 hectares of tobacco plantations in North Sumatra should remain with or revert to the plantation companies, whereas the other half should be distributed among the plantation workers. An Office of Land Distribution was set up in Medan to oversee the task, but it proved impossible to implement. Farmers, who had just acquired their land by occupation, were not prepared to surrender it again on a vague promise of future relocation (Ikhsan nd A, 3–6). Occupations became ever more widespread in the plantations.[12] The Communist Party, especially, saw this as an important vehicle for social change and engaged in the organization of occupations.[13]

The government was caught in a dilemma in North Sumatra, as well as in the rest of Indonesia, between fulfilling promises of social change with independence to the general population, and the protection of an industry that generated foreign income. The provincial government of North

Sumatra issued two different decrees. First, it determined that land ownership in expired concessions would revert to the state and not the nobility.
This was a way of instituting government as the ultimate landlord. Second,
government enacted what was known as a "standfast," first in 1953 and then
through the Emergency Law 8 of 1954. This decreed that all land occupations until that moment had to be resolved by negotiation, while any future
occupations would be considered a criminal offense (Pelzer 1982: 107). The
popular understanding among local people was that the land they already
possessed was now legally theirs and definitively excluded from the landholding of the plantation company. This understanding was further confirmed as their settlements were henceforth officially registered as villages.
Residency cards were issued and tax payment introduced in 1957. All land
held at this watershed moment seemed to have become legalized property.

While criminalizing further land occupations, the "standfasts" did not
put an end to them. The communists were increasingly active in occupations, and by 1955 the occupied portions of the plantations established
in Simalungung and Deli Serdang districts had reached between 37 and
58 percent.[14] The planters' association was increasingly active in pointing
to areas not used for plantations as such and therefore suitable for land
distribution, but by the end of 1956 the plantation companies had become
desperate and began direct negotiations with the national peasant union—
the Peasant Front of Indonesia—about which parts of the plantations to
release for peasant farming. By 1957, however, as these negotiations collapsed, the Indonesian military began to play an active role in the agrarian
conflict.[15] At his own initiative, the regional military administrator for North
Sumatra issued another "standfast," adding further confusion over which
occupations were legalized and which should be considered criminal. Both
the planters' association and the peasant movements protested against military interference in agrarian matters. But the military had stepped in to stay.

When President Sukarno began his efforts to circumvent parliament and
political parties through his "guided democracy" in 1957, he may not have
projected a vanguard role for the armed forces (McTurnan Kahin 2003), but
the military was to become "not only an enthusiastic partner but the main
driving force" in sidelining the political parties and taking over the Dutch

and other Western properties (Robison 1986: 70).[16] The army officers created the Pemuda-Military Cooperation Board (*Badan Kerja Sama Pemuda-Militer*), and more than seventy youth organizations and university student groups, as well as all the youth wings of the now-neutered political parties, made up this new force, mobilized and organized on an anti-Dutch nationalist diet (Ryter 2002: 80–84). When Indonesia faced a confrontation with the Netherlands in the United Nations over the future of West Irian/Papua in 1957, a wave of anti-Dutch sentiment overwhelmed the archipelago, and within a few days, Dutch property and infrastructure had been seized by unions and popular movements, but especially by the military and the youth organizations brought under their control.[17] Therefore, while this property was to be taken over by government, it first passed through the hands of the military. President Sukarno had declared the country in a state of war with the proclamation of martial law, meaning that military officers outranked their civilian counterparts at all levels (Pelzer 1982: 167). For North Sumatra, the military commander announced, all Dutch property would be nationalized and run by the military.[18] The national minister of defense followed suit and ordered that all regional military administrators should take control of Dutch possessions in the country. Thus self-legalized, the military took over the management of plantations. This was a far tougher and more resolute adversary for peasant squatters than the plantation companies had ever been. Massive evictions were the result, and the political space for negotiations contracted. By the end of 1958, the formerly Dutch-owned plantations formed the bulk of the new state-owned plantation complex, *Perseroan Terbatas Perkebunan Nusantara* (The Archipelago Plantations Ltd., PTPN). While this was formidable, nationalization meant even more than the actual takeover of Dutch property; it meant a definitive confirmation of the new state's territorial sovereignty and ultimate ownership of the nation's land.[19] It also meant that the military interests were conjoined with those of PTPN. Government institutions were now both legalizing and regulating property rights, as well as enjoying them.

By 1960, the Basic Agrarian Law was introduced for all of Indonesia. This was not only to establish a compromise between smallholders and plantation agriculture, but to create a uniform national legal framework to accommodate public and private interests in forestry and agriculture. The Basic Agrarian Law continues to be central in the regulation of landed property in Indonesia, but its comprehensive character lends itself to contradiction, a theme I shall develop further in Chapter 4. The law promises land reform, but also firmly establishes state control over the country's land resources and says that any local interests are subordinate to state interest.[20] The question therefore remains: whose interests translate into state interests?

New Order and Reformasi

Confrontations between peasants and planters continued during the early 1960s. However, the organizations that embodied the conflict had changed over the previous decades, and the field of agrarian struggle came to be populated by new actors in new alliances. Colonial planters, indentured labor, and princes and sultans were no longer the lead actors in the conflict. Instead, certain parts of government, with support from the military, the many nationalist youth gangs associated with the military, as well as rural Islamic elites and foreign capital now backed the concept of plantations, whereas other parts of government, and especially the peasant movements and the Communist Party, championed smallholder and peasant interests. In 1963, the peasant movements and the Communist Party began land occupations through what became known as "unilateral action movements" (*gerakan aksi sepi*) against landlords throughout Indonesia and especially the plantation belt of North Sumatra (Afiff and Lowe 2007: 89, De Groot Heupner 2016). These land occupations were cut short, however, by the coup d'état in 1965. Sukarno's reign and various government efforts at implementing the land reform elements of the Basic Agrarian Law were abruptly terminated by General Suharto's seizure of power. Suharto proclaimed a New Order, the name he gave his regime to mark its distance from Sukarno's "guided democracy" as the old order. In the name of restoring security and order, the government and the army orchestrated persecution of known and alleged communists amid an intense propaganda campaign to dehumanize the Communist Party and legitimate murder and detention on a massive scale.[21] The many farmers who had moved onto Dutch property in anticipation of land reform after independence were forced out, and their attempts to solicit government's active recognition and legalization of land claims failed abysmally.

Suharto's pogrom was largely organized and carried out by paramilitary and civilian youth gangs, Islamist militias, and even student alumni associations encouraged, equipped, and protected by the army (Farid 2005: 4, Huizer 1974, Kammen and McGregor 2012, Karina 2008, Melvin 2018, Robinson 2018, Ryter 1998, *Tempo* 2012).[22] Moreover, local scores of different kinds could be settled by denouncing one's adversary as "communist," thus turning him into an outlaw. For many years after, "land reform" bore the stigma of "communism," and the political category of "communist" became one of total demonization.[23] The pogrom not only dispossessed smallholders of land rights; for people labeled "communist," the very right to have rights was eclipsed.

The New Order regime stood on three pillars of control. Authoritarian rule was justified under an ideology of "organic unity" between state and society, and dissent was regarded as a direct assault on the nation. The memory of the violent persecution and murder of hundreds of thousands of alleged and actual communist sympathizers in 1965 served as a permanent deterrent against voicing opposition. Second, the political party, *Golkar* (*Golonkan Karya*, functional groups), became the political vehicle of the regime. All civil servants were expected to be part of *Golkar*, and to have no competing loyalties. The corporate nature of the organization and its comprehensive reach made the distinction between *Golkar* and the state somewhat academic in many instances. Third, the military had appointments in the legislature and in the bureaucracy at all levels, and, crucially, it had economic interests (Ascher 1998, Aspinall 2005, Crouch 1978, Lindsey 2001, McCulloch 2004, Robison and Hadiz 2004). The different branches of the military had interests in plantations, forests, and oil, and in all the industries connected to them. Thus, while the commercial sector formally became civilian and began to attract foreign investment from the mid-1970s, the military elite continued to have integral interests in the sector.[24] Many officers either went on "inactive duty" or retired to remain in the management and income stream. It meant that peasants, their movements, and their demands for land reform were directly antagonistic to the interests of the regime. Land occupations were seen as an outright attack on the state itself. The government never actually repealed the Basic Agrarian Law. However, it fundamentally changed its orientation. Policies favored large-scale plantation production, and politics favored political cronies.[25] While the government claimed to repossess land with law in hand, "it soon became evident that the new regime preferred a rule of law that was merely a façade for a system driven by political interests, patronage and nepotism" (Bedner 2016b: 25, see also Aspinall and van Klinken 2010, Lindley 2001). Land was distributed to companies controlled by military officers and to political friends under thirty-five-year commercial or plantation leases, and smallholders were forced off the land as squatters (Barber and Talbot 2003, Brown 1999, Gellert 2015, Robison 1986, Robison and Hadiz 2014).[26] Against the force of government and military, small-scale landowners had little legal remedy.

While police and military were often mobilized to subdue social unrest from workers, peasants, and students during the New Order, the youth gangs, the *pemuda*, were central players in street- or field-level politics, some with national coverage, others within a very local ambit. During the New Order, loyalties were with Suharto, the military, and the state party, *Golkar*. And the youth gangs were sometimes the extension of the regime; they worked as its unofficial service of intimidation. They operated in the twilight between racketeering and crime, on the one hand, and performed "regime maintenance chores" with nationalist zeal, on the other (I. Wilson 2015: 16, see also Bakker 2015, 2016, Barker 2001, 2007, King 2003, Lindsey 2001, Ryter 1998, 2002). Generally, from the 1970s the youth gangs became recognized as mass organizations, *ormas* (*Organisasi Kemasyarakatan*) or mass youth organizations (*Organisasi Kemasyarakatan Pemuda*, OKP).[27] This was a particular legal category for a range of non-government community, religious, ethnic, environmental, and welfare organizations engaged in social activities. This label gave the violent organizations legal respectability and, in principle, subjected them to government control. "During the New Order era, the border between paramilitaries and private muscle . . . groups [was] vague as military-trained paramilitary groups were used by the regime to carry out illegal violent and repressive actions against the civilian population. In exchange for their allegiance, these groups were allowed to engage in criminal activities and usually confirmed their loyalty by paying part of the profits they generated through violence, extortion, and other crimes to their patrons. Such . . . violence and criminality were normalized as practices affiliated with the regime and maintained through patrimonial alliances to the ruling elite" (Bakker 2015: 80–81).

From 1998, *Reformasi* opened a new path for democratization and a series of decentralization reforms that provided increased autonomy to local government. This appeared to be an open moment offering opportunities to transform society, including agrarian structures, and once again, land occupations accompanied the protests. A large number of student organizations, labor unions, and peasant movements were astir throughout Indonesia, putting democratic, social, and land reforms on the agenda (see Aji 2005, Anugrah 2015, 2018, Gilbert and Afrizal 2018, Ford 2009, Ikhsan 2015, Lucas and Warren 2013, Rachman 2011, Vu 2009, White 2016). While these movements acquired better access to politicians during *reformasi*, the agrarian movement never managed to garner sufficient support for a comprehensive redistributive land reform (Vu 2009: 180). Their ideology of anti-capitalist land reform did not enthuse the emerging political powers.

A plethora of political parties also emerged in a new, post–New Order situation of potential pluralism. Some parties were new and many were breakaways from the Suharto regime's corporatist party, *Golkar* (Slater 2010). Decentralization and democratization allowed for the furtherance of the "array of interests nurtured and incubated under the New Order's vast network of patronage. . . . North Sumatra demonstrates [that] elites . . . discovered that democratic institutions—run by money politics and violence—can be just as beneficial as the protection of an outright authoritarian regime" (Hadiz 2003: 121). Many of the politicians in North Sumatra who emerged during the *reformasi* came from local youth organizations and gangs, and the capacity of the *pemuda* to mobilize an electorate came to be valued.[28]

> Clearly, goons and thugs are particularly well-placed in a system
> of power in which the capacity to deploy, or at least threaten, vio-

lence is important in securing the control of the local apparatus of the state. They are particularly sought after given the enforced retreat of the military from an overt role in politics. Besides providing muscle for candidates, the leaders of youth organizations— because they preside over lucrative underworld enterprises—are able to fund political bids. With their muscle and money, they are also potentially capable of influencing policy decisions and debate in the local parliament, including those regarding allocation of contracts and other resources. They are thus an integral part of the workings of Indonesia's new democracy. (Hadiz 2003: 128)[29]

The past 150 years' struggle over land in North Sumatra has been persistent and changing at the same time. Plantations have remained a very dominant land use for most of the time, whereas actors, their interests, and alliances have changed. The broad brush-strokes of North Sumatra's checkered history show one thing very clearly: acquired rights and authority can be fickle. Rights can disappear with a regime, and regimes that promise to endure can dissolve very swiftly. This does not make legalization and its paperwork irrelevant; on the contrary, it produces layers of it.

The contrast between violently and radically changing regimes, on the one hand, and the persistence of plantation agriculture is stark. But the historical perspective offers a straightforward explanation. Plantation agriculture had been a colonial invention with all its racist and inhuman trappings, and thereby represented what people hated about colonial domination. Nonetheless, with independence it had become an *Indonesian* economic sector solidly grounded in new interests served by it.

Big pictures are made up of little ones. And an exclusive focus on the aggregated history will make us lose sight of the hodgepodge of dilemmas and challenges people faced in real time. The long run may be very important to people, but the short run holds the ace of immediate urgency. In order to better understand how people operated through radical change at the time without the benefit of divination, we take a closer look at how people and institutions operated to access and control land and legalize their possession. Here, we will see the unequal ability to effectively legalize possession despite opportunities through regime change and pro-peasant policies. The following is a detailed presentation of one case of long-drawn conflict.

Legalizing Land Claims on the Ground

The 699 ongoing conflicts mentioned earlier in this chapter are worth keeping in mind when we dive into the specificities of a single one of them. Events have not unfolded exactly in the same way everywhere, but this particular case fits into a general pattern. It is one of shifting but constantly strong interests in plantation rights. Between these a relentless struggle for possession involves physical presence, violence, and intimidation, and is accompanied by fervent attempts to legalize and illegalize claims. Finally, the conflict displays a remarkable longevity.

The village of Pergulaan, a drive of some three hours from Medan in Deli Serdang, is home to 3,500 people. Since 1968, when the land around them was taken by government for plantation concession, the village—a set of hamlets—has been an enclave inside large plantation complexes. Access goes through plantations on company roads. Over the years, people have seen what they believed to be their land taken over by plantation companies, and the emerging history of the village is one of push and shove. On one side are the plantation companies, government agencies, and the judiciary, together with various forms of enforcement—the army, the police, and private violent gangs. On the other side are the smallholders, their peasant movement, NGOs, Legal Aid, and various media.

The initial cultivation of the area dates back to the early twentieth century. In 1911, the company, London-Sumatra (LonSum), obtained a 75-year lease to produce rubber on approximately 5,400 hectares in the area.[30] The workforce was indentured labor blackbirded from Java. During the occupation, the Japanese encouraged a partial conversion of the plantation into food-producing smallholdings to support the war effort. The early years after Independence in 1945 were unstable. Workers-turned-smallholders continued to farm most of what had been plantation as well as what they had cleared themselves. However, LonSum recommenced its operations on the part of the plantation which had not been converted to food crops during the war.

The Emergency Law No. 8 of 1954 was meant to halt all agrarian conflicts by a "standfast." To the villagers, this standfast meant government acceptance of their claims to land they had acquired by occupation, and that this land would be part of a land-reform program. At the time, it seemed a way of legalizing the actual situation. However, LonSum contested this de facto expropriation of the lease in court, as acquiescence would, no doubt, have been seen as an invitation to further land occupation. The judge's decision was to confirm the status quo: LonSum could continue to operate the part of the plantation the company actually controlled, but it was not allowed to extend it; equally, the smallholders were allowed to continue to farm what they had already occupied and farmed, but they could not extend their possessions either. Lands were surveyed and registered by the District Agricultural Service, and from 1957 members of the community began to pay land tax to the district office. They received tax receipts and land use certificates (Land Occupation Registration Card, *Kartu Tanda Pendaftaran Pendudukan Tanah*).[31] Formally, none of the certificates entailed any land rights; they simply stated a "fact," that so-and-so resides on this particular land. Moreover, they were not supposed to be transacted to any third party. Nonetheless, they were seen as government legalization of individual land claims. People set great store by them, and these cards would keep turning up later and into the present, when card holders still attribute different forms of rights to them. Likewise, LonSum's part of the area was certified. Since Dutch-owned plantations throughout the country were all taken over, this compromise and its registration seemed to have saved LonSum from outright nationalization by a whisker.

So far, the confrontation between smallholders and LonSum had not been violent. Both parties seemed to have been probing claims throughout the 1950s within a government structure that lacked any distinct center. Old Dutch concessions versus Japanese permissions—both obsolete in all likelihood—were interpreted in a context of government and military standfasts, high-pitched cries for nationalization, and the physical presence of the opponent: they could produce any outcome imaginable. Such confidence in documents, held by both parties, may seem naive. It is worth recalling, though, that everyone was acting in the face of utmost uncertainty, with the future in the balance.

In 1959, however, LonSum claimed some 35 hectares in a smaller neighborhood of Pergulaan. The company managed to convince the local government of the legitimacy of its claim, and had a violent eviction organized by the police. By 1961 the area was planted with oil palms. This was the first openly violent confrontation between villagers and the company. It was not to be the last.

With Suharto's ascendancy to power in 1965, the company applied for a renewal of the lease and obtained a thirty-year extension running from 1968. This resulted in a series of larger evictions, and in 1972 LonSum and its subsidiaries had regained control over the 5,400 hectares making up the original concession from 1911. Moreover, another company, Harrison & Crossfield, acquired a concession of 4,000 hectares neighboring the Lon-Sum concession.[32] The village of Pergulaan was now effectively enclosed by plantations, even though the evicted smallholders continued to hold their Land User Registration Certificate proving land tax payment, and thereby some legitimate claim to the land. The evictions were part of the government's persecution of communists, carried out by army and police assisted by groups of youth gangs. Plantation security personnel threatened people who did not give up their land with garotting by steel wire, and some were detained in the company's warehouses. As one inhabitant of Pergulaan explained, "There is no fear worse than being accused of membership of the Communist Party."[33] The district administration further tried to collect all the villagers' land use certificates, making any future claims from smallholders more difficult to lodge because the paper trail of legalized claims disappeared. According to Harrison & Crossfield, some measure of compensation was offered to the smallholders who gave up farming, but this was consistently denied by our informants. The community's pleas to the provincial governor of North Sumatra, the chairman of parliament, and the district governor were all in vain. People had to abandon their farms. Some took up work as plantation labor; others migrated to town, or combined small jobs with seasonal migration.

In 1985, LonSum had people evicted from another 5 hectares adjacent to the plantation. The actual eviction was conducted by one of the most notorious youth gangs, *Pemuda Pancasila* (Youth of the Five Principles of the Nation), working as a private extension of the army.[34] This eviction prompted villagers to contact the National Land Agency to investigate whether the land in question was actually within the lease of the company. However, there was no response. In 1997, some ten years on, LonSum acquired and renewed a lease including the contested area for another twenty-five years. Just before the downfall of Suharto in 1998, the people of Pergulaan, like many others in Indonesia, formed a farmer's movement, Movement for the Struggle of the People of Pergulaan (*Badan Perjuangan Masyarakat Pergulaan*, BPMP), and demonstrated in front of the district governor's office in Deli Serdang. The people of Pergulaan and their newly founded movement received support from the neighboring peasant union (*Serikat Petani Serdang Bedagai*), local and national organizations such as Bitra (*Bina Keterampilan Pedesaan Indonesia*, the Activator for Rural Progress), Legal Aid, Medan, Sawit Watch, and the National Human Rights Commission, as well as one of the students' unions. This convinced the district governor to organize a stakeholder meeting, and, in the atmosphere of impending dramatic change, it was—once again—quite unpredictable what the outcome would be.

At the meeting, the representative from LonSum offered to hand back some 165 hectares that he acknowledged *could possibly* have been unlawfully obtained. However, a couple of months later, before any land was handed over, LonSum informed the police that the company still needed the land and could not give it up after all. This produced renewed anger among the villagers, and the district governor wrote to his superior, the provincial governor, to inform him that LonSum had reneged on its promise. Villagers even wrote to the British embassy in the hope that the British government would intervene, considering the name of the company. Receiving no replies, they occupied the 165 hectares again. They mapped and divided it into plots and began to farm in cleared spaces between the tree trunks. The farmers put up a sign that read,

> Farmers' ownership of this land is guaranteed by the Emergency Law no. 8 of 1955, and Decree of the Minister no. 36/HGU/1978.[35]

In December 1999, the company mobilized 600 men from the police mobile brigade, *brimob,* and from the youth gangs, *Pam Swakarsa* and *Pemuda Pancasila,* armed with clubs and dressed in army-style fatigues. Houses and gardens were vandalized as people were violently attacked.[36] LonSum replaced the sign put up by the villagers with a new one stating,

> Plantation.
> Squatters will be prosecuted according to the Penal Code 551.

From that moment and over the six weeks that followed, 50 *brimob* and between 20 and 100 members of *Pam Swakarsa* and *Pemuda Pancasila* stationed themselves at the edge of the village. Still, villagers stealthily moved back at night, poisoning palm trees by injecting them with insecticide. When the trees died, and palm oil production was impossible, people moved back into some areas. As a result, naked palm trunks would stand tall in certain parts of the plantation, telling the trained eye that this land was farmed by a stubborn smallholder. At this point, villagers also went to the district office of the National Land Agency to complain. The provincial office of the National Land Agency and the provincial governor had already confirmed the leases and dismissed the farmers' demands. LonSum dismissed all demands and suggested the farmers take legal action instead. In this period around the downfall of the New Order and the unsteady emergence of the *reformasi,* hopes were high among the villagers of Pergulaan, but the institutional uncertainty remained equally obvious.

Again, in 2001, smallholders tried to occupy land. This time more than 500 farmers attempted to settle on a substantial part of the plantation. The *brimob,* armed in riot gear, as well as squads from *Pam Swakarsa* and *Pemuda Pancasila* hired by the company, managed to push people off the land. This was repeated twice more during 2001. However, one achievement of the occupation attempts seems to have been that Pergulaan's resistance managed

Dead oil palm trunks, poisoned with insecticide, North Sumatra (Photo: Erwin Sipahutar)

to convince the National Land Agency to investigate the plantation land in order to look for evidence of village settlement in the plantation area. First, the National Land Agency found significant discrepancies between the map based on satellite imagery and the limits and boundaries of the lease.[37] Second, on the ground there was evidence of grave sites, wells, and other traces of habitation located among the oil palms. The argument was that since there was such evidence of settlement, the plantation could not have expanded without conflict, and if the land had been under dispute no lease should have been issued. This notwithstanding, the National Land Agency report did not produce any material change.

Five years later, in March 2004, 400–600 members of the peasant organization organized another occupation of 15 hectares. By this time, however, the government under President Megawati had passed Plantations Act No. 18 of 2004, criminalizing squatters in plantations. Squatting was no longer seen as a political act, but simply as a criminal offense. This response harked back to the Suharto years: the following day, seven leaders of the land occupation were arrested and sentenced to a year in jail. This was part of a wave of arrests in North Sumatra and elsewhere.[38] Following the sentence, a gang of armed men from *Pemuda Pancasila* was deployed to harry the villagers, destroying their vegetable gardens and spreading fear. Moreover, LonSum dismissed all casual laborers from the village, and 100 women lost their incomes. Another attempt at mediation was then initiated by the district governor. LonSum made a measured concession: it would hire villagers for road maintenance inside the plantation, and pay compensation for the destruction of village houses and the mosque by the thugs — *preman* — on its payroll.[39]

In 2006, two lawsuits were initiated in parallel. The population of Pergulaan filed a civil lawsuit against LonSum, the Indonesian National Police, the Armed Forces of Indonesia, the Ministry of the Interior, and the National Land Agency. As described in the introduction above, this eventually fell flat; but not without pettifoggery. The district court dismissed the villagers' land certificates as "issued by Communists during the Sukarno years," thereby, in principle, undercutting all government documents between 1945 and 1965. In the appeal to the High Court and the Supreme Court of Cassation, the judge dismissed the entire case as having expired despite the fact that there is no legal expiration limit in agrarian conflicts. The judge simply applied an element of Dutch law and nimbly closed the case. It was beyond the means of the villagers to unwind it again.[40] The other court case was conducted by LonSum against 11 people from Pergulaan on the criminal charges (now pressed again since the Plantation Act of 2004) of land occupation. Seven people were fined and sentenced to a year in prison. The two cases legalized the company's land claims and illegalized the villagers' attempt to vent theirs. The people of Pergulaan, who had expected the tables to turn with the post-Suharto *reformasi,* could ill disguise their disappointment.

Subsequent attempts at occupation took place in 2006 and 2007. In October 2007, a team of workers from LonSum, escorted by the *brimob,* began to dig a trench with bulldozers at the edge of Pergulaan. The trench — a veritable fosse, 4 meters deep and 3 meters wide — cut across the only access road to the village, and physically penned it in. People protested and tried to obstruct the excavation, but at the end of the day, a kilometer-long moat made children's access to school and adults' access to their fields within the plantation very difficult. The villagers made several further attempts at land occupation. These were all smaller areas of 5–15 hectares. Nonetheless, the picture was the same. In numerous confrontations, women formed human barriers to protect the crops and buildings. Security staff, often accompanied by plantation workers and chaperoned by *brimob* in riot gear, and different contingencies of *preman* from the various youth gangs, destroyed the crops and physically removed the farmers from the land. In 2006, the regional office of the National Land Agency organized a meeting with the participation of its legal team and the land tax office, the police, and police intelligence, as well as LonSum and their legal team, to meet with the peasant movement from Pergulaan accompanied by two local NGOs. The issue was the 165 hectares grabbed by LonSum's latest extension.[41] The meeting ended with reassurances that the district administration would set up a field team to investigate the facts on the ground. Yet no further steps were taken.

In the years that followed, trespassing and reclamation, as well as sabotage and vandalism, continued to fill local police reports. The Plantation Act was actively used in Pergulaan, across North Sumatra and Indonesia, to evict smallholders from what government agencies considered plantation land. As people were losing land, they became all the more dependent on salaried work; either far from the village or as workers on the plantation. However, working on the plantation brought its own problems. The leaders of the peasant movement considered it treacherous for local people to work for the enemy, even if it was the only source of income in the vicinity. And plantation workers from Pergulaan were indeed actively encouraged by the plantation foremen to inform on any seditious activity in the village. This was a dilemma some endured under pressure and humiliation and others tried to resolve by leaving the village altogether.

In 2011, villagers from Pergulaan (with the help of the Consortium for Agrarian Reform) managed to take their case to the Constitutional Court.[42] The objective was to undo the Plantation Act of 2004 that criminalized land occupations. This court had just recognized indigenous peoples' property rights to forests in a spectacular ruling (Fay and Denduangrudee, 2016, Rachman 2013, Rachman and Siscawati 2016, Wells et al. 2012), and the movement and villagers were hopeful. The Constitutional Court eventually ruled that several articles of the Plantation Act were contrary to the protection of indigenous peoples' land rights and that they were ambiguous and had been applied arbitrarily. The ruling concluded that the application of criminal sanction was excessive and that consultation and negotiation should be the path ahead. This was a small victory for the villagers of Pergulaan, yet their achievements through the legal system made the path ahead look awfully similar to the path of small incursions and brutal evictions already traveled.

Conclusion

The contrast between frequent regime changes and political unrest, on the one hand, and 150 years of plantation economy on the other, is a conundrum. Property contracts have been negotiated in North Sumatra at every rupture. Established rights have been temporarily suspended and turned into claims addressed to new authorities to whom the claimants would henceforth be beholden. Yet, mostly, these new authorities have had the power to define land rights with reference to state interests. In this turmoil plantation agriculture has proved remarkably resilient, and when we look at this dynamic historically a pattern emerges. While each rupture in the political system promised radical change, new dominant groups soon acquired stakes in the continuation of the structures against which they once fought. Although the actual protagonists changed, the structural interests remained. Moreover, the new stakeholders had the legal groundwork available to legalize and consolidate them. And for changing governments with different agrarian policies, revenue would ultimately appear to be much easier to capture from agriculture if capital was concentrated than if property was spread among hundreds of thousands of smallholders. Thus, plantation agriculture represented a target for resistance at one point, and a source of prosperity at another, for anti-colonialists, for the military, for youth organizations and gangsters—for all, it would seem, but the smallholders whose prospects for effective land rights have tended to dwindle.

At every turn, different actors have referred to the law when mobilizing documents and other evidence of their rights. All of these claims have been contingent, driven by interest, and essentially arbitrary. Still, legalization has served to bestow upon them an element of universal neutrality. The initial colonizers in North Sumatra endowed the class of sultans with land rights by what we might call "oriental natural law" backed by force. Since then, possession of land has become a right established by changing governments and their issuance of different forms of documentation. Hence, when governments fell and regimes changed because of social upheaval, war, or revolution, military coup, or democratization, the legal relics of past regimes retained some currency. Even during the most dramatic social change, when entire polities were made redundant, the idea of law's stability and trans-historical permanence seemed to prevail, and documents have been important to give claims an air of legality.

If law seems sometimes to have been applied without connection to specific interests—blind to the context—it is hard not to take the context into consideration, all the same. The court cases described above in the chapter's introduction, where certain government documents were invalidated and expiry dates were simply invented, are cases in point. People trusted government documents enough to keep them safe for decades, yet the judge could illegalize them on obvious political grounds. And at the time of the eviction in 1974, anyone would have known full well that a court case against the army and police, or against the company and the government, would have been foolhardy. Any such act would have incurred accusations of communism and brutal violence from the regime. Consequently, letting a case expire under such circumstances looks more deliberate than blind.

Despite law and legal proof, possession has often been secured by force. Property rights in land in the plantation belt in North Sumatra have more often than not started in illegality by thwarting the rights and rights holders of the time. Land occupations by peasant groups, youth gangs, and the military defied planters' rights in attempts to change the facts on the ground.

Sometimes they succeeded. In the earlier history, this resistance was driven by nationalist anti-colonial ideas, and for the peasant groups by outright anti-capitalist visions of peasant land control. More enduringly, though, plantation companies have organized evictions of smallholders even if the farmers held official documents in support of their claims. Sometimes, this was conducted by government agencies acting *ultra vires*, by the promotion of an unregulated process of violent dispossession of smallholders, and the subsequent confirmation of a new body of rights holders. Sometimes possession has been acquired by more amorphous providers of plantation security, such as gangs. Possession, violently acquired, was thereupon laundered as rightful property through the medium of law, and the last tenth of legalization consolidated the nine-tenths of possession.

Historically, plantation companies—public and private alike—have been the adversaries of smallholders. They have overcome several crises only through intervention by police and military, and with violence delivered by various contracted gangs. Outsourcing law and property enforcement to private gangs and militias has been an integral part of public authority, with the added feature of deniability for companies and government.

The legality of land claims has not been equally important at all times for companies like LonSum. In periods of turmoil, when nationalization was looming in the 1950s, or when the notion of land reform was reintroduced amid massive land occupations during *reformasi*, it was too risky to rely on the raw power of possession. During these moments of regime change—impending or real—LonSum and other companies would rely on documents, negotiation, compromise, and even accept the potential legality of smallholders' claims. During the New Order's hegemonic control when their possession was not in jeopardy, on the other hand, companies' concern for legality seems to have been secondary.

Despite numerous setbacks, smallholders have continually justified their land occupations and land claims with reference to the law. This is not because they were ignorant of the manipulation of the law, or its corruption by police, army, judges, and bureaucrats. Nor did they dream naively in the power of the law. But just as legalization has been seen by companies as an instrument to secure rights into the next regime, so for smallholders the preservation of certificates, documentation of claims through hearings, and recording of individual testimonies of violence and abuse have been ways of preserving the rightfulness, or at least the integrity, of their claims into the future. In this way, law lends life to the hope that injustice can be reversed.

The villagers of Pergulaan did enjoy several small victories along the way. No doubt *reformasi* and a more open political atmosphere in Indonesia, together with the relatively benign outcomes in recent Constitutional Court rulings, have stimulated hope among them. In the course of events, the villagers of Pergulaan have received support from important NGOs and political movements. However, while some success has been registered, fatigue has set in as well. The main characters in the village movement are second- or third-generation participants in this struggle, and even they are getting on in years. Many of the younger generation have left the village for brighter futures elsewhere, and even if conditions for footloose rural youth in North Sumatra were always tough, the fact remains: many have left. The prospects are rather cheerless for ordinary people in places like Pergulaan. Neither evictions, nor occupations, have been complete successes. Small fields of corn, cassava, bananas, and other smallholder crops alternate with larger patches of oil palm. This speckled landscape seems stabilized for the time being. Each opponent seems to keep the other in check—the plantation with vandalism and violence, and the villagers with more pointed nightly raids wielding syringes. Nevertheless, the story raises the uncomfortable question: who will be around to appreciate small legal victories if the community has already incurred defeat by attrition?

The next chapter focuses on how claims to land and identity intertwine. It shows how indirect recognition may offer a pragmatic substitute for impossible land rights and provide indirect legalization.

CHAPTER THREE

Indirect Recognition

Property and Citizenship Around Mount Halimun-Salak National Park

*J*ika negara tidak mengakui kami, maka kami tidak akan mengakui negara. If the state will not recognize us, we will not recognize the state. This was the slogan of 400 indigenous leaders
forming the congress of the Indigenous Peoples' Alliance of the
Archipelago, *Aliansi Masyarakat Adat Nusantara* (AMAN), in
March 1999. Customary law had been subordinated to statutory
law since colonization, and customary land rights had always had
to yield to national policy interests. A decade later, however, the
Constitutional Court ruled that indigenous communities did indeed have territorial rights, and that customary forests were not
state forests (No. 35/puu-x/2012). While this opened the legal possibility for establishing community control over forest resources,
the actual realization of recognized rights seems to have only just
begun. It foreshadowed a long process of pragmatic micro-politics
of recognition.

Mount Halimun-Salak was declared a national park (covering some 113,000
hectares) by the Indonesian government in 2003.[1] This meant dispposses-
sion and possible displacement of the local population. The area around
Mount Halimun straddles West Java and Banten provinces within three regencies (Bogor, Sukabumi, and Lebak).[2] Previously, the area around Mount

Halimun had been categorized as "forest" and was legally under the control of the Ministry of Forestry. Based on its gazetted status in the earlier Dutch colonial period, the Indonesian government had declared 40,000 hectares of Mount Halimun a "nature reserve" in 1979.[3] In 2000, a drought compromised the water supply to Jakarta, a mere 100 kilometers away, and the year after, flooding in the area left more than 60,000 people homeless and in need of temporary relocation. Studies showed, moreover, that forest cover in the Mount Halimun area had been reduced by 25 percent between 1989 and 2001 (JICA 2006). This became a national issue, certain government agencies joined conservationists in pressing for action, and the outcome was the decree in 2003. The reclassification of the area as a national park and its extension to cover more than twice the original area provoked a series of conflicts over territory, property, and authority.

Over time, during the colonial period and after, governments have exerted great efforts to control this land, and many people have had to give up land to plantation companies, to mining companies, and to different departments and companies within the Ministry of Forestry, all claiming territorial jurisdiction. As a consequence, many people have worked on the plantations, and over the last few decades, many young men and women have been forced off the land to seek work in towns.[4]

Displacement and relocation were therefore not new patterns in the area. The reclassification of Halimun in 2003 was so contentious because it happened in the course of a major regime change in Indonesia. Democratization and decentralization from 1998 had opened new spaces for political activities and changed opportunities for protest and territorialization from below. During the New Order, public administration had been centralized, militarized, and made upwardly accountable, while opposition was difficult and dangerous. With *reformasi*, social movements sprang up and voiced claims to land and rights in public ways, which had been impossible during the previous thirty years of authoritarian rule. Asserting sovereign power to order space, government was met by counterclaims from below. Many of these claims were directly territorial and focused on land, but others were expressed around identity and indigeneity (McCarthy 2005, McCarthy and Warren 2009). In practice, however, claims for property and citizenship often intertwine. They sometimes concatenate, where one successful claim leverages the realization of the next, which would otherwise have been futile.

I therefore develop the concept of indirect recognition as a key mechanism in acquiring effective land rights. This is followed by an analysis of government-citizen encounters in West Java and the dynamics of recognition in the fields of government territorialization, taxation, local organization, and identity politics. Finally, case studies of Nyungcung and Parigi settlements in the Nanggung subdistrict illustrate how people fashion their past and origin in order to create possibilities for indirect recognition of their property claims.

Indirect Claims, Indirect Recognition

Property rights and citizenship are fundamental to spatial control, and they intertwine in several ways. Conceptually, both are about recognition of a claim by a relevant authority or public. Claims to resources become property rights of different kinds and degrees when they are effectively recognized. Likewise, membership of an organized political body—the Indonesian nation, the indigenous community, or both—becomes citizenship in a broad sense when the membership and its entitlements are endorsed and enforced. Concretely, too, property and citizenship braid together. The recognition of one often effectively produces a recursive recognition of the other. This is indirect recognition. Simply put, property rights may entitle someone to full political membership of a polity. In fact, through time, many societies have reserved formal political participation for the propertied classes. Thus, claims to citizenship may be lodged by demonstrating landed property rights and tax payment. And the other way around works as well; property rights are often reserved for particular groups classified as rights subjects in a general way. Throughout the world, rights subjects have been stratified according to gender, race, and caste, as well as class, creed, and conviction. Hence, claims to property may be asserted by demanding rights-bearing identity or citizenship. Recognition of such indirect claims—indirect recognition—is peculiar in two ways. First, an indirect claim is usually a direct claim to something with an embedded indirect claim to something else. A direct claim to political identity may be an indirect land claim. It is usually addressed to the institution with the authority to recognize the direct claim. Yet, authorizing indirect claims can be effective, and sometimes even extend the institution's authority, as we will see below. Indirect recognition may be deliberate or sometimes more unintended. In a context of legal and institutional pluralism, different configurations can, no doubt, be expected. The other peculiarity of indirect recognition has to do with time. Indirect recognition can be effective immediately or it can hibernate. Just as unacknowledged claims can be stored for future more propitious moments, so can obsolete indirect recognition be retrieved from history when an opportunity emerges.

State projects of control, taxation, conscription, confiscation, and eviction make people suspicious of government authority, and have driven people into clandestine responses with good reason (Scott 2009). For many people, however, the grim reality is—to paraphrase Oscar Wilde—that there is only one thing worse than being seen by political authority, and that is not being seen. Not to be seen as a rights subject means that resources can only be accessed surreptitiously; it delegitimizes the claim from the person or group vis-à-vis government. Choices and strategies of visibility and obscurity therefore depend on the context, on the authorities' ambitions and resources, and on people's available options. The authoritarian regime under Suharto, thus, made direct land claims dangerous for ordinary people without connections to the regime (Aspinall and van Klinken 2010, Hefner 1990, Klinken 2018, Lucas and Warren 2013, Peluso 1992). Yet, total invisibility was not desirable either. Fortunately, total obscurity is not the only alternative to direct claims. Rather than direct claims to property or space, it may be safer to seek recognition as rights subjects whose claims are only indirectly tied to property. By payment of tax, and acquiring fiscal visibility, one way or another, one enters into the purview of particular institutions. One becomes visible. Such visibility—fiscal, cultural, political, economic, and so on—may be the first step to recognition as a rights subject with legalized claims. People improvise to present themselves and their claims in ways that are visible and meaningful to the appropriate institution of authority, as well as to a public for more general support. Maps, surveys, regulations and written settlements (customary as well as statutory), memos, tax receipts, fines, permissions, and authorizations all form traces of decisions peppering the political field as actual and potential reference points for spatial claims. They become signs of indirect recognition of land claims. Some of these fragments of recognition may have been insignificant and have had no effective meaning before, but now, in a new context, they become potent "proof" of the rightfulness of claims. They can facilitate the legalization of the claim they represent. Indirect recognition may not stand up in court, but most people live most of their lives outside the courtroom, and in everyday situations, indirect recognition can perform important work in delivering certain rewards of legalization.

This chapter examines ways in which statutory institutions categorized and ordered space around Mount Halimun in West Java, and how they dissolved and deleted prior rights and entitlements by the same token. This includes a focus on how local people operated within and around spatial and legal categories in order to reestablish recognized and legalized access to land and resources. Especially, the analysis centers on ways in which localized dynamics of spatial control took place *through* rather than *against* government recognition, and did so in indirect ways.

Government and Citizen Visibility

The first part of this section serves a dual purpose, namely as an analysis of the historical competition among statutory institutions, and as a context for the discussion of government's indirect recognition of land rights through collection of property tax, and the recognition of the local population as indigenous citizens. In order to be able to tax people, government must have a minimum of spatial control, and categorization of people inevitably accompanies such organization. However, taxation and categorization also carry an emancipatory potential to be harnessed from below. Hence, the first part of the section is a story told mainly from the perspective of the legislators and government administrators, who found it hard to control the facts on the ground and, as a result, found legalities piling up in multiple layers. By contrast, the rest of the section is told from the perspective of opportunities seized by the population.

Government Territorialization of Halimun-Salak

Codification of people's rights to resources and the establishment of government agencies to exercise authority over land use were fundamental in colonial rule in Indonesia in general, and in Java in particular (Breman 1983). A few significant legal instruments established the deep structure of tenure legislation and have informed much of the politics of land to this day. According to the Forestry Law (1865) and the Agrarian Law (1870), all land for which there was no civil law ownership or title was, by default, considered state land (Slaats et al. 2009, Wallace 2008). The territorial sovereignty expressed in these laws was "understood to include the state's right and duty to create, recognize, document, adjudicate, and protect all land and natural resource rights" (Peluso and Vandergeest 2001: 773, Peluso 1991, 1992).[5] This meant that all prior rights were overwritten and expunged, or at least reduced to practices that were tolerated as long as they did not go against state interests.

Forest policies dispossessed local people of rights to the forests they inhabited. The Forest Service enforced policies of exclusion with varying degrees of zeal. Principles of what was known as scientific forestry were used to justify government-managed forest plantations where production and extraction were the primary aims. From the early twentieth century, new concerns about nature conservation were added to the rationalities of production, and the Forestry Service began to declare upland areas for Forest Reserves. The declared intention was to protect lowland agriculture, control erosion, and preserve water resources. By 1932, some 1.7 million hectares had been marked out as State Reserved Forest in Java (Peluso and Vandergeest 2001: 782, see also Peluso 1991, 1992). From 1865 till 1927, a series of ordinances were passed, tightening the government hold on the resources and, with increasing precision, criminalizing local people's very presence in the area (Peluso and Vandergeest 2001).

Between 1904 and 1939, the Dutch colonial government gazetted some 48,000 hectares of the area around Mount Halimun in West Java as forest reserve.[6] The many people who lived there and farmed the area were thereby legally dispossessed. For some administrators on the ground, this presented intolerable dilemmas that asked them to choose between securing people's livelihoods and enforcing government spatial planning. Thus, the "Resident of Banten took an initiative by legalizing [local people's] land [rights] through Resident Decree No. 10453/7/1924. This decree allowed the cultivators to farm their lands based on rent right with unlimited period, but with restricted area. Furthermore, it gave an authority to village leaders to allocate and distribute land to the shifting cultivators. [Between] 1901 and 1925, the Banten Residency distributed about 100 hectares of land for shifting cultivation" (Galudra et al. 2008: 24).[7]

The colonial Forest Service, on the other hand, did not pay heed to any such rights accorded to shifting cultivators by the Colonial Resident. In the conflict over jurisdiction between these colonial institutions, the Forest Service ordered jail sentences for large numbers of farmers. In 1922 alone, 3,000 people were reported jailed for farming within the boundaries of the forest reserve (Galudra et al. 2008: 25). During this period, a further 93 hectares of dwellings and farmland were included in the reserve and the local population was compensated and forced to move. The records do not say whether people actually moved out but reports on continued "infringement" of the gazetted state forest zone would suggest that eviction was incomplete. The turmoil of the Japanese occupation and Indonesian independence in 1945 may explain why no clear settlement was reached in the following years.[8] As a result, there are many places in the Mount Halimun area where contradictory claims can find backing in statutory legal decisions.

The Basic Agrarian Law of 1960 was an attempt to develop a uniform legal system of land administration. Yet, while the Basic Agrarian Law putatively covers Indonesia, no governments, and especially no ministries with responsibility for forestry, have ever recognized the law as valid for areas declared "state forest." Instead, each resource has had its own law, and each "of these laws seems to create an independent regulatory system implemented by autonomous state agencies" (Safitri 2010: 71, see also Sahide and Giessen 2015). The Forestry Law of 1967 categorized over 70 percent of Indonesia as "forest" and under the jurisdiction of the new Ministry of Forestry. The many categories of "state forest" represent an equivalent number of government agencies with jurisdictions, such as the Forest Service, the State Forest Corporation, and National Parks.[9] Thus, the greater part of the national territory came "under the direct jurisdiction of the Forestry Service and [was] considered by administrative convention, but not by law, to be excluded from the jurisdiction of the National Land Administration and the Department of Agriculture" (Colchester et al. 2003: 135). This basically confirmed the colonial legislation from 1865, and was a measure to claw back "forests" from the jurisdiction of the Ministry of Home Affairs and the National Land Agency responsible for the Basic Agrarian Law.

Administratively declaring an area as "forest"—and thus overlaying community lands with different zones for logging, plantation, and protection—effectively disenfranchised the resident population. However, the legalization of the classification of "forest" suffered from significant formal deficiencies. Especially, the delineation was incomplete. As a result, around the year 2000 as much as 90 percent of Indonesia's "State Forest lands [had] uncertain legality" (Colchester et al. 2003: 141). Nonetheless, the ministry was strong enough to control state forest land with uncertain legality during Suharto's New Order, and only in 2011, more than a decade after the end of the New Order, did Constitutional Court rulings challenge its jurisdiction. As a consequence, the area of Indonesia claimed by the ministry was reduced from almost "70 per cent to a mere 14 per cent of the country's land mass" (Bedner 2016a: 76–77). As Bedner explains, *designating* land as forest rather than going through the full process of *gazetting* it was ruled insufficient to bring it under legal control of the ministry.[10] It is a remarkable example of how government authority when dressed in a sufficient air of legality may stick in one context if not in another.

Different government and government-owned institutions tried to territorialize at different scales in the area around Mount Halimun in the 2000s. At the central level, the Planning Agency of the Forestry Department, the Law Bureau in the Forestry Department, the Department of Nature Reserve and Forest Protection, and the State Forest Corporation lodged competing claims to control the area. Two main claims emerged. On the one hand, the first three agencies strongly supported the idea that the area should be classified as a national park. On the other hand, the government-owned commercial enterprise—the State Forest Corporation—saw its logging opportunities dwindle with the proposed new classification, and accordingly was against it. Historical documents studied by Galudra et al. (2008: 11) indicate that the land could be considered state forest, yet the legal status lacked clarity. When government pushed for the reclassification as a national park in the early 2000s many assumed that the extended area had not previously been gazetted as state forest. Even the Planning Agency of the Forestry Department had demarcated no more than 10 percent of the area. In fact, most of the forested area around Mount Halimun had already been gazetted by the Dutch between 1905 and 1930 (Galudra et al. 2008: 12–13). What emerged most clearly, though, was the incomplete availability of relevant information to relevant authorities.

The history of government territorialization of the Halimun area shows three important aspects of the process. First, there has been rivalry between government institutions over spatial control. Not only has control shifted between such institutions, but there has often been a wide gulf between a formal set of rules and actual practice (Bettinger 2015: 255–56). Second, the documentation in terms of registration, gazetting, and delineation is often incomplete and difficult to find; not merely for researchers but for government agencies at different levels and citizens of different stripes. The status of space—whether it is to be viewed as territorialized or as an unsettled frontier—is anything but clear. Hence, current territorialization and legalization rests, to a large extent, on actual practice, including legitimation with reference to what is *believed* to exist in terms of documentation, rather than what documentation can actually be produced. Third, *reformasi* opened up new spaces for political action. Land occupations became frequent in West Java and other parts of Indonesia and were no longer clamped down upon quite as systematically. This provided time to consolidate land holding and engage in strategies that would legalize land use. This means that spatial control was made up of contemporaneous interlacing processes of erasure and elimination of systems of rights and use, on the one hand, and the creation of new institutions, jurisdictions, and spatial representations, on the other. Historical claims from below allow us to examine this. Local people have sought recognition and legalization in two cross-pollinating ways: as taxpaying citizens and as indigenous peoples.

Fiscal Visibility

Taxation is rarely popular. Historically, levies have been imposed rather than welcomed, and they have represented the capacity of rulers to extract resources and control the population. Indonesia is no different. Yet, in authoritarian societies, taxation may be one of the few ways in which government recognizes the presence of people and their access to resources. However unfair the tax, it leaves a trail of acknowledgment of the existence of fiscal — if not legally enfranchised — subjects. Hence, while taxation does not prove property rights, it strongly suggests that someone was there in an open and legitimate way. It holds the potential to become an indirect recognition of something more and adumbrates a social contract.

Indonesia's modern land tax system dates back two hundred years. Initially, the land tax level resulted from a negotiation between the colonial administration and the village leadership, and the contact between the colonial administration and the individual was mediated through local nobilities. From 1810 a land tax was introduced on Java, linking the peasants to the colonial government rather than to indigenous rulers (Elson 1994: 24).[11] While the integrity of the land surveys was doubtful, and a good measure of arbitrariness prevailed, the point is that people now paid directly to government, which recognized and recorded their land use. Although the tax was, in principle, calculated as a proportion of the harvest, in practical terms it translated into a function of the area, and people considered the tax receipt proof of ownership and legalization of their property (Breman 1983, Doorn and Hendrix 1983, Hoardley 1994, Hugenholtz 1994: 141 and 151, Kano 2008: 311–43, Peluso and Vandergeest 2001: 771–79, Svensson 1991, Zanden 2010).

From the 1950s onward, villagers in Java paid tax to the village office, which would transfer the collected tax to the district. Tax receipts were popularly known as "Letter C," after the ledger section in which village administration books would record "land farmed." Such tax transaction was not proof of land ownership in a formal legal sense; nor was it a manifestation of the village administration's authority to control land use. All the same, it was a government acknowledgment that the taxpayers had an income from land, and the popular understanding was that it was legal proof of land holding (Bedner 2016a: 86, Leaf 1994, Simarmata 2012: 61). It was a basis for use-right claims known as *hak girik*.[12] These use rights were treated as tradable commodities among farmers. "Letter C" documents, and the rights perceived to be represented by them, were transacted for money in West Java and in the villages presented below. What this meant in practice would vary, yet it did form an indirect recognition between ordinary people and government.

The system of "Letter C" was managed at village level with significant variation, and it was not until 1985 that a uniform tax for land and buildings (PBB, *Pajak Bumi dan Bangunan*) was introduced. The collected taxes were transferred to the central state for subsequent redistribution to provinces and districts, while distribution to villages was decided by municipal and district government. This was a powerful political instrument for Suharto's central-ized government; it could reward clients and punish areas where the opposi-tion was strong (Slater 2010). From 1999 (but only effective from 2011), the PBB tax was collected and remained at the district and village level.[13]

People's presence in what was later to become a national park around Halimun could hardly be a surprise to the government: taxes had been col-lected from the area since colonial times. The area could not reasonably be considered an unpopulated wilderness when farmers were administratively visible taxpayers. During the 1950s and 1960s, land politics was in turmoil in Indonesia. People were encouraged by government to occupy (especially Dutch-owned) plantations. Smallholders acquired a variety of land certifi-cates of more or less enduring value (Afiff and Lowe 2007, Lucas and Warren 2013, Pelzer 1982). In the area around Halimun, smallholders were invited to have claims legalized as land ownership rights during that time (Galudra et al. 2008: 16), and the local administration issued Land User Registration Certificates (*Kartu Tanda Pendaftaran Pemakai Tanah*, KTPPT). This ran counter to the interests of the Ministry of Forestry, which considered the entire area as Forest Reserve. However, the Ministry of Forestry pursued two—contradictory—strategies to manage this overlap of claims. On the one hand, it contested the validity of the land certificates in court. On the other hand, the Ministry of Forestry engaged in contracts with local farmers who were to pay 25 percent of their harvest profits to the ministry to have access to farm. While the arrangement was legally dubious, the payment of rent certainly strengthened smallholders' claims and sense of tenure security. However, with the reclassification of the forest reserve as a national park in 2003, the Park Authority contested the rent-payment-for-land arrangement.[14] And yet, only a handful of village hamlets — *kampungs* — were officially acknowledged within the national park (in 2012), whereas more than 300 settlements were known within and at the edge of it.[15] These communities enjoyed no direct recognition of land rights from the ministry with territorial jurisdiction (Forestry). But their tax payment served as an indirect recognition of their long-term presence — a voucher to be cashed in if and when the communities gained political visibility as rights subjects.

Adat *and Identity-Based Visibility*

Fiscal or political visibility as an individual taxpayer can be compounded to good effect by visibility as a collective, a community, or a movement. After *reformasi*, the political field opened up for indigenous movements, peasant movements, environmental movements, student movements, workers' movements, and so on.[16] To understand the significance of indigenous movements in the Halimun-Salak area, it is necessary to take a step back and briefly sketch out the politico-legal phenomenon of *adat*.

Adat, or custom, or customary law, is often referred to, not as a coherent system and form, but as a common term for "customary" as applied to "a wide range of varied institutional arrangements found among the diverse indigenous populations" in Indonesia (McCarthy 2005: 58, see also Li 2007). During the colonial era, government, working through indirect rule, selectively elevated certain customs to official customary law if they fitted well into the categories of the colonial enterprise (Benda-Beckmann and Benda-Beckmann 2011: 179). Indeed, formalization and intervention were the salt of colonialism and state formation, and the official idea that statutory and customary law were two distinct, separate, and internally coherent systems, and that *adat* law was an authentic expression of Indonesian legal principles, untouched by the colonial power, was an idealized simplification. As Lev (1985: 66) puts it:

There was . . . the irony that an *adatrechtpolitiek* [a policy of *adat* law], intended to keep local law in local hands, actually reinforced the authority of Dutch-controlled institutions over that law. As *adat* law was understood theoretically to persist best in the closed community, the *adat* researchers tended to write as if local communities *were* closed. Reading . . . studies from the 1920s and 1930s, thorough as many of them are, one is seldom aware of the surrounding Dutch presence of administrative authority, economic enterprise, commercial power, social influence and cultural example. The writers . . . often even seem to deny that they themselves are there. But the villages were not closed communities; and the *adat* law was peculiarly theirs but not theirs. The degree to which it had become a product of Dutch authority was evident in the establishment of *adat* courts by the colonial administration, in the review of *adat* decisions by the *Landraden* [district *adat* courts], in the rendering of decisions in *adat* issues by Dutch *Landraad* judges, in the presence of Dutch officials at *adat* court sessions, in the remarkable research on *adat* that was done by Dutch scholars and by Indonesian scholars trained by Dutch teachers, all of whom wrote in Dutch. Once written, moreover, the *adat* research violated a primary principle of *adat* law theory, that the *adat* lived in local tradition. Now written, it lived in books, which Dutch judges, and Indonesian judges, half a century later, used as if they were codes.

State courts have consistently had immense difficulties in dealing with customary law, especially in land matters. State court judges have tended to act in a formalist manner and rely on codified rules, and the contextual and procedural nature of customary law has looked to them as arbitrary rather than rule bound. The two legalities may not even agree on what are legally relevant facts, and the interface between statutory and customary law has proved to be a minefield of incompatibilities. Hence, whenever it was expedient, statutory categories of property and new political identities were imposed and reproduced through the colonial administration's everyday power to categorize, regulate, and exclude.

After independence, successive Indonesian governments worked to unify the administrative structure and reinforced the philosophy of state owner- ship of land (Wallace 2008: 192). This reduced *adat* to more of a cultural folkloristic expression of identity than a political legal system. In practice, however, government's reach into people's affairs varied greatly throughout the country, and local ways of going about everyday matters in the name of *adat* intertwined with formal government regulation. Thus, while *adat* and statutory arrangements may seem to stand in opposition, the actual practice has been more pragmatic (McCarthy 2005: 79).[17]

The political rupture of *reformasi* gave significant traction to strategic es- sentialization and revival of *adat* as a political rallying point for claims to re- sources and indigenous sovereignty (McCarthy and Warren 2009, Moniaga 2007, Rachman and Siscawaty 2016, Urano 2010). In 1999, the first national congress of indigenous peoples was held, and a federation of indigenous peoples' movements formed as the *Alliansi Masyarakat Adat Nusantara* (Alliance of Indigenous Peoples of Indonesia's Archipelago, AMAN). Their radical rallying call was a refusal to recognize the authority of the state of In- donesia until it recognized theirs (Bakker 2009, Henley and Davidson 2007b: 14). Emboldened by the new situation, these claims for property rights, citi- zenship, and territory were very direct. Since then, a number of remarkable steps have been made by the Indonesian government to recognize indig- enous communities as rights subjects. The Constitutional Court decision of 2012 to recognize communal rights of ownership to forest, and to no longer consider community-owned forest as "state forest," was seen as a watershed— especially since it gave jurisdiction to local government to recognize *adat* communities (Affandi 2016, Arizona 2010, Arizona et al. 2015, Bedner 2016a: 76–85, Rachman 2013, Rachman and Siscawati 2016, Wells et al. 2012).[18]

Difficulties remain, however, in defining what an *adat* community is— even with the issuance of official guidelines—and government agencies and plantation companies have remained more than reluctant to cede au- thority and resources. Hence, while the watershed changes at the national level demonstrate the significance of *adat* in recent resource politics in In- donesia, the realization of the embedded promise of recognition still needs to be hammered out in local everyday politics. Indirect claims to resources and indirect recognition of them as rights play a role here.

In the Halimun area an indigenous group formed in 1999. SABAKI (*Kesatuan Adat Banten Kidul*, Indigenous Unity for Banten Kidul) became a founding member of AMAN and began to lobby with the district governments to implement the increasingly progressive national policies, decrees, and legal rulings. However, they met with procrastination and inaction, as boundary committees and "integrated teams" were formed to produce the legal and cartographic basis for the establishment of *adat* territories (Vitasari and Ramdhaniaty 2015: 22–29). From 2006, SABAKI engaged with the province and district governors to become recognized as an *adat* community. At this time, there was no mention of the land rights attached to the collective identity, but this process stalled as well. However, by 2014, a public hearing of testimonies was organized in Lebak on the momentum of the Constitutional Court decision, and the following year SABAKI, together with a handful of NGOs, the vice-regent, and the Lebak parliament chairman, produced a joint statement to recognize indigenous territories in and around the national park (Vitasari and Ramdhaniaty 2015: 29–33). Whether it will eventually materialize in local *adat* ownership and control over the resources is too early to say. While national legislation created openings for identity-based claims, their actual realization on the ground depends on many small steps. It is therefore worth going into the details of indirect recognition through the incomplete, unfinished, partial, and pragmatic micropolitics of claims making. At this level, selective compliance and partial recognition draw up the contours of everyday resource control.

Cases of Selective Compliance and Indirect Recognition

In the following, I present and discuss the spatial strategic dynamics of recognition in and around two settlements in Nanggung subdistrict, Nyungcung and Parigi, located inside the national park and on the edge of it, respectively. Both cases demonstrate how the boundary between legal and illegal was reworked and claims were legalized by indirect recognition. The cases also differ. The first one shows how the population, through mapping and negotiations with the park authorities, managed to invent new territorial categories. In the second case people made alliances with statutory institutions other than those holding territorial jurisdiction. In both cases, the population claimed indirect recognition in the gray area of partial and pragmatic spatial claims based on a mix of tax payment and indigenous identity in order to continue to reside and farm in what they considered to be their land.

Nyungcung

The settlement of Nyungcung dates back to before the first colonial attempts to establish a forest reserve (Writers Team 2011). While people lived under the threat of eviction, it never materialized in a permanent way during colonial rule. The Provincial Forest Service, which exercised territorial jurisdiction over the area after independence, tolerated some settlements and acknowledged people's land claims to some degree.

From 1978, part of the forest reserve, including Nyungcung, was transferred to the State Forest Corporation, the timber company owned by the Ministry of Forestry. The transfer of territorial authority meant that the corporation created forest plantation plots and curtailed villagers' land use. In settlements such as Nyungcung all forms of agricultural production, save paddy rice, were actively forbidden, and farmers had to pay rent to the corporation for their rice fields in addition to the village land tax ("Letter C"). This practice was not legal but quite common.

When the area was recategorized in 2003 to become part of the national park, the State Forest Corporation's operations ceased and new opportunities arose for the people of Nyungcung. With the departure of the corporation, the inhabitants reclaimed the land they had lost to the corporation's forest plantations. Local people uprooted the mahogany seedlings and began to farm the slopes. The park authorities soon confronted them and prohibited their use of the land. At this point, however, the political context in Indonesia had changed dramatically. With *reformasi*, a broad range of movements and civic organizations had seen the light of day and could operate relatively freely. The inhabitants of Nyungcung contacted one such NGO, the Indonesian Institute for Forest and Environment (*Rimbawan Muda Indonesia*, RMI).[19] During the next eight months a process of participatory

mapping was launched.[20] Rice fields, dry-land fields, settlements, and cemeteries were mapped and areas of possible expansion were marked out. As
part of the mapping, a historical description of the land use, a *kronologi*,
was also established. This included documents such as tax receipts, and
extraordinary permits to farm in plantation areas (*Kartu tanda pendataran
pemakai tanah perkebunan*) issued by different authorities through time.
Some documents did not have a direct relation to the specific claim, but
they documented a long-term presence in the area.

Once the mapping was finalized, the inhabitants and RMI invited the
newly elected village government of Malasari for a field visit.[21] In 2004 the
Ministry of Forestry introduced a policy on collaborative forest conservation in conservation areas (Ministry of Forestry Regulation P/19/2004), and
RMI used this policy to leverage community claims. RMI organized a workshop with other NGOs, with the Agricultural University of Bogor (*Institut
Pertanian Bogor*, IPB), and with the Forest Service advisers, to invent and
establish a new category of forest and land use: *Kampung Dengan Tujuan
Konservasi* (*kampung* with conservation purpose) (see Galudra n.d.). This
category was a new invention and counterintuitive to a park administration that equated "conservation" with "no people" (Kubo and Suprianto
2010). At the same time, RMI worked with the people in the *kampung* to
specify what rules of access and use this would entail in practice. As a result of these consultations, Nyungcung formed a group of "*kampung* forest
guards." They patrolled the area of the park surrounding the village on a
regular basis. The idea was to make sure that no one from the village farmed
outside the boundaries established through the mapping exercise, and, just
as important, that no one from outside the village used the space. Crucially,
though, it demonstrated active governance — NGO-fortified governance, to
be sure, but not government governance.

The village government was positive toward the idea of recognizing the
farmers' land claims. It was, after all, land they had cultivated historically,
and the prohibition was connected to the recently departed New Order.
Moreover, several of the newly elected members of the village assembly belonged to the recently created indigenous peoples' movements AMANAT
(*Alliansi Masyarakat Nanggung Transformatif*, the Transformative Alli-

ance of the People of Nanggung) and saw village rights to land as a legitimate claim.

Subsequently, a series of negotiations began between the hamlet of Nyungcung and RMI, the village government of Malasari, and the park authorities. In 2010 the negotiations resulted in an agreement.[22] It legalized the population's presence on the land the people farmed. This even included the production of trees. The park authorities and RMI addressed the Conservation Division in the Ministry of Forestry to have the new categories of land use endorsed, along with the principles according to which the zoning would reflect that actual land use: 1) it was decided that categories should be based on actual conditions; 2) there should be a public consultation (to be overseen by the newly elected district government); and 3) importantly, people would have rights to the trees they themselves planted in the area.

Thus, villagers of Nyungcung, assisted by an NGO, managed to make visible claims to their land in the park. The community became established as a politically visible rights subject when it organized as an *adat* hamlet with a mapped-out territory. The community built an effective argument by mobilizing land tax receipts to document historical land use in their *kronologi*. Moreover, creating a *kampung* forest guard not only demonstrated the people's intentions and capabilities to be responsible stewards of the natural resources with which they wanted to be entrusted; by patrolling the perimeter of their *adat* territory, the forest guard also demonstrated the exclusivity of their claim.[23] Thus, the relative success of the participatory mapping depended not merely on the inhabitants' capacity to wrest land rights from the park in a compromise. It equally depended on their capacity to exclude others. Continuous land use, *kampung* forest guards, and maps effectively produced property rights and a degree of privatization or exclusivity of the space in question.[24] The most striking achievement of the people of Nyungcung was their success in inventing a new administrative category in anticipation of the later Constitutional Court ruling. Government recognition as a "*kampung* with conservation purposes" with certain rights turned squatters into citizens with rights to exclude others. The recognition legalized their presence and completed their nine-tenths of possession of the area. The community of Nyungcung had not (yet) acquired formal *adat* territorial rights by the beginning of 2017. Yet different forms of indirect recognition had put its people in a position of relative control of their territory. The internal property arrangements within the community—whether communal, and to what degree, whether alienable, and to what degree—remained internal. The direct claims to recognition as an indigenous territorial community indirectly provided recognition of property rights defined and enforced by the community itself. Pragmatism and indirect claims, as opposed to foolhardy pursuit of direct claims to property, also characterized the strategies of people from Parigi.

Parigi

Parigi is a *kampung* of 350 households in Cisarua village, situated between the perimeter of the Halimun-Salak National Park and a rubber plantation enjoying a lease. Historically, people had lived and farmed in what had become the park area in 2003. After independence, the community had occupied the neighboring Dutch-owned plantation. Although there had been a history of confrontations with evictions and reoccupations during the early 1960s, the villagers had managed to hold on to some land. In the 1980s, the National Land Agency initiated a land allocation and registration program, PRONA (*Proyek Operasi Nasional Agraria*, National Land Registration Project), sponsored by the World Bank. The objective was to title land to individual farmers (Wallace 2008: 195). In 1983, 338 Cisarua farmers received around 82 hectares of land inside the former plantation area.[25] However, the village leader apparently collected all individual certificates, and none of the landholders had seen them since.[26] Despite the fact that the National Land Agency had issued land certificates under the PRONA program, it also issued a 25-year plantation lease of 360 hectares including the PRONA-titled area the same year. It was leased to a private company for cultivation of cloves and tea. The smallholders were evicted from the land, and some began to work as laborers on the plantation. In 1993, the company lease was sold on to a large rubber-producing company, Hevea Indonesia. The new company did not cultivate all of the land for which it had a lease.

In 1996, people from Parigi and two other *kampungs* occupied around 200 hectares of the rubber plantation. Rubber trees were initially left largely untouched while people began to cultivate a more complex composition of crops in the spaces between them. Hevea Indonesia attempted to have people evicted but failed and resolved to continue to farm the unoccupied part of the plantation. However, after three years, at the downfall of Suharto, villagers began to build residential houses and remove the rubber trees in the areas they had occupied. Subsequently, the areas controlled by villagers and the areas controlled by Hevea Indonesia began to look distinctly different.[27] At the same time, the company began to issue contracts to the occupying farmers sub-leasing the occupied land for money. Even though such sub-lease contracts were quite illegal, some farmers accepted them because they documented and seemed to legalize their presence.[28] In fact, the contract represented an official—albeit illegal—mutual recognition, the substance of which remained somewhat opaque. The farmers had not purchased the land outright, and the land, in any case, was not the company's to sell. But people paid for a right to farm, and this right was as robust as the company's ability to transfer it—illegal, but effective. At least, their land use had been acknowledged by a relevant party: the official lease holder. By the same token, the company's right to lease it out was recognized: not by law, nor by government, but by the lessee.

The inhabitants of Parigi had long regretted the shortage of school facilities for their children. After the occupation of the plantation land, livelihoods seemed more secure, and people were determined to stay in the *kampung*. The neighborhood associations therefore conceived of a plan to establish a rural secondary school in the area.[29] In the beginning, leading figures of the community, including the primary school teachers, contacted a local NGO in order to conduct a participatory mapping exercise and establish Parigi's *kronologi*. The results of the mapping exercise were used in an application to the Provincial Educational Department in Bandung for a secondary school. In 2008, the community applied for the construction of school classrooms, and the Provincial Government's Educational Department granted it. The school's first classrooms were built the same year, and the following year, two additional buildings were constructed. Leveling the ground for the construction was heavy work, and the villagers contacted a local mining company. The company lent the villagers two Caterpillar machines for a month. There were many reasons to be on friendly terms with the neighbors, and no doubt community assistance also looked good in the company's corporate social responsibility accounts. The opening of the school in 2010 was marked by the participation of the district mayor from Bogor and all the pomp the *kampung* could muster. A monument with photographs of the opening and a stone plate was erected to commemorate the event. The location of the school was right in the middle of the occupied plantation land. The inhabitants of Parigi had sought—and obtained—recognition from different quarters. The old agreement with the plantation company receded into the background, whereas recognition from government institutions became central.

When the inhabitants of Parigi had contacted the District Educational Office and the Provincial Ministry of Education for permission and funding for the school, they had gone through the normal bureaucratic procedures—only they had failed to mention that the land on which the school was to be erected was, in fact, occupied and in dispute. The plantation company had not actively farmed the land, however; and it had now been farmed for years in small plots by occupying villagers. To the educational authorities, it looked like a landscape of smallholders, and when the district governor was finally made aware of developments, the process must have seemed too far gone to reverse. After two years, the National Land Agency granted the land rights to the grounds to the school, which was now a legal entity belonging to the district.

Obviously, Hevea Indonesia protested against the construction of the school on what it considered to be the company's land. Hevea had a lease to 360 hectares of land, and while the occupation by villagers had been a nuisance, the effective recognition by the provincial government of this claim by the occupying community severely jeopardized the legitimacy of the company's entire claim. The company hired surveyors and put in boundary markers to signal what it considered to be the area it legitimately leased. The boundary markers were all issued with a metal plate with the name of the company and of the National Land Agency.[30] In 2011, the *kampung* of Parigi began the construction of a mosque and Islamic boarding school in the area. While this served a local demand, it also established a valuable connection with the Ministry of Religious Affairs (*Kementerian Agama*

Inscription: With the grace of a great God, the rural secondary school of Nanggung in Bogor district was opened. Unveiled by the District Governor, Rachmat Yasin. 24 June 2010, West Java. (Photo: Christian Lund)

Republik Indonesia), which sponsored the construction in part. Moreover, it made eviction politically difficult. Anyone in search of public support in Java will think twice before demolishing a religious government edifice.

Over the years, the official status of the land had changed significantly. What was now the school grounds had been state land inhabited by people with weak property rights after independence and until the 1980s; it had become state lands under the jurisdiction of the Ministry of Agriculture, some of it leased out to private companies, overlapping with some government-titled land through PRONA. Then smallholders had occupied the land, initially without government recognition of their land use. And then, in 2013, after the school construction, it had again become state land, now owned by the District Government. In a certain way, land was still (or once more) "public," but the challenge to its control by the Ministry of Agriculture and the leaseholders not only paved the way for a much-desired school, but also unsettled the status of the wider plantation as such. In 2010, the village applied for funding, provided by the World Bank, for a small feeder-road project. Two years later, a small network of macadamized roads connected one end of the settlement to the other. Again, the villagers had gone through the District and Provincial Governments that would administer the grant, and before the plantation company was able to put a stop to it, the roads were a settled fact in the plantation. Hence, during the census in 2010 people's ID cards read: Country, Province, District, Village, and *Kampung,* and under *"Kampung,"* it stated "(Block) HGU"—that is, "the land under plantation lease *(hak guna usaha)*"—thus recognizing that these Indonesian citizens officially, though maybe not legally, resided on land which had been allocated to Hevea Indonesia on a plantation lease.

The local population's efforts at territorializing space were a mix of physical presence and claims to citizenship—to some degree an *adat* citizenship with their membership of AMANAT—and to public service. As citizens in need of a school and an Islamic boarding school, and as a disadvantaged community in need of roads, the inhabitants of Parigi managed to become visible citizens and legitimate their presence to get a tighter hold on the space they inhabited.

Conclusion

For the past century or more, the area around Mount Halimun-Salak has been the object of competition over property and territory. Government interventions have been ambitious and comprehensive. Previous orders and rights have been erased, and government institutions have imposed classifications of space, along with the juridical authority to control this frontier. The discourse of government-engineered territorialization has been powerful, yet competition between statutory institutions had made it possible for local populations to align with one set of government interests against another. Sometimes, people had obtained a partly tolerated presence in the landscape by tax payment, thereby gaining indirect recognition of their property claims. If it did not legalize the claim directly, it produced an indirect legalization of the claim. With *reformasi* and the creation of new political space, the field of opportunities expanded. Established authorities were unsettled, and it became possible and less dangerous to explore and exploit legal and institutional contradictions, while social movements, NGOs, and elected local politicians could pilot local interests in new energetic ways. People's organization as *indigenous* expressed a claim to both enfranchised citizenship and rights to land. At the local level, these claims were pursued as a series of direct and indirect—as well as individual and collective— claims, each leveraging the next in small steps of legalization.

Reformasi undid prior rights and weakened authorities, but it also created myriads of new social contracts involving indirect claims and their recognition. While the land claims inside and outside the national park differ in detail, they share a central common feature. The element of indirect claim and indirect recognition is significant. Payment of tax is not a legal claim to property, and the tax receipt even states this explicitly. Nonetheless, the tax payment connected the citizen to a particular piece or size of land and was an indirect claim to its control. Indeed, the tax receipt indirectly acknowledged it. This may not constitute full, unencumbered freehold (which few people have in Indonesia), but even limited property rights are property rights.

The deliberate and demonstrative organization of identity-based movements reveals a comparable consideration. Self-identification as an *adat* community was promoted with a discourse of sovereignty at the national level. At the local level, however, pragmatic, piecemeal maneuvers characterized the intercourse with government. People's selective compliance with regulation and their official solicitation of acknowledgment as rights subjects indirectly voiced a claim to land. Schools, roads, and *kampung* patrols were indirect territorial claims. They most of all said: "We are *officially* here."[31] The echo of indirect recognition from particular parts of government responded, "We know." Nationally, *reformasi* may have been a "big bang" of democracy and decentralization, but locally, rights and legalization have been acquired by increments. Law's emancipatory potential was realized little by little.

Residence and farming depend on different registers of legitimation, and access and control over space follow different paths. Residence and public services such as schools and road infrastructure depend on ministries that do not control—or depend upon—space as a natural resource for conservation or exploitation. Local people, enumerated and registered in the census, put forth demands as *citizens* in legitimate need of service. They complied with the statutory institutions' fields of intervention in selective and opportunistic fashion. This legitimated residence and made eviction more difficult. These direct claims to citizenship had *indirect territorial and property effects*. The conflicts over residence engaged the boundary between legal and illegal and reworked it in the process. In the end, land holding was indirectly legalized through the recognition of legal references of people's identity-based right to presence in the area. The communities' possession was consolidated by legalization.

In Nyungcung, located inside the national park, residence and land use were closely connected, and while occupation and presence were illegal according to some ministries, agreements, and the invention of a new category for a community that claimed *adat* status, legalized the settlement. In Parigi, people's presence had hitherto been tolerated, but they now aimed for more visible recognition. By establishing connections of recognition with the Ministry of the Interior, the Ministries of Education and of Religious Affairs, and even the World Bank, people were no longer simply undesired squatters in the eyes of the "resource ministries." They had become *citizens* with the right to have rights.

The questions of who belongs where, and what belongs to whom, seem to be of perennial concern. The intensity with which people and governments have deployed efforts to make, unmake, and remake their own and each other's claims over the past century has reworked what is legal at Mount Halimun. Governments' territorialization policies and local people's direct and indirect claims have prepared new layers of historical facts for future struggles to revive. And since exclusion and dispossession, violent protests, and evictions are still frequent in Indonesia, people should not romanticize successful legalization, or trust acquired rights to endure by themselves.

The next chapter focuses on land occupations by peasant movements in West Java. Here, too, identity is an important trope through which to express land claims. However, as we shall see, the stigma of "communist" was a leverage for exclusion rather than access. The chapter focuses on the inner workings of land occupation and the implications for property and authority relations when peasant movements were the vehicle for land claims and their legalization.

CHAPTER FOUR

Occupied!

Property, Citizenship, and Peasant Movements in Rural Java

Pak Amin once owned a rice field. His tax receipt [*Surat Pemberitahuan Pajak Terutang*, SPPP, payable tax notification for land and buildings] shows it to be part of about 10 hectares of rice fields. About 20 people at that time owned the land. The confiscation by KODIM (*Kommando Distrik Militer*) 0613 in Ciamis of ABRI (*Angkatan Bersenjata Republik Indonesia*, Armed Forces of the Republic of Indonesia) was made at the request from the plantation. At that time, it was said: "Now this land should not be claimed property right again, it belongs to the plantation." At that time, the tax receipts were all collected. The confiscation was done in 1965. The confiscation of land lasted for 35 years. When the New Order collapsed, the owners occupied and reclaimed the rice field. During the 35 years, all rice fields were leased, rented, and mortgaged by the plantation supervisor, after being divided between the crooked foremen, ranging from the lowest to the highest rank. Their names are: Agung, Bagus, Cahyono, Darma, Elang, Gunardi, Ismaya, Joyo. The village police, Kadek, and Mr. Panutra. In essence, all the leaders of plantation workers got a share of the 10 hectares of rice field. Depending on the rank, each received 100 bata, 200 bata, 300 bata, 500 bata. Even the village police received 1 hectare. This was at the time when Ramelan Sukamuljo was bupati [*district mayor*]. He never defended the people.[1]

Land occupation sounds as simple as it is radical. You move on to land held by others and announce, "This is ours now!" In fact, while it is radical, land occupation is not simple at all. In recent decades, land ownership and control have been significantly challenged in most parts of Indonesia. Not only have new groups of land users occupied land from which they were formerly excluded; the institutions to which these people are beholden for their land rights are also new. During the late 1990s, as the New Order spiraled into decline and finally collapsed, agrarian protests became ever more frequent. From 1998, different social organizations, groups, and movements formed in a period of political transformation. The fall of the Suharto regime opened a path for democratization and a series of decentralization reforms that provided increased autonomy to local government. This appeared to offer opportunities to transform society, including agrarian structures. Land occupations by smallholders accompanied the protests. Often they seized—from state forests or private and government plantations—land that in previous periods had been farmed by smallholders. The land occupations were controversial. On the one hand, they were condoned and even hailed by popular movements as the realization of the long-awaited land reform that was embedded in the Basic Agrarian Law from 1960 but never fully implemented (Bachriadi and Wiradi 2011). On the other hand, forest and plantation owners, as well as local government institutions, frequently condemned the occupations as theft. Whether occupation was "reclaiming" lost land or "theft" is one issue. Another, underlying one is how this fundamentally challenged and reworked the social relations of property, citizenship, and political authority.

Since property and citizenship are fundamentally relational, and intimately related to public authority in their constitution, recognition of claims to land and other resources, and of political identity with various entitlements, simultaneously invest the institution that provides such recognition with recognition of its authority to do so. Claims to rights are ways to invoke public authority and governing capacity in different institutions, be they statutory or not. And conversely, categorization and legalization of property and citizenship is a way to acquire and exercise public authority. In Indonesia, this is not reserved for statutory institutions alone. Social and political movements and customary institutions may claim to be "non-state," yet in practice govern and control political subjectivities, resources, and space.

The chapter engages the processes through which property, citizenship, and authority are produced, fabricated, or sometimes conjured up, and the dynamics through which they are reproduced, challenged, undermined, and possibly eliminated. I attempt to do this while remaining mindful of the uncertainty experienced by the protagonists themselves. The following sections analyze how governing institutions in Indonesia have dispossessed different groups of people, and how the categorization of property and citizenship has structured exclusion in rural Java.

The chapter outlines the configuration of recognition and misrecognition of property and political and economic identity claims that effectively entitle actors to possess land. In the process, established categories and entitlements are destabilized, and public authority itself is put on the line. By following the actual relationships, the historical and contingent shifts, the multiple logics and the tensions between them in the two case studies of occupation, the chapter shows how property and citizenship have come about, and how public authority in these domains has been produced as a consequence.

Modern History of Property and Citizenship in Java

The end of Dutch rule in 1942 and the vigorous efforts to decolonize and take charge of Dutch possessions did not mean an immediate end to Dutch law (Lev 1985: 66). For the government of the newly independent nation, the notion of state domain and government land control was, no doubt, too tempting to let go. Throughout the 1950s, government tried to work out a post-colonial land legislation, but only by 1960 did the Basic Agrarian Law reveal its promise of land reform, together with political and legal visibility, to the Indonesian rural population. In principle, the Basic Agrarian Law regulates land tenure and property in Indonesia (Fitzpatrick 2006, Slaats et al. 2009). It constitutes a legal framework for government control of space and acquisition of land, and stipulates rules for land use. In principle, it also provides for land reform and land registration. The law builds on the premises that land is fundamentally inalienable, must have a social function, and belongs to the Indonesian people, whose interests are represented by the state of Indonesia. This last element resonates with the colonial laws of 1865 and 1870 and opens a wide interpretative scope.[2] The "right to control by the state" in all matters pertaining to land, water, and air gives the Indonesian government agencies a very large formal measure of control over property (Leaf, 1994: 15). And as long as the state has not granted any rights on state land, it "holds direct right of control over" it (Reerink 2011: 61).[3] The actual implementation of the Basic Agrarian Law and the institutional empowerment that the law has occasioned have been contentious throughout its existence, however, and emphasis has shifted with political regimes since 1960. The New Order government policies favored large-scale plantation production, and politics favored political cronies. Government used the law to dispossess landholders by recategorizing their political identity as communist, by delegitimizing their claims, and by removing them forcefully. Once occupiers were stigmatized as "communists" or "political prisoners," during the New Order, rights to property evaporated.

Toward the end of the New Order era, a large number of organizations, NGOs, and movements began to carve out political space in the increasingly pluralist context, and even the youth gangs proliferated in search of new political and economic underpinning (Bachriadi et al. 2013, Li 2000, Lucas and Warren 2003, 2013, Peluso et al. 2008). Land returned to the political agenda through various actors. During the same period, land occupations began to occur once again on Java and elsewhere in Indonesia. Farmers occupied land in plantations and forests from which they claimed to have been evicted earlier. Many of these plantations had been Dutch-owned during the colonial era and had already been taken over by farmers once or twice before, in the 1950s and 1960s. In West Java the occupations came about as a result of interaction between community leaders and student and other activists. They challenged the ownership and control of the land by the plantations that had been established since the mid-1960s. However, naked land occupation only meant possession, whereas legalization—the last tenth of property—was still to be accomplished.

Peasant Movements in the Rupture of *Reformasi*

A large number of peasant unions appeared in the 1990s; many federated in the Indonesia Peasant Union Federation (*Federasi Serikat Tani Indonesia*). In West Java, the Sundanese Peasant's Movement (*Serikat Petani Pasundan*, SPP) emerged gradually in the 1990s. The social basis of the organization lay among the landless and smallholders in association with urban activists and students, who also began to form unions around that time. The main tactic was land occupations of State Forest Corporation or plantation land, and in this they echoed the "unilateral operations" of the Communist Party in the early 1960s (Rachman 2011: 9). The philosophy was that the land had originally belonged to smallholders, who had been dispossessed by colonial and post-colonial government policies for the benefit of private and government companies. This may explain why, once evicted, smallholders and their descendants had returned to the same location time and again. For many, the claim was on what they saw as their specific land; it was not an abstract claim to just any land. Soon, SPP was seen as a political force to be reckoned with by the Garut, Tasikmalaya, and Ciamis district governments and the National Land Agency (Bachriadi 2010: 291–319, Rachman 2011).

The political atmosphere was positive toward land reform in the first years after *reformasi* and decentralization. All the same, land occupations take tremendous courage and a good deal of cunning; courage to take possession, and cunning to legalize it. During the 2000s, movements like SPP encouraged and organized land occupations while urging government institutions and politicians at different levels to acknowledge the cause of occupiers, recognize the legitimacy of their demands, and legalize them (Rachman 2011: 10). It seems clear that the smallholders' demands were to get back land they believed to be theirs and have their rights to it recognized. If government refused, the public and collective recognition of themselves as rights subjects by themselves as a movement would have to do.

Land occupations were widespread. As Lucas and Warren (2003: 88–90) explain:

> These "reclaiming" actions included occupation of plantation estates, golf courses, and neglected "sleeping land" acquired by

investors for speculative purposes. In East Java alone, according to Legal Aid Foundation sources, there were more than fifty actions by dispossessed farmers reclaiming disputed lands. At Jenggawah . . . local people occupied the estate [a former Dutch plantation covering more than 3,000 hectares], after a decade-long struggle. In North Sumatra, two thousand farmers demanded the return of 100,000 hectares of plantation land controlled by a state company.

For good reasons, there are no comprehensive membership lists for SPP, though membership cards were issued. Moreover, "membership" or adherence was qualified by "active participation" rather than by payment of a membership fee. Different sources estimate SPP to have numbered anywhere between 25,000 and 700,000 people (Aji 2005: 42, Andéer and Jelmin 2004: 27, see also Anugrah 2015). Numbers may also have fluctuated over time. SPP appears to have been firmly rooted in some 50 villages, where 30–50 land occupations of different sizes had been organized.

In West Java, in Garut, Tasikmalaya, and Ciamis districts, some 14,000 families occupied 9,000 hectares of land in 41 locations in early 2003 (Afiff et al. 2005: 4). During this period, the State Forest Corporation, plantation owners, and armed forces violently opposed occupations. Corporate landholders and occupying smallholders engaged in many confrontations throughout Java—some more violent than others, and some very violent indeed. The occupations remained modest in relation to the extensive territory of the districts, but as a challenge to the existing order they were very significant. To the thousands of occupying farmers, they were dramatic, transformative events.

Land occupations involved several aspects, not least competition over terminology. In 1998, a plantation owner in Cilawu in West Java engaged an Islamic national celebrity preacher, Zainuddin MZ, to give a speech denouncing land occupation on religious grounds. In a passionate performance, he described land occupation as theft, or land looting (*penjarahan*), and therefore a sin. Immediately after the speech, the vice president of SPP— who was also imam of a mosque in Garut—called together the imams of

Sign at SPP's office in Garut, West Java (Photo: Christian Lund)

the subdistrict of Cilawa for a debate. The result was a counter-declaration to be pronounced in all mosques at the following Friday prayer. The declaration recognized theft as sin. Yet the land occupations by smallholders were not to be seen as theft, the clergy argued, but rather as repossession (*reklaiming*) of land, which had initially been stolen from the people by the Dutch and subsequently "fenced" to plantation owners. In this light, repossessing the land by occupation actually meant absolving the plantation owners of their sins of theft. Land occupation, therefore, according to the SPP imam, represented new livelihood options through legitimate repossession of property, as well as a good deed. The irony was not lost on people, yet the significance of the semantics was more than wordplay. Reframing the different stages of possession gave occupation an appearance of justified reappropriation. Labeling the operation with the language of ethics—understood and respected by ordinary folk—removed land occupation from the simple category of formal illegality in which it had been placed.

Land occupations did not concern questions of land access alone; they had wider implications for property and territorial control. The peasant movement, SPP, managed to have many of its members elected to the newly established democratic village councils. They thereby played a political part in Indonesia's new government institutions. However, SPP also established elements characteristic of autonomous governing institutions. As noted above, members of the movement did not simply take out a "subscription" to a movement. Active participation and mobilization were the salt of SPP membership. The readiness to act was the "membership fee" or "tax" that they paid, enabling them to rely on the reciprocal protection of their own land claims by SPP's mobilization of fellow members in times of need. When an eviction was looming, SPP would mobilize all its members, and thousands would go to the occupied plantation in question. This averted many forced removals because the turnout outnumbered the police, soldiers, and plantation security personnel, even when these coercive forces were reinforced with thugs from the youth organizations. Even though this mutual recognition of occupants' land claims and SPP's authority to command the members' presence did not entail a financial exchange, the cost of participation incurred by mobilized smallholders was not negligible. In addition to the danger of violence and arrests, the costs of transport, food, and absence from one's own farm were often a considerable burden for people on a tight budget.

Finally, although land acquired through such occupation was not subject to an actual cadastral registration, imitations of formal registration of plots in occupied areas were common. Government stationery and instruments, such as ledgers, registration forms, and cadastral maps, were replicated and improvised. The format of the ledgers of the National Land Agency was copied, and the occupying smallholders kept the books. Names, locations, crops, and membership history were recorded. Paperwork was carried out in order to apply to the National Land Agency for recognition of ownership. The idea was not to forge government papers as such but to make them as authentic as possible so that in the event of officialization, it would be a simple operation. Acting in anticipation of government regulation long before any was adopted, people tried to conjure up rights by legalization. By organizing their settlements in conformity with the formal technical norms, as if they had already been recognized, smallholders entered the orbit of the National Land Agency in anticipation of a "contract." In order to establish a "contract" of mutual recognition, the inhabitants acted and organized as they anticipated the agency would expect proper citizens to act. To my knowledge, however, only exceptionally was the process of registering the land with the National Land Agency carried through. Various explanations for this were offered in interviews with SPP members and cadres. One was hostility on the part of the National Land Agency. A more convoluted version was that SPP cadres would explain to the members that procedures for land registration had been engaged, but because of some new appointments in the National Land Agency, the whole procedure had to start over. Some members suggested that the SPP leadership itself was in fact stalling the process to keep its members exclusively beholden to the movement for their land. Consequently, they were kept from establishing property relations with Indonesian statutory institutions.

The property rights produced in this relationship between successful squatters and an active movement were circumscribed. In the ideology of SPP, it was important that land was not a commodity to be transacted and accumulated in capitalist dynamics. As a consequence, land transactions within occupied areas were, in principle, limited. According to SPP's philosophy, land rights could be bequeathed to heirs but could not be subdivided, rented, mortgaged, or sold. Thus, beholden to SPP, smallholders could farm the land, but not transact it. When people actually did so anyway, tensions would loom, and the question of what institution guaranteed such transacted land rights would arise.

Adherence to the movement meant that small conflicts between occupying smallholders were dealt with by SPP cadres. In fact, card-carrying members of SPP would proudly brag how their membership gave them more than land: Members enjoyed a status which meant they would no longer be physically harassed by police and others at the market, and people could even wriggle their way out of the odd fine for a traffic violation by producing an SPP card or claiming to be "citizens of SPP." Police, foresters, and even the officers of the State Forest Corporation acknowledged that contrary to the situation during the Suharto years, they had, in practice, less effective jurisdiction in areas with a strong SPP presence, and less jurisdiction over the movement's members. SPP could even make it difficult for people *not* to be members in an occupied area.

SPP enjoyed a sovereign moment in the areas where it had a strong membership base. It controlled land allocation in these pockets; it defined and enforced rules of land tenure; it taxed and protected people in its occupations; it created a school; and it successfully established a terminology that combined the radical seizure of property and authority with the propriety of an honorable Muslim life. Finally, paperwork and procedure gave the whole operation an air of legality. Land occupations and the relations between movement and members were not without tensions, however. While SPP defined and enforced new property relations, statutory institutions remained in the imaginary of occupying smallholders as desired institutions with the power to recognize and legalize land claims. Different land occupations all had their distinct trajectories, but case studies of two emblematic examples from the southern part of "occupied" West Java will invoke the broader picture.

Two Occupations

Banjaranyar

In Banjaranyar, a village in Ciamis district, current land occupations marked the latest in a long series of shifts in land control. The area around the village had been a 348-hectare Dutch-owned rubber plantation.[4] People in the area were very active in the colonial resistance, and with the flight of the Dutch in 1942 the local population, including plantation workers, moved onto the land and began to cultivate it. At independence and the definitive departure of the Dutch, all plantation buildings and material were set ablaze, and the remaining rubber trees were uprooted.

In 1960, after the adoption of the Basic Agrarian Law, the area was to be distributed through a land reform program that included the entire

348 hectares. In 1963, a local government leader challenged the land reform plan and the smallholders' occupation of the land; he applied instead for a plantation lease to convert and renew the colonial lease. The dispute went to the Agrarian Court (also known as the Land Reform Court) but no settlement was reached.[5] At the time, intense political conflicts were raging, mainly between Communists on the left and the army (with support from Islamic parties) on the right, with the Nationalists caught somewhere in between.

In 1965, after the coup that brought the army and Suharto to power, Banjaranyar was targeted in the anti-communist purge, like thousands of other villages in Java.[6] The land was effectively "freed up." Smallholders were evicted; some were arrested; their houses in the plantation area were destroyed; and land was handed over to a private plantation company with a 30-year lease. From 1967, the village was categorized as a forced-labor camp. The villagers, now prisoners, were forced to work on the plantation without pay. Some of the area was farmed with paddy rice, and the political prisoners were given plots to farm on the condition that 80 percent of the harvest went to the local military commander. The surviving prisoners were freed in 1979—the same year in which thousands of prisoners were released from the notorious Buru prison island. However, for years after their release they had to report to the police every month, their ID cards were stamped with "ET"—"Ex-TaPol" or former political prisoner—and they and their children were barred from holding government jobs.[7] Only in 1999, with President Habibie's general amnesty, did the "Ex-TaPol" stigma cease to be seared into their public identities.

After their release from the forced-labor camp in 1979, villagers attempted another land occupation in 1986, but they were immediately evicted. At the downfall of Suharto and the end of the New Order in 1998, villagers formed a committee and went to the new district administration to get the land back. The answer was somewhat ambiguous; people could rebuild their houses on the plantation land, but they were "not to bother the plantation" (*tidak mengganggu perusahaan*). By the end of 2003, however, local inhabitants had seized 160 hectares of plantation land, and the committee became a recognized local chapter of the Sundanese Peasant Union, SPP.

Faced by smallholder membership of SPP, the plantation company em-
barked on a new strategy. Instead of resorting to violent evictions, it entered
into negotiations with the land occupants. In the end, local smallholders
were to retain some 69 of the 160 hectares they had occupied, which had
anyway not been actively farmed by the plantation company. The company
would sign over the land for "land reform" so that the National Land Agency
could take steps to issue land certificates to the smallholders. In return, they
were to give up the remaining 91 hectares of occupied land, leaving a total
of 215 hectares for the plantation. They did so, for a time. However, much
of the plantation land was, in fact, not used as a plantation. The plantation company rented out around 100 hectares to smallholders for a fee of
100,000 Rupiah (about U.S.$10) per 1,400 square meters and eight days of
labor per year plus 30 percent of the harvest. Such arrangements—subletting leased land—were not legal but were, and remained, quite common,
and smallholders received receipts from the company for the rent they paid.
The final 115 hectares were used for rubber and worked by plantation workers who lived on the plantation lands in two small settlements.

As for the occupied 69 hectares, it was decided by SPP that all members
should have a share in it, and the association began to map and divide the
land. As a consequence, each plot was a mere 1,000–2,000 square meters.
People used their plots for building houses with a garden. In the following
year the community of occupants applied to the National Land Agency for
land titling of the 69 hectares with the help of SPP. After some six months
of field investigations, the National Land Agency issued land certificates
(*hak milik*) for more than 500 plots. However, land certificates were not
given directly to the land occupants but were handed to the local chapter of SPP to distribute to its members. SPP, and not the individual farmers, was the rights subject of government, and the farmers were the rights
subjects of SPP.

SPP organized a meticulous ceremony. Each landholder—generally
a family—presented itself to the chairman of SPP for an interview. Four
questions were asked and answers were recorded. People were asked to:
(1) account for the history of their land in the village; (2) give evidence of
their participation in the land struggle; (3) explain the meaning of the land

certificate; and (4) explain what they felt about receiving the certificate.[8] Below are some excerpts from the interviews.

> With the certificate, we will not be pushed off the land. We will
> be free to farm. The certificate is valuable — it means that
> there is power.
>
> I wanted to get land, so I joined the SPP. My father was a ma-
> chine operator in a tapioca processing plant. We rented land
> from the company, but it went broke in 1984.
>
> I came to Banjaranyar in 1945, to become a tapping laborer. It
> paid a cent per day, sometimes a little more depending on the
> amount of rubber. I worked as a tapper for 20 years. In 1965,
> we were chased away. Now we can get the land.
>
> After we entered the SPP, there is always someone saying all
> sorts to weaken it. For example, there is the saying, "anyone
> who enters the SPP, will later enter the Communist Party."
>
> The existence of a certificate means there is power, so it should
> not be sold.
>
> By joining SPP, we often take action and now we know many
> people. We often participate in education. There is much to
> know about the land, plantation leases, and agrarian history.
>
> I feel happy to get a certificate, but I feel the burden of having
> to pay taxes. Moreover, there is a sanction from the SPP. It is
> so heavy. I worry that if at one moment I am unfortunate and
> need money, I will have to sell the certificate.
>
> I have been fighting to farm. Previously, I had to rent. I joined
> SPP's struggle to work on the land; this is a proof of the suc-
> cess of the joint struggle of all the SPP. It is a precious paper.
>
> There was a demonstration to Banjarsari, to the village, to
> Ciamis. I joined the demonstrations. Never cheated. To Ban-
> dung, to Jakarta. To Jakarta twice.
>
> In the past, before the certificate, GIBAS [*Gungan Inisiatif
> Barisan Anak Siliwangi*, Siliwangi Youth Organisation, a
> youth gang] was always terrorizing us. They did not say it

> directly but they said that the plantation had to be cleared of
> communists.
>
> Certificate means a proof of ownership. If you already have a
> land certificate, no one can interfere.

These are voices of villagers who applied for land and who shared their histories and understanding of the significance of the land allocation as well as their faith in the procedure and documents. This was a very intense ordeal, and left them in no doubt about the importance of SPP's decisive role in authorizing their land access.[9] To receive papers for the land was one thing, but the fact that the documents bore no indication of their Ex-TaPol status was quite another. With land certificates in hand, people were now fully enfranchised, taxpaying citizens beholden to the government of Indonesia for the (admittedly tiny) plot of land they had occupied. The certificate legalized their citizenship as well as their property.

After obtaining certificates on the 69 hectares, a second phase of occupation was initiated in Banjaranyar in 2008. SPP members occupied another 150 hectares of land to farm. Of these, 65 hectares represented simple defections (rather than new invasions) on the part of those leasing land directly from the plantation company: SPP members had encouraged these tenants to suspend their payment to the company and join their organization. SPP threatened to report the plantation's illegal practice of subletting leased land to farmers to the National Land Agency. This could jeopardize renewal of the lease.[10] By 2012, the plantation company had ceased to charge rent for the land.

The change from a tenancy arrangement with the company to landholding guaranteed by SPP was very significant for the villagers. Statutory certificates were not issued for any land beyond the initial 69 hectares. No government institution recognized the smallholders' possession of this land as legal or legitimate, leaving the smallholders exclusively beholden to the SPP. Mimicking statutory procedures, the movement had established a land register in which the landholding of each member was listed, its location indicated, and the payment of the land fee recorded. Each member paid 3,000 Rupiah per year per 1,400 square meters of land held. In addition, each family contributed 10,000 Rupiah if there was an SPP activity such as a meeting to which the organization needed to send a representative. Finally, ad hoc contributions could be required. The support for SPP was not unanimous among the land occupants. Some farmers had occupied land alongside the SPP members and were farming it in the same manner, but they did not mobilize to protect other squatters from eviction at the behest of SPP. The movement leadership frowned upon this behavior and let it be known to the plantation company that selected and targeted evictions of these non-members would not be opposed by the movement. SPP's practice of disassociating itself from free-riding occupants left the latter exposed and put pressure on them to join the movement.

The democratic and decentralized political system that emerged after the fall of Suharto offered new possibilities for local politics. Thus, the village of Banjaranyar elected an SPP member as village head in 2008. When a new school was built in 2010, it was situated on the plantation company's leased land: The village head negotiated with the company and eventually convinced it to write a letter granting land to the school project. The company's legal right to transfer leased land like this was quite uncertain, and the wording of the letter quite opaque. However, the fact remained that village infrastructure, which facilitated settlement within the disputed area, had been constructed.

The history of land conflicts in Banjaranyar is long. It extends over at least three or four generations and alternates between government control—either directly or through concessions to plantations—and control by villagers themselves. In later years, this control was structured through the SPP. Villagers' membership of SPP gave them land and simultaneously gave SPP authority; a social contract of property and authority was established. This period included several significant moments. First, when the initial occupation of 160 hectares was reduced to 69 hectares, the path to obtain certificates issued by the Indonesian government was opened. While depending on SPP's protection and committing themselves to its actions, smallholders sought recognition from government institutions as well. By applying for statutory land rights people attempted to make themselves visible to the National Land Agency, anticipating the requirements and language of government acknowledgment of their claim. By obtaining land certificates from the National Land Agency, smallholders held property with legal recognition from the Indonesian government. They were thus beholden to the government for this property and, most importantly for the people of Banjaranyar, they had been elevated to full citizenship by that token. They were no longer Ex-TaPol with curtailed civil rights. The recognition of property rights by the Indonesian government went hand-in-hand with obtaining recognition as full, unadulterated citizens of Indonesia; property led to citizenship. In this light, the size of the individual plots mattered little.

For the remaining 150 hectares, different dynamics of recognition emerged. Here, the smallholders remained invisible to government but beholden to SPP as rights subjects. SPP had not been delegated the authority to control this land from government and was essentially acting as a sovereign authority. It was not property that gave access to citizenship, but the reverse. It was their membership of SPP—effectively a form of citizenship—that entitled people to a piece of land recognized as theirs by this organization. The SPP's efforts seemed to prepare for the recategorization of the occupied land from "plantation land" to "land for land reform," ideally paving the way for the government's legalization of the farmers' property rights. As of 2018, it still remained to be seen whether SPP would actually relinquish its authority over land by transferring it to the National Land Agency, and whether the agency would recognize the occupants' claims as rights. Meanwhile, the people of Banjaranyar effectively hold two kinds of citizenship and hold property as part of two different social contracts.

Harumandala

Harumandala is a village in Pangandaran district.[11] The village consists of several sub-villages or kampungs and is located in a steeply sloped landscape. After independence, the area saw many armed confrontations between the Indonesian army and the Nahdlatul Ulama (literally Revival of the Ulama, a traditionalist Sunni Islam movement). The confrontations died down around 1961. The area was formally under the territorial authority of the

Provincial Forestry Service of West Java, and the entire area was classified as "forest." However, most of the area was, in fact, populated with villages and *kampungs*. Generally, people were farming paddy rice on terraces, as well as different crops on forest plots (trees, fruits, vegetables, spices, and more). In practice, people could clear land for paddy rice farming and other activities without much interference from the authorities. No legal rights ensured people's access to land, but the Provincial Forestry Service tolerated farming and people regarded the land as their own.

In 1978, all of the forest land controlled by the Provincial Forestry Service in West Java—close to a million hectares—was transferred to the State Forestry Corporation, which had previously operated only in Central and East Java.[12] As a parastatal institution with its own uniformed "forest police," and as a part of an authoritarian regime, the State Forest Corporation was inaccessible to ordinary people seeking to argue or negotiate their case. The corporation established boundaries to create teak and mahogany plantations, clearing the area of any farmed fields that might be in the way. Moreover, it started to act as a government landlord, charging rent for the fields people cultivated in the area. These farmers thus became tenants of the corporation, and in the process consolidated its land control. The State Forest Corporation officials appointed individual villagers as rent collectors and gave them rent-free land in return. The rent consisted of 33 percent of the villagers' rice production: there was no legal basis for it, and it was never registered as official company income. Illegal logging activities increased steeply in Ciamis district after 2001, with teak and mahogany as the targeted species. Accusations and counter-accusations between villagers and the corporation were frequent. The villagers claimed that the corporation and police officers were colluding with loggers, who also hired villagers to work for a daily wage, while the State Forest Corporation, on the other hand, accused the SPP of being behind the illegal logging.

In 2006 the villagers created a local chapter of SPP, and 186 people joined. During training sessions farmers were told that the Forest Corporation's collection of rent was illegal, and actions toward land reform could be launched in the area by occupying land the corporation claimed to control. Forest land was never earmarked for land reform, however, so SPP cadres may have overstated the opportunities in their attempt to galvanize support. The first move, nonetheless, was to refuse to pay rent to the State Forest Corporation. Instead, people paid 10,000 Rupiah per month to SPP and turned their presence into a land occupation.

Some villagers were summoned to the Forest Corporation office where they were interrogated and accused of logging in the area, but the occupation continued. Information about the occupation reached the West Java police commander and the corporation director in Jakarta. They decided to reestablish the corporation's control over the occupied forestlands by launching a forest security operation funded by the Ministry of Forestry. The operation was preceded by a joint reconnaissance for forest security control conducted in March 2008.[13] The State Forest Corporation provided the reconnaissance team with a detailed map that indicated "forest security disturbances." The team reported that approximately 290 hectares of forestland were occupied by nearly 1,600 villagers from four villages in the Cigugur subdistrict. A detailed report from Forest Unit 89 stated that permanent crops such as cocoa, vegetables, herbs, and wood species, as well as a small mosque, nine houses, several monitoring posts, and an SPP office, were located on the occupied lands.[14]

Three months after this reconnaissance report was issued, the West Java Police, the Ministry of Forestry, and the State Forest Corporation launched the forest security operation. This was a joint effort to combat illegal logging and timber trade, the first of five policies prioritized by the Ministry of Forestry for 2005–9. The main objectives of the operation were to reestablish control of the state forestland and to evict the people occupying it. The operation invoked the military terms Security Operation (*Operasi Keamanan*) and Dangerous Area (*Daerah Rawan*), echoing the Suharto era. Similarly, the use of terms like "illegal loggers," "illegal occupiers," "subversive," and "anti-state" established an association between land occupation and organized crime.

Officers from the State Forest Corporation and the Provincial Police in Bandung came to Harumandala and its six *kampungs*. More than 300 police officers set up camp on the local soccer field and began to prepare the evictions. The operation was initiated by a ceremony in which the police commander, the head of the corporation's forest police, and representatives from the local government Forestry and Plantation Unit went through the objectives of the operation—namely, to find evidence of illegal logging, to evict illegal occupants and destroy their farms, and to remove any illegal construction from the area.[15] First, the police and the corporation officers made house-to-house searches for timber.[16] Then, fields were ravaged and houses were burned to the ground. Some houses were left standing, but the police marked them with chalk "This house must be destroyed by yourself" (*Harus dibongkar sendiri*), or "This house and land is not yours but the property of the state" (*Rumah dan tanah ini bukan milik kamu tapi milik Negara*). Finally, the police forced the villagers to sign a statement in which they renounced their membership of SPP and declared they would never join again. It is well worth recalling that this took place almost a decade into the post–New Order democratic era, and that SPP was a legal organization. During the operation, some ten villagers were arrested and subsequently sentenced for "destruction of forest by illegal occupation." They all spent between one and two years in jail.

After the police operation, people resumed the cultivation of their plots in the area but moved to live in *kampungs* outside of the State Forest Corporation area for a couple of years. By 2010, people had begun to move back to one of Harumandala's abandoned *kampungs*, Pasir Pilar, inside the corporation-controlled area. They reconstructed their houses, and within six months some 34 families had reestablished themselves in the *kampung*. The local SPP chapter drew up a map of the area, registering each plot and its owner.[17]

The State Forest Corporation contacted the settlement, but now with a new approach. They announced a planting ceremony of mahogany trees and invited villagers to witness. An area was cleared and 1,000 seedlings were planted in rows. Each row was publicly named after a government institution. Thus, the first row was named "the row of the provincial governor," the next, "the row of the police commander," "the row of the Indonesian army," and so on. The intention, no doubt, was to impress upon the people of the area that these resources belonged to and were under the protection of the entire government structure of Indonesia. Moreover, the State

Forest Corporation had the whole episode filmed.[18] The following night, however, all 1,000 mahogany seedlings were uprooted. A few days later, the corporation agents returned to mete out punishment for the destruction of the plants. In the fighting and commotion that followed, the agents destroyed the local mosque. This provoked people from Pasir Pilar and other *kampungs* to go to the local police in Cigugur to complain about the wanton destruction of their religious building. The presence of several hundred angry farmers seemed to make an impression on the police, who promised to investigate. Although nothing ever came of the investigation, the situation calmed down; people remained in their *kampungs* on the disputed land; they resumed farming their plots and rice fields, and they continued *not* to pay rent to the State Forest Corporation. They were not beholden to the corporation or the Indonesian government for their land rights. Instead, they held land thanks to "the republic" of SPP, with the opportunities and dangers this implied.

As people moved from Cikares and other *kampungs* outside the corporation area and back into the *kampung* of Pasir Pilar, they asked the official local territorial administration—the village office—for new ID cards that would reflect this change. This was done. By that token, Pasir Pilar became an official *kampung*, situated in the area that the State Forest Corporation claimed to control as forest. Moreover, as people registered to vote for the 2014 elections, officials from the subdistrict would visit all houses and place an official government sticker on the door with the name of the voter, and place of residence—their new official *kampung*.

The system of payment to SPP remained provisory, but with the smallholders' return to the contested lands in 2010, all *kampungs* of Harumandala also began to contribute to the Village Office to the tune of 1,000,000 Rupiah annually. At first, the Village Office, its mayor, and its elected parliamentarians were reluctant to receive the funds. They were unsure whether they were entitled to them, and what it would mean to accept them, but after some negotiation the Village Government of Harumandala accepted the contribution at a public ceremony.[19] While still perceived as illegal occupants by the State Forest Corporation, smallholders were beginning to be seen as taxpaying, voting, registered Indonesian citizens. The contributions were not from individual members but from SPP, and people generally saw the "contribution" as related to the issue of land. This "contribution" established a new substantive and formal relationship between landholders and the Indonesian government at its lowest level, the Village Office. It remains to be seen what this new relationship represents. One might argue that it not only established the SPP landholders as owners of property in the eyes of the Village Office; it also established the Village Office as a public authority on questions of property in land that was classified as forest. As the smallholders made claims to resources, they also invoked public authority in the Village Office. Tax payment attributed to it governing capacity and the authority to legalize land claims. This may, eventually, put the Village Office in competition with other statutory institutions.

Conclusion

Rule has never been uncompromised in rural West Java, and for the occupied areas, this is especially true. The confrontation between governments, powerful landholders, and more or less organized rural masses has been driving agrarian change in Java and the rest of Indonesia throughout its modern history. The upheavals following the end of the New Order are thus not the first but simply the latest in a series of dramatic claims following political ruptures and new possibilities.

Order and resistance have been woven into one another as competing actors have tried different combinations of force, governance, and legalization. The actual land control—by government agencies and corporations, or movements and farmers—depended on their respective abilities to dig in their heels and evict or exclude rival claimants. The mobilization and organization of large numbers of smallholders was a decisive step for smallholders toward control of space against the military force and hired muscle used by the plantations. In one of the cases analyzed above, a plantation company ceded its land; in the other, government claims in the form of the State Forest Corporation's demand for rent failed to prevail. Instead, the social relationship between smallholders and the SPP was the dominant structuring dynamic of resource control in these spaces.

On the large scale, successful land occupations have remained the exception, but they represent elements of political and theoretical importance. The struggles over land challenged more than the existing land rights; they challenged and suspended government's very authority to define them. Land occupation produced a sovereign moment for the peasant movement. The SPP was not beholden to government for the land it controlled. Rather, it had established a new relationship of mutual recognition with its members, the local smallholders. The SPP recognized their claims to land on the basis of active adherence, and the smallholders, in turn, recognized the movement's capacity to recognize and defend these claims as rights. SPP members recognized the movement's authority to govern. This formed through land struggles at the rupture of the New Order. The mutual recognition between peasants and their movement effectively produced an alternative path of legalization, even if the Indonesian government did not recognize it. Land occupations of the past 20 years continued to be defined as illegal by government. On the other hand, the on-the-ground local reactions of statutory institutions to land occupations ranged from violent opposition through tolerance, to acceptance and approval. In the situation of the 1998 regime change, many government institutions, as much as other institutions, seemed to be searching for a long-term tenable position. However, in its public discourse, government persisted in its efforts to discredit land occupations, to classify them as illegal, and to criminalize their perpetrators.

Land occupations gave the peasant movement political and legal visibility. By forming a movement, people resisted and averted evictions, and continued access to land for the smallholder went through the movement rather than through the recognition of a right by statutory government institutions. The occupations articulated social identity. Active membership and readiness to be mobilized for more than one's "own" plot of land defined the relationship. The culture of being part of a movement—a member of a class with a shared project of progress—was crucial, as statutory legalization of land occupations remained rudimentary. In contrast, SPP mapped out space, distributed land, collected tax, resolved disputes, schooled its members, and provided other services; in short, it took on the mantle of a governing institution to legalize the land under its control. SPP also worked to exclude non-members, and the transfer of its control to statutory institutions seemed not to be very urgent. The movement harnessed and organized discontent, protest, and interest in the twilight between contentious and routine politics. It vacillated between being a movement embodying a "collective will," and an organization with bureaucratic and service operations for its members, and hints of institutional logics. Even if SPP cadres saw themselves as distinctly outside government, they defined and enforced collectively binding rules and effectively governed. Hence, just as government institutions may be stakeholders with specific interests *as well as* authorizers acting in the name of the commonweal, so may social movements be able to authorize and govern fields of property *as well as* representing interests within them.

Clearing an alternative path of legalization was both the generative opportunity for SPP and, subsequently, its bureaucratic mainstay. This may help to explain why the SPP leadership was sometimes irresolute about approaching statutory institutions such as the National Land Agency. While ultimately success would be confirmed by having claims to land recognized as rights by statutory government institutions, battle-hardened activists of the peasant movements knew it was dangerous as well as difficult to trust government institutions. Moreover, such success could eventually make the movement redundant. Whether and how the relationships of mutual recognition between smallholders, movements, and government institutions will consolidate politically, institutionally, and legally over time is an open question. For the moment, the smallholders walked a fine line. They adhered to the movement to secure the collective protection and legalization of their settlement and their property. Yet in anticipation of future statutory recognition, they also continued to engage with government institutions through demands for land registration, or with ostentatious tax payment to hesitant local governments—institutions to which they had hitherto remained barely visible citizens, without even the right to have rights.

The next chapter focuses on a thoroughly violent confrontation between public authorities and farmers, and among the authorities themselves. The civil war in Aceh may well be an extreme case of land conflict and legalization, but it also shows the odds faced by ordinary people if they are denied the opportunity to organize.

CHAPTER FIVE

Predatory Peace

Dispossession at Aceh's Oil Palm Frontier

*D*ilarang melintas garis polisi [Police line. Do not cross].
The yellow plastic police tape stretched out of sight, separating the oil palm plantation and land farmed by smallholders.
On smallholder territory Caterpillars, bulldozers, and other large
machinery stood around, their advance temporarily halted. They
had been clearing the ground for the extension of the plantation
when the smallholders blocked their way, threatening the invad-
ing force of workers and stilling the roar of their machines. Three
truckloads of police then descended on the area. They declared an
embargo on the land and positioned the official yellow tape. Soon
the bulldozers roared again, while police kept people out. "After
the peace, peasants lose their land to plantations everywhere,"
was the explanation offered by local villagers. "Companies spray
farmers' fields with pesticides and herbicides to make work here
unbearable. Companies simply move big equipment onto our
land, uproot plants, and dig canals for oil palm cultivation."

When regimes change, policies, laws, and the institutions they undergird
are suspended. Sometimes just for an instant. Sometimes for good. The
civil war was a serious rupture of Acehnese society. Violent conflict raged
from 1976 until the peace treaty in 2005.[1] With peace in Aceh, the stars

Police tape, Aceh (Photo: Christian Lund)

seemed aligned for profound change; peace held the potential to rework property relations and strengthen smallholders' claims to land. The Free Aceh Movement (*Gerakan Aceh Merdeka*, GAM) had impressive support to back its forceful rhetoric of rural transformation. Moreover, legal instruments of land reform (both land redistribution and formalization of rights) were available to enact such a program. The end of the war also offered an opportunity for the integration of Aceh into the project of the Indonesian nation—something more than 100 years of colonial occupation and post-colonial nation building had never fully accomplished. Historically, Aceh has remained culturally and politically distinct from the rest of Sumatra and Indonesia, and there has always been an underlying tension between the central power in Jakarta and Aceh. And, finally, even the tsunami that devastated the coast in December 2004 had turned provider, bringing an inflow of resources in the wake of tragic destruction (Green 2013a+b). The open moment of peace held promise of a new social contract.

Yet the violence of war was followed only by the violence of peace—and, although this was on an entirely different scale and much more localized, its broad effect was to disrupt the new spirit of resistance to plantation land acquisitions. Indeed, the intense security situation during the last decade of the war made it possible for agrarian violence against smallholders in the ensuing "peacetime" to be presented as routine security operations. A decade on, although Aceh may now accept integration into Indonesia, bringing with it a booming palm oil economy, smallholders' hopes for secure land rights seemed dashed.

Despite occasional and transitory alignments between political interests and peasant interests in the course of Indonesia's modern history, lasting political recognition of the legitimacy of smallholder claims has remained a pipe dream. During the early 1960s, strong political interests championed land reform, but then came the 1965 coup. The New Order favored large-scale plantation agriculture as well as high-volume concessions for oil, gas, and timber extraction in Aceh (see McCarthy 2006, 2007, Ross 2005, Schulze 2007b). The new window that opened briefly at the fall of Suharto in 1998 quickly shut, and large-scale interests soon dominated again. Indeed, for Aceh, war, martial law, and generalized unrest largely obscured the subtler political opportunities brought about by *reformasi*.

Instead, more profound frontier dynamics of dispossession prevailed. Peace made it tempting for planters and politicians to latch on to the global oil palm boom and facilitate the development of large-scale production.[2] Natural conditions for oil palm cultivation are nearly perfect on the coastal plains: a hot, humid, and rainy climate, and wet, swampy soil in lowland areas. Across this terrain a broad new frontier opened, as smallholder claims to long-term access were obliterated and new rights were created and favored.[3] Leases and location permits were the instruments that laundered violent dispossession as legal and legitimate change. It became possible for planters, government, army, and police to dismiss potentially political action as simply criminal. By characterizing smallholder claims to occupation as criminal trespass, prior social conventions and the practice of smallholder access yielded to the new rights of companies purchased and legalized through concessions.

Aceh is an extreme case of something general. It is a story of smallholders' alienation from land and the social contract of property. In many ways, it is an old story continued, yet the context of a conflict and post-conflict frontier provides a particular dimension to the institutional architecture, and to the emergence and consolidation of new social contracts of inclusion and exclusion. Recalcitrant landscapes have been brought under the control of capital, while citizenship rights—the basis for objecting to theft, predation, and exclusion—have been undermined and silenced through political violence. This frontier was forged in war, and the instruments of dispossession—political power and institutional manipulation—were conjoined in a context of overwhelming violence. The conflict initially undermined smallholder claims, and the peace subsequently consolidated the dispossession by strong government interests in the plantation and palm oil sector, violence, and the fraudulent legalization of land concessions. This chapter focuses on how land for plantations was acquired from smallholders, and how control over it was secured by force, administration, and law. It focuses on how large-scale land acquisitions have been legalized and smallholdings eliminated.

In what follows, I sketch out the idea of frontier dispossession for the analysis. I then outline the specific configuration of the political and agrarian structure in Aceh during the conflict and after. Then follow two analytical sections. First, an analysis of the general land politics in Aceh during and after the war is presented, tracing GAM's development from a rebel movement with a nationalist and popular base to a political party with a rent-seeking practice and an interest in the palm oil economy. This is followed by an analysis of the institutional mechanisms of dispossession through land lease allocations. Empirical documentation from two different locations in Aceh illustrates the smallholder-plantation land conflicts. By turning space into a frontier under weak claims, new actors were able to seize it through violence, political power, and the paperwork of legalization.

Frontiers as the Crucible of Property Rights

The struggle over land in the post–peace accord context in Aceh can be seen in terms of a frontier. While the word *frontier* suggests a savage space, untamed and unclaimed, to be harnessed for progress, it covers a more sinister process. Frontier spaces are not empty.

> Frontier spaces are where the, often violent, destruction of previous orders takes place, and the territorialisation of new orders begins. . . . [T]he discovery of new resources to control often takes place in populated places and leads political authorities like governments to disconnect people from place and to disenfranchise them as bearers of rights. When "frontiersmen" rearticulate the connections between places and the centers of power, and reframe their relative importance, ordinary people often find themselves abandoned or violently excluded while fighting for renewed recognition of vested rights. When frontier moments offer new opportunities of wealth capture, where institutional competition is intense, and where political power is skewed and livelihood precarious, old social contracts give way to the struggles for the reconstruction of new ones. (Rasmussen and Lund, 2018: 396)

In the crucible of the frontier, rights and authorities are challenged, suspended, eliminated, and ultimately recreated and re-territorialized (Li 2014, Lund 2013, Peluso and Lund 2011, Tsing 2005). The frontier constitutes a rupture—an open moment—particularly propitious for observing and analyzing how people rough out new social contracts of property and citizenship. We therefore need to see how old rights were underpinned, challenged, extinguished, and replaced by new ones. This is sometimes, but not always, represented in law, and sometimes, but not always, defended and enforced by statutory institutions. The effective existence of rights defined and promised in statutory law, thus, depends on the powers and interests of the authorities to enforce them.

A claim to land is always essentially political. It entails a claim to be seen as a rights subject and a corresponding recognition of the institution's power to recognize the claim as a right. Legal and political visibility as social beings is central to recognition of rights and enactment of social contracts. Yet, in a context of post-conflict where violent terror has been meted out by all sides—even if unevenly so—claims are not trivial. They are lodged with a heightened sense of risk. The presence of terror makes it very likely and understandable that political action will suffer intimidation and atomization (Arendt 1969, Sundar 2016, Taussig 2005). In fact, the interest in visibility as a rights subject may be canceled out by the interest in the relative safety of obscurity. This dilemma varies with the context, with people's courage, fool-hardiness, and desperation as well as their caution and despondency—all well demonstrated in Aceh's recent history. The central question for small-holders in Aceh was whether peace and the political ascendancy of GAM would enable them to claim land successfully, whether peace would prove favorable to their plight, or accelerate their dispossession.

In what follows, I take a closer look at the period of conflict in Aceh, focusing on institutional competition, transformation, and violence. I then sketch out how the post-conflict agricultural politics has actually operated on the ground, vis-à-vis the benefit accrued by plantations and the detri-ment sustained by small-scale farmers. This forms the context of current claims to land where smallholders have become all but abandoned insti-tutionally, while planters' claims align visibly with current policies of the province and country.

War and Postwar Land Politics

The inclusion of Aceh within Indonesia has always been a point of con-tention. The Acehnese resisted Dutch colonization and the area was never totally under Dutch control. After independence Indonesia was character-ized by turmoil and violence, and in Aceh the rebellion led by *Darul Islam* (House of Islam) was the first expression of resistance to centralized Indo-nesian rule (van Dijk 1981). In 1959, Aceh obtained special status, but it meant little in reality. However, when a local businessman, Hasan Tiro, was bypassed in subcontracting for the large hydrocarbon contracts that went to Exxon, he formed what was to become GAM in 1976. For many years, GAM did not pose a serious threat to Indonesian rule, but from 1998, when the rest of the country experienced the relatively peaceful *reformasi*, resistance grew more intense. Martial law was declared for Aceh in 2003, and GAM intensified its attacks on civil servants and administrative buildings representing the Republic of Indonesia (Schulze 2006). Following the tsunami in 2004, a peace accord was worked out in 2005.

From 1998, GAM's assassinations of civil servants and those whom they saw as collaborators instilled a fear among people matched only by the anxiety produced by army-organized disappearances and brutal incarcerations at a much greater scale. The conflict produced a generalized and well-founded terror of being seen as associating with, let alone organizing for, any political program that would hint at opposition against the Indonesian state. The individual victims of violence were surrounded by an entire society consumed by angst. The armed conflict with its random acts of terror was not over simply because peace came to Aceh. And, as in many post–civil war situations, neighbors who became enemies had become neighbors once again—only now with a poisoned history. Moreover, the peace accord left a considerable number of entrepreneurs trading in violence now looking for gainful employment. Young men who "used to be ordered around by their social betters suddenly found themselves with weapons, at the center of an exciting political venture, and with the ability to tell others what to do" (Aspinall 2009b: 12). In essence, the conflict and the modus operandi of the military and GAM left a legacy of imminent arbitrary violence, forceful extortion, and fickle protection. Consequently, property rights on all sides were tenuous.

Much of the original leadership of GAM had gone into exile in Sweden, and from Stockholm they issued the broad political orientations for the struggle, canvassing a discourse of nationalism and Islam.[4] In Aceh, on the ground, field commanders developed the military strategies. GAM also recruited among rural Islamic teachers, urban student activists, and especially village youths. The "*Ulama* served as administrators, advisers, teachers, and judges, while activists served as publicists, administrators, and teachers, and encouraged popular participation" (Barter 2015: 227). The general popular uprising against Suharto in the late 1990s took a nationalist turn in Aceh, and with the collapse of the New Order, GAM began to mobilize extensively. Some of its members were former soldiers and many hailed from backgrounds as small-town toughs. As Barter puts it, this "transformed the secessionist organization, which gained military capacity . . . but sacrificed reputation and discipline" (2015: 230). Young men, already quite familiar with the use of violence, flocked to GAM, and "local *preman*—small-time gangsters, petty criminals, and thugs—as well as the porters at markets or bus stations, whose job was to hustle passengers and cargo and whose work was sometimes legally dubious" (Aspinall 2009a: 165) made up an important element in the swelling ranks of the movement.

GAM gained ground from 1999, and targeted Indonesian government officials. Many were killed, more fled, and many village leaders resigned and handed in the stamps they used to officiate documents (Aspinall 2009a: 159).[5] Many village leaders simply switched to GAM and continued to perform their duties, though under the authority of a different "state." GAM, thus, began to register—legalize—land sales, resolve minor disputes, and even issue marriage licenses, often through the local *Ulama*. In such areas, smallholders held their land as part of a new social contract—however weakly specified—with GAM. Moreover, GAM took over those of the local schools they did not destroy.[6] They also began to extort "tax" from the population—especially ethnic Javanese plantation workers, companies, transporters, and even Indonesian civil servants and village officials. Especially, contractors were levied 10 percent of the construction budget as tax or protection money (Aspinall 2009a: 179–84, Schulze 2007a: 91–93). GAM targeted ethnic Javanese as they were seen to represent the invasive imperial power, with no future as citizens and rights subjects in a free Aceh. Hundreds of thousands of ethnic Javanese lived in Aceh as a result of historical work migration. GAM intimidated, harassed, and also killed Javanese farmers, and some 120,000–176,000 people are believed to have fled to North Sumatra during the war (Schulze 2006: 236). The forced displacement peaked between 1998 and 2005 as a result of the army's strategy of winnowing out rebels by dividing the landscape into "security zones," on the one hand, and GAM's attempt to intimidate ethnic Javanese on the other. Ethnic Acehnese of different stripes usually returned to their homes after weeks or months of displacement, whereas Javanese often left their homes never to return (Aspinall 2008: 127). The purge of the Javanese was the outcome of "deliberate violence, intimidation, and attacks, which, in turn, were in keeping with GAM's ethno-nationalist construction of Acehnese territory as the historic and exclusive property of the Acehnese" (Aspinall 2008: 133). Javanese transmigrants were depicted by GAM as the categorical enemy of the nation of Aceh. In terms of scale, however, the counterinsurgency was the main driver of displacement.[7]

In Aceh, during the war, this basic structure of the military's role and actions developed significantly. Successive security operations legitimated a massive presence of aggressive soldiers, and the absence of any accountability allowed them to conduct plunder at all levels (Aspinall 2006, Kingsbury and McCulloch 2006, McCulloch 2005a: 9 and 20, 2005b: 214, Robinson 2001: 226–31). The army was engaged in all sectors from logging, plantations, and construction to imposing traffic fines and controlling prostitution and drugs, and it provided protection for those who could pay. This included the oil production facility, but also plantations and other enterprises. In certain areas, the military organized proxy armies — gangs of militias prepared to do (even) dirtier work for them.[8]

Following the peace accord, GAM transformed into *Partai Aceh* in 2007, and the party won the following provincial election and governorship, most of the districts, and countless subdistricts (Aspinall 2014, IPAC 2015a). *Partai Aceh's* ascendance meant that a new circle of power emerged, but it did not change the conventional Indonesian power game of local politics.[9] Leaders of GAM soon captured the top positions in Aceh through *Partai Aceh*, and the GAM elite became active and influential in all kinds of business "backed by their freshly acquired political positions and connections" (Ansori 2012: 35, see also Aspinall 2009b, 2014).[10] The strong support for *Partai Aceh* and the party's subsequent conquest of the majority of political positions made the new elite virtually unassailable. Political office gave executive power and access to the immense reconstruction funds flowing into Aceh after the tsunami (McCawley 2014).

Two developments conjoined here. First, the level of unaccountable resource appropriation — corruption — had been on a steep rise, and even if cases had been taken to court, the public prosecutor's office had been known to stop them (Fadillah 2016; see also Aspinall 2009b, IPAC 2014, for variations of corruption). And second, the palm oil plantation complex had become a priority for any Acehnese government, regardless of its affiliation

(AICB 2015). The profitability of palm oil production made it tempting to promote plantations, illegal as well as legal, and legalize the operations in any perfunctory way available.[11] Consequently, while *peasants* had been the nation's salt in GAM propaganda, and small-town and rural populations had been the social base during the struggle, the interests of *Partai Aceh* had now shifted base. While GAM and *Partai Aceh* had promised radical change, the new dominant groups soon acquired stakes in the continuation of the structures against which they once fought. In power, they tended to align with those of the emerging elite (Ansori 2011, 2012, Aspinall 2009b, 2012, Firawati 2014).

Legalizing Dispossession in Postwar Aceh

Governments in Indonesia have consistently operated as if all land ultimately belongs to the state. They have remorselessly abrogated any current uses, however time-honored, by invoking "state interests." Moreover, despite recent legislator attempts to weed out inconsistencies, historically, legislation has backed competing rights and established overlapping jurisdictions for rival authorities (Bedner 2016a, Fitzpatrick 1997, Slaats et al. 2009). Concretely, land reform targeting the rural poor has been part of the political and legal promise—largely unfulfilled—since 1960, while, at the same time, the legislation also accommodates large-scale plantation agriculture through a lease system.

After the peace accord and the end of open, generalized violence, a new phase of land struggle began in Aceh. Small-scale farmers tried to reclaim land that they had previously cultivated with or without government consent. Alongside this, the Aceh government also initiated land allocation to smallholders in different ways. On the other hand, however, large-scale land concessions for plantation agriculture—especially the palm oil industry—were also reactivated and expanded on the coastal plains. Companies with leases began to claim back land holdings they had had to abandon during the conflict, and to extend them if possible. Hence, the peace accord allowed for old patterns of land acquisition and conflict to reemerge, but now in a new political context.

While there were competing, sometimes countermanding, political imaginaries for the future of Aceh (McCawley 2014, Phelps et al. 2011), investment in palm oil production has been an important carrier wave of the economic policy in the region in the past decade (AICB 2015). Oil palms can be farmed by plantations and smallholders, and in Indonesia the smallholder share varies from region to region, with a national average of approximately 40 percent in 2013 (Potter 2016: 320). Since the early 1980s, different schemes emerged that combine plantation estates with smallholder farming. In the early schemes, companies with land concessions ran a core plantation, while up to 80 percent of the land was farmed by smallholders who would get legal title (*hak milik*) to their land after they had reimbursed government or company loans for seedlings and other inputs. The Plantation Law of 2004 reversed the proportion between core plantation and smallholders to 80/20 in favor of the company and opened options for contract farming with decreased control of land for the participating smallholder (Julia and White 2012, Li 2015, McCarthy 2010, McCarthy and Cramb 2009, Pichler 2015, Potter 2016). While usually quite unfair, these schemes often proved an offer difficult to resist for the smallholders, since their land rights outside such schemes were very weak. Outside the scheme, people would only hold customary rights, which would yield to any government interest. The question in Aceh was which form of production to promote and which social contract of property the new political leadership would privilege. The policies for small- and large-scale agriculture intertwined with the peace process.

A two-tracked program for land allocation to smallholders was initiated in 2005, but neither option could show more than modest actual and durable success after the first few years. The first land allocation program was in fact part of the Peace Accord.[12] Former GAM fighters and former pro-Indonesia militias were to be reintegrated and victims of the war were to be compensated with land.[13] This program ran into problems in different ways. First, there was a conflict between the need to know and register the names of the beneficiaries and their desire to remain anonymous for fear of identification and subsequent assassination. Second, there were plans to transfer entire plantations owned and managed by government to ex-fighters. This scheme was halted by fear that government control and surveillance would be facilitated by the physical concentration of beneficiaries. Moreover, the practical challenge of identifying and parceling out and distributing the land seemed insurmountable to the Aceh Re-integration Agency.[14] As a result, compensation was paid in cash rather than in land to most ex-fighters.[15] The fact that GAM leaders were seeking to finance impending election campaigns no doubt also motivated the cash-in-hand approach.[16] Individual smallholdings were not part of the new government's vision of a social contract involving property in Aceh.

The other land allocation track was part of a more conventional program already familiar in the rest of Indonesia, and part of the new Aceh government's policy to promote palm oil production.[17] Here, government would invest part of the extra resources from the special share in the oil and gas resources established by the peace accord. In contrast to the program managed by the Aceh Re-integration Agency, this land allocation track was to be implemented by the regular Forestry and Plantation Office of the Aceh Province, and it formed part of the provincial program Green Aceh — Economic Development and Investment Strategy for Aceh (Shohibuddin 2014: 26–28, see also Lakhani 2016). Government would supposedly supply reform beneficiaries with seedlings and other inputs in addition to land, and the formal target group was smallholders, the original constituency of GAM and *Partai Aceh*.[18] However, large tracts of the designated public land were either already occupied by smallholders or situated in the vicinity of existing oil palm plantations that could integrate the land. Government policy soon evolved toward linking virtually all land redistribution programs to plantation agriculture in one form or other. Thus, in reality this land reform program dovetailed with the policy to expand oil palm plantations. First, rather than redistribution or new allocation of land, the reform consisted of a registration of land people already farmed. Furthermore, only 2 hectares could be registered, and it was expected that this land would be integrated into the plantation. If people farmed in excess of 2 hectares, no rights to the "excess" land would be recognized.[19] The irony was that in order to receive government recognition and legalization of land rights, the farmer had to surrender his property to a scheme where he lost control of it. Thus, passed off as land reform, the "redistribution" program in Aceh was, in fact, support to oil palm production and the integration—absorption—of smallholder property into plantations, as in many other parts of Indonesia. No wonder many farmers were more than skeptical about the idea.

Generally, local communities have rarely fully understood the implications of entering into a contract farming scheme with a company that had obtained a lease. They have often believed that the land would revert to them as individual holdings once the company's lease had lapsed. Smallholders would give up their land for a 25-year lease period, expecting it to revert to them after completion of the lease. However, according to the government administration in Aceh, local people only had valid claims to the land *as long as* they farmed it in a *traditional* manner.[20] Once they gave up the land for oil palm cultivation, any prior claims pertaining to the (essentially public) land terminated, and land reverted to being public land only. Thus, once the leases expired, the land would become public again, under the control of the government, now unfettered by the prior rights of smallholders who thereby disappeared from the equation altogether (Colchester and Chao 2013: 118–22).[21] In fact, contract farming schemes seemed to offer smallholders a form of indirect recognition of *their* property rights, but the price was to forfeit control of the land, and, ultimately, lose it for good.

In the field research areas in Aceh, contract farming was not configured to benefit smallholders. To sign a contract with the plantation company, smallholders would in principle have to join cooperatives created and controlled by the companies, which also appointed and paid the cooperative leaders. Payment to the farmer would then be channelled through the cooperative. Smallholders would have to borrow the capital for the initial investment in plants, drainage, and other capital costs, and the company would, in principle, offer such loans. Reimbursements would be deducted from crop earnings.[22] Some accepted in the vain hope that, somehow, this would secure their access to land and entail acknowledgment of their rights.[23] The reluctance of smallholder consent did not prevent companies from acquiring land through the lease system, however.

The plantation policies require a little more detail, because that is where the devil resides. The Basic Agrarian Law regulates plantation agriculture and operates with concession leases of 25–30 years. Plantation company owners need such leases in order to operate.[24] For a company to obtain a lease, it has to proceed through a number of well-defined steps (Sirait 2009: 32–36). After registration with the Board of Investment and application for a tax number, the company can apply for a location permit (*izin lokasi*) with the district and provincial governments (Wallace 2008: 195). This allows the company to search for, and subsequently acquire, suitable land within a specified area. The location permit will delineate an area of, say, 10,000 hectares *within which* the company can identify, say, 3,000 hectares for its operations. The location permit is, thus, not the actual lease, but the preliminary step to acquire one. The company must subsequently submit a business and land-use plan to the district government. The proposed land-use plan must align with the district and province development policies and specify the spatial outline of the plantation. At this stage, the Forestry Department must confirm that there is no overlap with existing forest use, and a fact-finding mission with participation from the district administration must ensure that smallholders are not already farming the concerned area. Then, an environmental impact assessment must be made, and finally the company can apply for the actual lease. In theory, that is.

During the New Order, these decisions were managed from Jakarta, but the post-Suharto decentralization reforms allocated authority to decide on the location permits to the district mayor. The fact that the issuance of the actual *lease* remained with the central government did not reduce the local incentive to issue *location permits* for money. As Pichler (2015: 525, see also Li 2017) points out, from a narrow administrative point of view at local government level, plantations are much easier and more lucrative than smallholders, who require all kinds of additional service. Moreover, whereas lease revenues go to the national coffers, the fees for location permits go to the district (Miller 2009: 167 and 177–82, Potter 2016), and since issuance of location permits is a one-off form of revenue, it is tempting for district governments to constantly issue new permits to plantation companies. After the war, the districts in Aceh thus began to issue location permits on a larger scale to companies again. By the end of 2010, some 200 permits had been issued to initiate the process of obtaining concession leases.[25] Issuance of location permits had become a serious source of income for district administrations.

Hence, while officially plantation companies must go through a long process to obtain a lease, in practice, more often than not, the companies did not obtain the full suite of necessary documents. Moreover, of those papers that they did have, some would often have expired, or been acquired in the wrong order, or were otherwise lacking in strict legal application. Most importantly, companies rarely verified that the land was not already farmed by someone. Mostly, it was.

Consequently, the companies often operated outside the law for most or all of the time. They operated *as if* they had the right and all the necessary papers. Usually, no one in the district office challenged the companies' rights to proceed, as long as illegal fees were forthcoming. Once the process started, the companies acted *as if* it was already completed. They legalized their illegal land acquisition by letting the inappropriate document—the location permit—masquerade as the actual lease and endow the operation with a luster of legality.

By acting *as if*, companies created and legalized an established fact for their purposes.[26] When companies with a location permit could act *as if* they had obtained the lease, they began to coerce and intimidate smallholders into abandoning their land. Companies would offer to buy land at a third of the going rate, or less. If that did not work, other tactics of intimidation were deployed.[27] When they were met with protest, they called on the police to stop the "unruly farmers." The companies would again argue that the land in question was within the leased area. It would be quite difficult for people to prove the opposite. As one informant explained:

> There are frequent spatial overlaps between land reform land and plantation leases. The authorities do not bother to verify on the ground, and the government [*Badan Pertanahan Nasional*, BPN/ National Land Agency] has little knowledge of what goes on in remote areas. People may well farm with customary rights, and they may also have SKT [*Surat Keterangan Tanah*, a document of the history of land rights and use] and even *hak milik* [exclusive transferable rights] through the help of their local *keucick* [village head] and *camat* [subdistrict head], but the land may still be within

the boundaries of plantation leases or *izin lokasi* [location permit] areas. In such cases the companies are much stronger. They [the companies] have the right to have people evicted if they are within the land of the plantation lease, but not if they are merely within the *izin lokasi*. Still, if they successfully evict people, the land effectively becomes part of the land under lease, and what was not legal in the morning has become legalized in practice in the afternoon—especially since there is no actual control of the surface area involved. This is measured—estimated—at the beginning, and then approximated as the plantation expands, but not in any detail. Thus, people become squatters and can be evicted as the plantation lease expands. The plantation companies pay the police to evict people and to ensure security within the plantation. Strictly speaking, this is not legal, yet it is current practice.[28]

Aceh's oil palm frontier has challenged smallholders' claims and rights, customary and informal as they may have been, and replaced them with others as new social contracts emerged. As the war ended in Aceh, peasants and planters expressed competing rights claims, and the new political leadership was called upon to engage in the reestablishment of a new social contract of rights. Who was going to enjoy property rights, and to whom would they be beholden? GAM had often relied on support from rural communities, and it could have been expected that relations between the new political powers and the peasantry would consolidate. Yet the support for GAM was uneven. Some areas inhabited by non-Acehnese, and especially plantation areas with transmigrant Javanese and their descendants, had been targeted by GAM for violence. Here, experience had taught the population to be watchful in dealings with either side.

Two Cases of Dispossession

Most conflicts between planters and smallholders display a common pattern. Yet they also have long histories and specific combinations of violence, political power, and paperwork. A close look at micro-processes allows us to situate agency, choice, and negotiations in the historical circumstances where hands may be dealt in advance but are not played mechanically. The following two cases capture this.[29]

A Case from East Aceh

After independence in 1945, a cluster of hamlets was unified and formed the village of Bawang.[30] The population was mixed, with Acehnese, Batak, and Javanese as the major groups. During the 1970s and 1980s the population grew and the farmed area increased. However, around 1990, the security situation deteriorated sharply as fighting between GAM and the Indonesian army intensified in the area. Many of the inhabitants fled the violence to other parts of Aceh and to neighboring North Sumatra.

The plantation company Bumi Flora was established in 1987. By 1989 the company had obtained a location permit setting aside 6,500 hectares in the area for oil palms. The company marked out zones for its plantation and included areas partly abandoned by the villagers of Bawang. Bumi Flora, in concert with the military, approached the *kampung* leaders who had remained in the area and coerced them to destroy and level the abandoned hamlets, making the land suitable for planting. There was some open resistance, with villagers blocking the access roads, but the presence of the military made any opposition imprudent; the military commander declared that all those who had fled the area were associated with GAM and hence were enemies of the state. Whatever land they had farmed was now unencumbered state land. Bumi Flora proceeded to have the new borders of its plantation established in 1990 and 1991. The National Land Agency and the District Agency for Forestry and Plantations conducted a field survey to establish that the area was "clean and clear." However, the report stated that 3,500 hectares of the total were, in fact, used by smallholders, and that signs of long-term residence remained in the area. Although houses had been razed to the ground, mosques and gravesites remained in the landscape amid the forlorn flotsam of foreclosed families.

A new report soon replaced the first one, however, and the National Land Agency stated that Bumi Flora was the only legal occupant of the public lands in question. Moreover, the company was beholden only to the government for its land. No other actors had legitimate legal claims to it. Nonetheless, in 1991, Bumi Flora invited the villagers to receive some compensation. A ceremony was organized at the army barracks where each farmer was photographed as he was handed an envelope of 100,000 Rupiah. Once the photo had been taken, the overseeing officer purloined some 20,000 Rupiah from each envelope while explaining that this was a fee, and the money was not compensation for the land but payment to the farmer for having cleared it. Around this time, villagers from Bawang created an association. However, a week later, the association's three leaders were detained. Some five days later, their brutalized bodies were found in a ditch.[31] In the following years, Bumi Flora obtained a series of authorizations and dispensations for past and future expansion of the plantation. By 1994—a few years into its operations—the company obtained its lease and its land acquisition was thereby legalized (Darusman 2010).

When Suharto's New Order crumbled in 1998, and land occupations multiplied in Indonesia, villagers in Bawang occupied some 1,000 hectares of the contested land. They blocked access routes used by company workers and organized a system of patrols. One month into the occupation, the military was called in to clear the area, and in a public ceremony replicating the one staged four years earlier, each of the four *kampung* leaders was presented with 30 million Rupiahs. In addition, some villagers were cajoled into signing two receipts: one for 700,000 Rupiah and another on which the figure had been left blank. No money ever accompanied these receipts.[32] The mood of *reformasi* soon evaporated in Aceh and a more intense state of emergency reigned, during which opposition or protest could be deadly.[33]

After the peace treaty in 2005, repression eased and people organized again. A rally invited speakers from various NGOs and popular movements in Banda Aceh. The night before it was due to take place, however, eight human rights activists were arrested and later convicted for seditious speech. Nonetheless, the organizers managed to enter into dialogue with the newly elected district mayor, M. Hasballah from *Partai Aceh*, about possible land redistribution. Hasballah had been a member of GAM and was generally seen as sympathetic toward smallholder demands. However, no concrete steps toward redistribution resulted. On the contrary, from 2008 the provision of plantation leases seemed to resume in Aceh, and, in the name of "development," Bumi Flora was able to add 3,000 hectares to its existing plantation.

In 2011 the farmers organized an occupation of part of the plantation. A thousand hectares were occupied, some oil palm trees were destroyed, and equipment was vandalized. It led to a public meeting at the district mayor's office with participation from the farmers' organization, representatives from Bumi Flora, the police, the army, lawyers, journalists, and public administration officials from the National Land Agency and the District Agency for Forestry and Plantations. The mayor decreed that a fact-finding team should be established to investigate the possibility of releasing some plantation land for the purpose of land reform. In 2013, the national land distribution program PRONA (*Proyek Operasi Nasional Agraria*) issued land certificates to 40 farmers in the area.[34] However, as these plots were inside the area under dispute, the National Land Agency refused to give effect to the final requisitions, arguing that it would be necessary to await the report of the district's fact-finding team. As one of the farmers explained, "I showed them the [PRONA] certificate as proof that the land is mine. But the police think it is a fake because it is a photocopy. But I will never give them the original. If I do, I will never get it back. It has been stamped and signed by the *camat* [village leader], so if it is fake, the *camat* made a fake document."[35]

The fact-finding team never got to finalize its report.[36] Following the elections in 2012, a new district mayor had taken office. Bumi Flora and other companies had generously supported his campaign, and upon taking office he put an end to the investigation. In addition to the financial support for his campaign, the new mayor received a few favors from the company. First, Bumi Flora and the other plantation companies subcontracted his private company to clear grounds in the plantations when they needed replanting. Second, they provided legal guidance to ease his acquisition of a personal location permit for a private plantation. They paid and instructed someone in the Agency of Forestry and Plantations to prepare all the necessary paperwork legalizing a private land acquisition in the name of the district mayor.[37] This form of "capacity building" was in all likelihood not directly illegal, but it facilitated the subsequent manipulation with location permits and actual leases. The upshot of these adjustments was that *Partai Aceh* did not push for land reform as promised, but effectively aligned itself with old elite plantation interests in East Aceh. There was a general mood, it was explained to me, that "things have moved back to the Suharto years, where politicians, military and companies were one."[38]

The case from East Aceh shows how the plantation company and the military initially forced the population of Bawang off the land and subsequently made an effort to make it look legal and fair. Moreover, despite promises of land reform and even the issue of empowering papers, any real reversal of plantation land control was delayed, sidetracked, or blocked.

A Case from West Aceh

During the war, villagers from Pisang began to clear an unused swampy and forested area near their village. The clearing was very gradual because of the danger of provoking either the army or GAM. By 2002, they had cleared some 20 hectares. After the peace accord, the clearing of land continued, and by 2008 the farmers had cleared 40 hectares and established a farmers' association with 60 members. However, the same year, the plantation company, PT PAAL, began to put up boundary markers, dig drainage ditches, and uproot the rubber trees planted by the villagers. Company workers and its security service—a motley crew of off-duty policemen and GAM ex-fighters—carried out the operation.

The farmers and their association protested. First, they addressed the district mayor, but to no avail. Then, in 2009, the villagers contacted the National Land Agency at the provincial office. As a part of the peace settlement, a land redistribution program had been initiated and it included the group of villagers who had cleared the swamp. However, land redistribution was not attractive or possible for all. Some villagers were offered land so far from their homes that they simply refused. For others, their identity proved a problem. To be eligible in the program, one's ID card had to read "Farmer." However, during the conflict, many GAM fighters had forged ID cards reading "Farmer" to blend in. As the Indonesian army targeted "Farmers" in the hunt for insurgents, many ordinary farmers responded by having their ID cards changed to "Worker" so as not to be mistaken for an insurgent (McCulloch 2005a: 18). Ironically, this disqualified many from benefiting when the land reform came.

At the same time, PT PAAL obtained a location permit covering the villages concerned. The permit—of some 8,300 hectares—entitled the company to identify suitable, unoccupied, and uncontested land for its plantation. Once such land was identified, the company could proceed to apply for the actual lease. While the location permit allowed the company to search for land *within* this area, the company and the district administration in practice considered the location permit *as good as* the possible resulting concession lease. PT PAAL therefore mobilized big machinery to construct drainage canals, to uproot local farmers' crops, and to spray their vegetable gardens with herbicides, making their crops inedible. After this, the land was physically incorporated into the plantation. In July 2011, a second batch of land reform certificates was issued by the National Land Agency to the villagers. This encouraged people to resume their protest, and they went to the land in question to destroy the newly planted oil palm seedlings. Called in by the company, three truckloads of police officers then descended on the area and put it under embargo. In principle, this meant that no one could farm it; yet in practice PT PAAL continued to operate on the land. The villagers contacted the National Land Agency and a field survey was conducted in January 2012. The National Land Agency declared that the redistributed land was, indeed, located within PT PAAL's concession area. No further action was taken.

The company called for a meeting with the villagers at the police station with the police commander as chair. At this meeting, the company offered three alternatives: the farmers could swap the land for land somewhere else; they could sell the land outright to the company (that is, they would sell or give up their claim); or they could allow their land to be part of a subcontracting scheme. Any one of these options would deprive farmers of control over the land. Even though no one wanted to swap their land for land of uncertain location and unknown quality, a handful of people agreed to sell their land to the company. As for the rest of the farmers, their land, too, was equally incorporated into the plantation, and they then faced unpleasant alternatives. Either they could join the cooperative and sign up for contract farming, or they could refuse to do so, with a slim chance of ever recovering their fields again or receiving any other benefit. Around half of the 60 farmers submitted to joining the scheme, and later explained their regrets in the course of several interviews.

The company had initially promised to train the smallholders, and to provide fertilizer and pesticides. Moreover, the company undertook to buy the harvest at a price fixed by the government. However, the actual experience was quite different. Instead of farming their own two hectares under the guidance of the company, each farmer's land was absorbed into the plantation, and all physical markers of that particular field were gone. The landscape was changed. A farmer usually knows that his land stretches from this ditch to these trees, and then from this rock to this farmhouse—from mark to intimately known mark. However, once the land was included within the plantation, all such recognizable physical characteristics disappeared. During one of the visits to the area with one of the "included" farmers, he pointed to the endless rows of oil palms and explained to me, "my land is in there, somewhere." His property had faded into perfect impalpability.[39]

In principle, the farmers who signed up for the contract scheme would get a 40/60 cut of the production profit. However, of the 40 percent, 10 percent would go to administrative costs and the remaining 30 percent was supposedly paid through local government into the cooperative account of the farmer. All of the farmers we talked to had yet to receive *anything*. The farmers who signed up ceased to be farmers and instead became a kind of *lumpen* rentier class, with no control over their land. They might own land and pay tax for it, they might even be registered as smallholders in national statistics, but they had no say in what to farm, nor could they retrieve their land.[40] Some relinquished their claim to the company for money. Others simply resigned. As for those who stayed outside the cooperative, their land was still absorbed into the plantation, perforce, and could no longer be identified in the landscape.

The farmers in Pisang had gradually broken new land and were hoping to have their rights to it recognized. Especially after the peace accord, recognition seemed realistic. However, the case from West Aceh shows how the plantation company managed to incorporate the village land into its plantation and legalize it by deliberate misrepresentation of the location permit. This second case further shows how equal measures of attrition and fear wore down the villagers. Violence and intimidation from police and the company, and indifference from local government, left the villagers alienated from their land and without political recognition. Despite peace, promises of land reform, and the arrival of *Partai Aceh* at the head of the province, they had effectively been severed from the social contract of property.

Conclusion

Frontiers are characterized by the suspension of old orders and the opportunity to create and territorialize new ones, and the entire war period in Aceh can be seen as a frontier struggle over what should become the prevailing agrarian order. While smallholders had high hopes that GAM, transformed into *Partai Aceh*, would act in their interest, peace instead paved the way for expansion of the oil palm plantation sector. The initial policies in favor of smallholders combined with the practice of plantation lease policies and resulted in the absorption of smallholdings. It could, indeed, be argued that this, more than anything, made Aceh look like the rest of Indonesia, even if the historical background of war was specific (Anderson 2014, Colchester and Chao 2013, Colchester et al. 2003, Colchester et al. 2006, Sirait 2009, Tiominar 2011). Oil palm production was already a part of the agricultural repertoire, but, with peace, interests and powers realigned anew to reinforce plantation production.

The frontier dynamics in Aceh combined violent evictions and subtler forms of erosion of competing claims. Smallholders' history, identity, and property were often used to disqualify them as rights subjects or render them politically and legally invisible. Javanese plantation workers turned land occupants and smallholders may structurally have looked like Acehnese smallholders, but politically they did not. They attracted no support from GAM or *Partai Aceh*, who could not reconcile their presence with a nationalist project. Many were disqualified as rights subjects and, facing precarious citizenship in the new Aceh, they left. To this must be added the perverse effects of wartime accidents such as identity card manipulation, which rendered entire groups invisible as entitled smallholders. Victory, indeed, delivered the hardest blow. *Partai Aceh*'s political ascent after the war did not produce effective change in overall policies in favor of plantation agriculture. Instead, legalization of plantation expansion through leases—genuine and adulterated alike—multiplied.

The lease acquisition system for plantations included ambiguous measures to protect smallholders. However, district administrations and other government institutions generally allowed location permits to pass for fully acquired leases, and smallholders were turned into squatters constantly on the back foot when it came to confrontation. The dual policy of smallholder and plantation development may look balanced and progressive, with potential for providing smallholders with secure tenure and a good livelihood. However, the "integration" of smallholders into the operation of plantations took the form of absorption in many places. No spatial feature of smallholder property remained distinct after "integration," and the smallholder's labor was no longer tied to his own land: the embrace of the production of oil palm was total. The dispossession and alienation of smallholders through the conjuring trick of contract schemes thus worked to legally dissolve the spatial properties of their holdings. Only occasionally were the contracts between smallholders and plantations established in writing. Such ephemeral contracts further exposed smallholders to dispossession by the companies, which could simply ignore their side of the bargain. In contrast, photographic "documentation" was used by companies to record, and misrepresent, "fair" compensation. Again, this illustrates the fundamental paradox of this book, namely, that law is neither disregarded nor respected in a narrow sense. Instead, law is deployed to legalize and lock in settlements by invocation of state power. Adding the last tenth of legalization to company possession secured state enforcement as well as durability to make rights outlast the current moment of simple superiority and relative success. Even with the overwhelming military force prepared to evict those who had not already fled their village, a public spectacle of compensation was carefully staged and documented to legalize the dispossession. All of this occurred in the lingering shadow of violence and fear from the preceding war. Perhaps this explains why the organizational potential of smallholders as a class to be reckoned with has remained in abeyance. Violence, actual or present as a pervasively credible threat, prevented the effective organization of small-holders' claims. Smallholders' claims to landed property have weakened over the last two decades in rural Aceh. In the postwar frontier moment, smallholders' land rights have been suspended in a violent rupture, allow-ing the growth of plantations. In the areas studied for this chapter, GAM and *Partai Aceh* supported peasant land occupations only sporadically and ineffectively, leaving people ever more vulnerable to dispossession as local government and capital legalized the creation of plantations by fair means and foul.

Violence has been prominent in the land struggles in Aceh. Sometimes, however, more subtle maneuvering and ostentatious civic compliance may dominate—as the next chapter on Bandung demonstrates.

CHAPTER SIX

On Track

Spontaneous Privatization of Public Urban Land

In 2013 and 2014 two mysterious fires damaged the office of the Assets and Financial Management Agency in Bandung. They destroyed the office building of the city's Integrated Permit Agency of Municipal Government, and an unknown number of land planning documents and certificates were lost. It happened after elections in the interregnum between two mayors. The old mayor had to leave office after he was detained by the Anti-Corruption Commission, put on trial, and prosecuted at the state court for bribery and corruption. The newly elected mayor had not yet established control of the municipal bureaucracy and administration. For all its paucity, the paper documentation of land rights in Bandung became even more rudimentary after the fires. As facts on paper were flammable and became harder to produce, facts on the ground became all the more important.

Large populations in urban Indonesia live at the margins, with precarious rights to property and citizenship. Since colonial times, government has been able to declare land as state property and thus, at the stroke of a pen and with the backing of force, turned residents into squatters. Dispossessed, they became legally and often politically invisible to government. Their rights were expunged and their claims rendered incompatible with government's own property rights. Residing at the margins within the planned city, urban *kampung* dwellers often have good reason to be suspicious of public authority and prefer to keep open the option of obscurity. Political visibility cuts two ways, however, and to be *invisible* as a rights subject inevitably delegitimizes any claim to legal rights and makes such legalization impossible (Arendt 1973: 296, Somers 2008: 21). Therefore, careful choices of visibility and obscurity have to be made on a daily basis. While judiciously avoiding certain governing agencies, people simultaneously try hard, using imagination and flexibility, to be seen by others instead. People improvise ways in which to present themselves and their claims that are visible not only to the appropriate institution of authority but also to a public from which more general support may be forthcoming.

The competition over space seems especially tense in urban areas where the effects of marginalization are dire. Urban areas have been objects of attention from very different angles. De Soto's influential book, *The Mystery of Capital,* focuses exclusively on the absence of recognition of private property as the single decisive feature that keeps people at the margins of society (de Soto 2000). It is true that property rights are important and that the exclusivity of ownership represented by government-recognized deeds is often something people aspire to have. However, Santos's work from Brazil in the 1970s (1977) demonstrates how the marginalized may construct and reproduce their own legalities in parallel with government regulation. And in later work Holston (1991, 2008) shows how government institutions manipulate the law, while ordinary people are forced to create legality for themselves. I therefore suggest that a fixation on government-recognized *private property* blinds us to other relevant forms of acquiring space, securing access to land, and gaining recognition and legalization of claims, livelihoods, and residence. Furthermore, I argue that claims to space are made up of a web of specific relations of recognition, and that sometimes formal private property need not be part of what makes rights effective and land tenure secure and certain.

This chapter examines these different claims and relations of recognition in detail. Specifically, it analyzes struggles over urban space in Bandung, a city of some two-and-a-half million inhabitants. A significant amount of land in the central zone of the city has been public land since colonial times. Thus, the municipal government claims to have the "authority to exercise a direct right over 51 per cent of the city's land" (Reerink 2011: 95). Large swaths of these public lands are now under informal settlement, however, and land is effectively privatized while its formal legal status remains turbid. The unclear status of the areas has not prevented those who live there from actively claiming effective rights to be there.

The chapter focuses on a particular piece of land, a strip alongside a now inoperative railway line. Approximately 30–50 meters wide and 5 kilometers long, it stretches through the central parts of the city. As infrastructure, it falls within the ambit of government spatial control. Yet the area has become a settlement for ordinary people through an intricate combination of claims. The selection of this urban setting for our study is not a claim that spontaneous privatization is generalized in Indonesia, in its urban areas, or even in Bandung. Instead, it is an example of how privatization *can* take place even where one would suppose that government control over space is rather strong. If privatization dynamics nonetheless unfold under the nose of government, these are dynamics worth studying in many other places. The analytical argument is developed in the following section. Thereafter, a brief outline of the history of informal, unplanned urban settlement in Java is provided as a context for this study of the spontaneous privatization of a stretch of inoperative railway track in Bandung.

Property Bundles and Representation

Privatization of public land generally means the transfer of property rights to land hitherto held by public institutions or agencies to private individuals or companies. In deliberate privatization policies, the transfer of property can be done in one swift move, so to say. It may thus look as if we are witnessing the transfer of a single, consistent, and absolute right to one single thing. Indeed, it may even look as if the property is the thing— the land—itself (McPherson 1978). However, in the case of Bandung (and many other places), such transfers from public to private take place in informal, non-guided, incremental, incomplete, and non-consensual—sometimes even contentious—ways. In such contexts, it becomes obvious that, in fact, many different claims are being "expressed" at the same time through people's privatization of public lands. It is therefore necessary to break down the overall claim into its constituent parts. It makes sense to see the rights to space as a "bundle of rights" (Benda-Beckmann, Benda-Beckmann, and Wiber 2006). Such bundles include rights of different consequence, such as rights to access, to be present, to reside over time, to construct a house, to extract benefit, or to conduct business, as well as the rights to transact all of those rights, by renting out the right to reside or selling it outright. People often refer to such transactions as buying and selling land. However, this is inaccurate. What is bought and sold is not land, or even government-recognized land rights, but the *imperfect* bundle of rights, warts and all. The seller sells the imperfect rights s/he has, and the new landholder or house owner will hold the land and house under similar conditions of legal imperfection and possible uncertainty. What is transacted are *land right opportunities*—that is, the opportunity to legalize possession as property. Sometimes, this works better than at other times, and the realization of this opportunity probably lies as much in the context and circumstances as in the nature of the right in question.

Rights are, basically, claims that are recognized by some form of authority or the surrounding community (Macpherson 1978, Sikor and Lund 2009). And as we break down the overall claim to space into its constituent parts, we see that these claims are not all addressing the same kind of authority for recognition. Many claims are recognized as rights by statutory institutions, but in a complex institutional environment—such as a city—there are many competing government institutions with which people can lodge claims. Sometimes, claims fall outside an institution's formal mandate or jurisdiction. But appeals to institutions to recognize claims even beyond their formal mandate can actually work to extend the institutions' *effective* jurisdiction. In Indonesia, the state's ultimate authority in land questions is widely recognized. Yet determining which of the many government institutions will actually represent this state authority is more open to political contestation. People's claims invest the institution with an *expectation* of public authority, and the extended jurisdiction may become effective if the

claims endure as effective rights. Institutions that are not statutory or part
of government also operate in ways to define and enforce claims as rights.
They may be companies, religious institutions, social movements, or gangs.
By appealing to such institutions, people may actually invest them with
public authority as well.

In contexts of multiple claimants to space, and multiple possible authorities to recognize them, it is difficult to talk of rights as unequivocal. Rather,
we are looking at competing attempts to make a case for the rightfulness of
different claims (Rose 1994). And rather than looking for one overarching
recognition of a single claim as property, we face a dense, dynamic web of
relations of recognition between claimants and institutions. Some of these
relations align with and reinforce one another. Others compete, challenge,
and suspend one another. In such situations, the practical question is not so
much whether rights to property exist or not, but rather with what security
and certainty land is held. It is possible that there is no single dominant
rights claim but rather a mix of more or less compatible claims backed more
or less effectively by different institutions.

Concretely, different documents, artifacts, and physical edifices represent
the relations of mutual recognition and hence legalization. In this particular case, there are land tax receipts for residential structures, and quittances
for payment of business tax on workshops and restaurants on the railway
tracks, suggesting some form of legitimate presence. There are visible census stickers on windows showing residence. There are signboards from the
railway company and others signaling ownership, and physical structures
such as voluntary community police sentry boxes on the land demonstrating authority, as well as other buildings such as houses, mosques, schools,
and local communal infrastructure established by government agencies.
Many of these material representations are props and paraphernalia of the
state, and by invoking the idea of statutory authority, a simple census sticker
bestows an air of legality on the house, its occupant, and the occupation
itself. Which of these many representations are most persuasive as rightful
claims to the space is, indeed, an empirical question.

This chapter therefore inspects the broad range of claims to space and
the connections of recognition they constitute along the now abandoned
rail tracks running through Bandung municipality. Claims and rights often

develop by contingent increment. Therefore, a historical perspective—
from the first claims to land along the then-active railway line, up to the
present—is useful. The railway line cuts through nine *kelurahan* (sub-
sub-municipalities) in the municipality of Bandung over approximately
5 kilometers. First, however, we need to situate this space in the context of
planned and spontaneous urban development in Java.

History of Informal, Non-Planned Settlements in Urban Java

Urban landscapes develop in a mix of government plans and more spontaneous activities driven by individuals and groups. At some moments,
plans and legislation are "ahead" of demography and economy; at other moments, demography and economy drive development. Hence, urban spaces
can be defined in administrative and political terms as municipalities with
specific legal and developmental attributes, or in terms of demographic
density and economic agglomeration. The modernization of the Indonesian cities has been a constant struggle between, on the one hand, a government planner's ambition of order and progress through standardization,
structure, and adequate infrastructure, and, on the other, a more unwieldy,
opportunistic, provisory pragmatism (Colombijn and Coté 2015). Bandung
represents both developments. Focus in this chapter is on urban spaces in
Bandung, where spontaneous land acquisitions, settlements, and use have
challenged government-planned land use. Hence, the chapter investigates
an urban space that supposedly is fully under the control of government and
its planners, but effectively is only partially controlled by it. Such areas are
not new but have history.

During the early stage of colonization, the Portuguese and the Dutch
built their trade and military bases in towns within the coastal area. In the
late nineteenth century, Bandung grew as a commercial town in the center
of plantations in the Priangan area, and earned its fashionable sobriquet,
Parijs van Java. At one point, the Dutch colonial government even considered making Bandung the capital of the Dutch Indies (Reerink 2011: 26). As
the city grew, Bandung absorbed surrounding villages, and they developed
into urban neighborhoods, *kampungs*. As Reerink (2011: 27) points out, these
"*kampungs* were allowed a high degree of autonomy, which mean[t] that

the population could apply its own customary administration, and administration of justice, also in relation to land."[1] Consequently, in terms of demographic density, professional occupation, and general economy, Bandung and other cities in the Dutch Indies developed as urban areas. Bandung officially became a town in 1906. Administratively and politically, however, much of the urban area remained "rural." While geographically engulfed by the expanding cities, administratively and legally many *kampungs* remained rural settlements (Reerink 2011: 29). Some municipalities of large cities like Semarang, Surabaya, and Medan began to undertake "*kampung improvement*" before the *kampungs* had been integrated administratively into the city, thus infringing on village autonomy. In Bandung, the last rural *kampungs* were integrated into the city in 1964 (Colombijn 2013: 186). This process of urbanization was far from smooth.

Many Dutch and other Western residents abandoned their properties in urban areas during the Japanese occupation from 1942 to 1945. At the same time, agricultural production in the rural areas was redirected to support the Japanese war effort. Famine hit rural areas in many parts of Java and, as a result, migration to urban areas increased. The Japanese military encouraged local people in urban areas to cultivate any available vacant land without seeking permission from the tenured owner (Colombijn 2013: 168, Tunas and Peresthu 2010). This was the beginning of widespread squatting of urban land. In 1943, the Japanese introduced a system of neighborhood unit association, which later was refined as *Rukun Tetangga*, or RT (smaller neighborhood association) and *Rukun Warga*, RW (greater neighborhood association).[2] It functioned to control the population and, at the same time, to support mobilization for war purposes (Jellinek 1991: 106, Reerink 2011: 33).

After the war, flows of people pulsed from and to urban areas, while policies vis-à-vis informal settlements in urban areas went through cycles of "tolerance and repression" (Colombijn 2012: 233, 2013: 207–27). During the Indonesian revolution and fight for independence, Sukarno and the Republican leadership encouraged squatting on public land and Dutch plantation land in defiance of colonial rule (Abeyasekere 1989, Colombijn 2012: 232). The Dutch military chased suspected freedom fighters in the urban *kampungs*. The colonial government even issued a law that made illegal occupation of urban land a criminal act (Reerink 2011: 33).[3] After independence in 1945, the conflicts between Islamic separatists, communists, and nationalists created significant insecurity in the countryside, once again propelling large numbers of refugees into urban centers (Cybriwsky and Ford 2001, Reerink 2011). They often settled on public lands such as cemeteries, on the banks of rivers and canals, and, as in the present case, along railway tracks.

In this chaotic political and economic situation, land occupations organized by the Communist Party as part of its challenge to the government were widespread. Other political groups and different professional associations, such as the Association of National Entrepreneurs, and the Association of Small Entrepreneurs and Traders in Jakarta, also supported the informal settlements and argued against evictions (Colombijn 2013: 218). In 1958, the government nationalized properties and assets of Dutch individuals and companies in Indonesia. Many vacant lands thereby became available in urban and rural areas. The first 20 years of independence were characterized by significant violence and unrest. When Suharto came to power after ousting President Sukarno in 1965, and the Communist Party was banned, alleged communists and sympathizers were persecuted as government began to exercise tightening control over the population. In this climate, military and civilian officials, as well as private individuals backed by youth gangs and paid thugs, seized the opportunity to evict people from informal settlements for their personal benefit. Land, property, and spatial control were central features, Colombijn (2012, 2013) suggests, in the struggle between communist organizations, on the one hand, and land owners and the military on the other. After 1966, conflicts over space frequently ended with forced evictions "for public benefit." Yet none of this stopped the irregular occupation of vacant urban lands (Davidson 2015, Tunas and Peresthu 2010, Winayanti 2010).[4]

During the New Order, government considered land to be crucial in attracting foreign investment, and it issued the first of a series of decrees on land acquisition to secure "land for development." However, as Winayanti points out, "while new regulations were being produced to support private investment . . . there was no clear town planning law to guide urban development. . . . Town planning was being steered *de facto* by ministerial decrees and regulations produced by the Ministry of Home Affairs and the Ministry of Public Works. Subsequently, town planning became a source of rivalry between the two ministries" (2010: 60).

Moreover, corners were cut for developers who had permits for construction processed with the planning authorities (Hudalah 2010: 38, see also Dieleman 2011). During the New Order, small-scale urban landowners were in a weak position vis-à-vis government, and tenure security for people considered to be squatters by government was especially precarious. Importantly, the legislation did not allow for the acquisition of rights through uninterrupted adverse possession (Fitzpatrick 1997: 197). In other words, no matter how long people had been settled on the land, the law did not see that as a way to acquire rights to it.

The measure of democracy and decentralization that followed the defeat of the New Order after 1998 had two significant consequences. First, people—even informal settlers—now constituted an electorate, which politicians could not afford to neglect entirely. Second, land administration was first decentralized, then recentralized, and its basis was reworked four times in 10 years. Inevitably some confusion resulted from different competencies at different levels of government. For example, Moeliono (2011: 191–299) points out that the Spatial Planning Law of 2007 is inconsistent in its allocation of planning powers between levels of government.

Therefore, when communities settled on urban land, their rights remained opaque, to say the least. Security of tenure was less a question of right and wrong, and more a matter of actively building a contextually persuasive argument and establishing as many relations of effective recognition by significant institutions as possible. The interaction between government agencies with their (often incoherent) policies and local strategies to secure valuable rights to the urban space are best approached through a detailed case study.

History of the Railway Company Land in Bandung

The still visible if long-silenced railway tracks of the line between Bandung and Ciwidey tell a story of the gradual appropriation of space. Here

Mosque on the tracks in Bandung, West Java (Photo: Ari Nurman)

and there, the tracks are above ground, but then they disappear under a house, a car workshop, a mosque, or a community police station, only to reappear some meters behind the building, now paved as a street, encrusted in a badminton court or a schoolyard, disappearing again under a restaurant or a shop. The ghostly tracks are there. Yet the space looks like most densely populated neighborhoods of the city.

This section presents a brief history of the railway line that once connected Bandung and Ciwidey, and of the changes in the management of the train company, and describes how this has affected the changes in land use along the decommissioned railway line. The section shows the gradual transfer in control of the land along the non-active line from the Railway Company to residents, and how people have tried to make persuasive claims to legalize their presence on that land.

The Railway Line

The history of railways on the Bandung plateau starts with the colonial period and the need to transport goods for export. The Dutch colonial government had the railway between Bandung and Ciwidey built in the period 1918–24.[5] From independence in 1945 until early 1970, the railway was the main connection between Bandung and Ciwidey, with three services daily. Road transport improved during the 1970s, however, and by 1980 the line, now considered unprofitable, was closed for good.[6]

The company also underwent a series of changes in its institutional setup. Shortly after Indonesia declared its independence, the Train Youth Movement (*Angkatan Muda Kereta Api*, AMKA) took over the railway system in September 1945.[7] This was one of the thousands of youth gangs and movements engaged in the struggle for independence. The movement tried to secure the country's infrastructure for the republican government, and declared the establishment of *Djawatan Kereta Api* (DKA), a state train company.[8] With its central office located in Bandung, this train company operated mainly in Java and Madura. Meanwhile, *Staatspoorweg* and *Verenigde Spoorweg Bedrijf* (SS/VS) managed train operations in Sumatra, still under Dutch occupation.

The international recognition of the sovereignty of the Republic of Indonesia in 1949 brought the nationalization of the company. The DKA became *Djawatan Kereta Api-Repoeblik Indonesia* (DKARI) in 1950. This meant that the train service was directly under the control of—and managed as part of the services overseen by—a government ministry of transportation.[9] Since the 1960s, however, the train service has evolved, first into a company owned by the Ministry of Transport and then into an "open company"—open to private investors and not eligible for government subsidy. In 2007, the government privatized the train company and abolished its monopoly on train operation. In a nutshell, this meant that all operations had to be profitable or else they would be discontinued.

In terms of ownership, the railway land was state land when the railway was first constructed. State land—*tanah negara*—implies that the state "administers" all land on behalf of the Indonesian people (Bedner 2000). The authority over state land was delegated by the National Land Agency as right to manage (*hak pengelolaan lahan*) to various state and state-owned companies. When the railway company was privatized, the land under the actual tracks remained public land and was now rented out to the company, whereas the company owned the land upon which its buildings stood.[10] With the Decentralization Law of 1999, the authority over delegated state land became rather unclear. What levels of government represented the "state" entrusted with public land? In cases where such lands were not effectively controlled by the company but ceded to settlements of ordinary people, the situation was hardly any clearer. Who held the rights to the land was far from a settled fact; it became a fact to settle.

Occupying the Land

The landscape alongside the railway between Bandung and Soreang was once dominated by rice fields and scattered settlements, but gradually, during the late 1970s, it was transformed into residential areas. The first housing complex, the Buah Batu Baru, located at the western side of the railway, was built during this period. The land east of the tracks was divided into housing plots and sold by the farmers who had cultivated rice on the land. In fact, what was transacted was the use-right, the *hak garapan*.[11] Several other housing complexes were built—some by the railway company for its workers. As the housing development emerged alongside the railway land, the first buildings were erected on the actual railway land by residents very close to the then still active tracks. It included food stalls—*warungs*—serving people in the emerging settlements, and confirming the popular Javanese stereotype that you can always fit in a *warung*, even in the smallest empty space.

People gradually began to settle on the unused railway land and cultivate it when the trains ceased to run in the 1980s. Generally, each new settler chose the size of his or her plot. Only in the village of Kujangsari did the village official divide and allocate the railway land. The settlers first put marks on the land by planting certain trees and cultivating the land with cassava, taro, vegetables, banana, and other rain-fed crops. Some people simply occupied the land, while others asked for permission from the nearest official, either the stationmaster or the railway controller.[12] It would appear that none of the controllers ever forbade or prevented the occupation. In the early phase of occupation, the residents paid informal rent to the stationmaster and the controller of the railway. The amount and the terms varied. Those near Cibangkong station, for example, paid rent to the train master, the amount being decided by him. Meanwhile, residents who occupied land farther from train stations paid rent to track controllers. In some areas, the occupants said that no one had obliged them to pay anything. Usually, however, the controllers would come to visit people living on the tracks once a year, during Ramadan, to extend *silaturahim* (an Indonesian Islamic term for renewing social relations). This was the occasion when the residents would offer small amounts of money to thank the controllers for letting them stay on the land.[13] At first, the stationmasters and controllers allowed the residents to cultivate the land as long as they did not erect any buildings. This "prohibition" seems to have been effective only briefly, however. The size of the plots varied. Some had 20 square meters, but others took 200 square meters. One particular settler took about four hectares. It would have been obvious to stationmasters and controllers that the intention in all cases was to build and settle.

Consolidating the Occupation

In the period between 1981 and 1984, the land along and on the inoperative railway came to be completely occupied. The rice fields along the railway land were converted to housing, first as non-permanent houses made of bamboo. Verbal agreement and tacit understanding between the house owner and the stationmaster were common, but, more importantly, the surrounding community, neighbors, and the head of the neighborhood association also acknowledged the legitimacy of the building by assisting in its construction. Soon, some residents with small parcels of land expanded their holding by buying their neighbors' land, and residents with larger plots of land started to divide, sell, and rent out land to third parties. From around 1990, residents gradually started to improve their housing. They invested in construction and transformed the non-permanent bamboo structures into semi-permanent houses. Bit by bit, people cemented their floors and built brick walls; some began to put in a second story. According to our interviews, no one ever prevented people from improving their houses. Hence, over a period of five years, the land along the railway tracks was completely taken over for other purposes. Following the occupation, the new residents began to further consolidate their residence by a range of different activities. The railway land was absorbed into ordinary neighborhood settlements and began to look like other *kampungs* in Bandung. Few features were visible to distinguish them from the more regularized structures, irrespective of the legal status of the land. The railway land had become part of their space. This did not happen overnight, but by many combined increments.

Obtaining an Address

One of the most obvious forms of recognition is an officially accepted address. Residents in a new, informal residential area had addresses that did not exist prior to the settlement but were produced as a part of it. They made the residence visible. There were several alternative ways of obtaining an address, depending on the local situation. When the occupied land was located in the extension of an alley or street that already had a name, people simply put a number on the front of the house. If their house was located far from an alley, they made their own alley, named it, and put a number on the house. Very often, the number was not merely a continuation of the sequence from the neighbor's house, but rather the number of the house across the street with a letter added, such as 123B. Sometimes, if there were not yet close neighbors, people would form their own neighborhood and often use a single number for the cluster of houses and add an "S," for example 10S. The number would be taken from the closest house in the alley that connected their neighborhood with the nearest road. The letter "S" was for *sementara* (temporary). Later, residents would number the houses individually. The litmus test of this form of officialization was whether the postman could find the house with the address. New residents therefore systematically asked relatives in their hometowns to write to them, and during our interviews they proudly produced letters that had found their way to their houses.

As a part of obtaining an address people affiliated themselves with the nearest *rukun tetangga* (RT), to become recognized residents of the neighborhood.[14] In some areas along the railway line, residents decided to form an RT on their own, and obtain recognition from the *rukun warga* (RW). Usually, this worked. It meant being counted in the regular national census, as the census staff would liaise with the RT and RW structure. People received a small sticker from the government to put on the window acknowledging their presence. Once official recognition from the RT was established, it was possible to apply for various formal letters. The head of the RT had the authority to issue statement of residency (*surat pernyataan domisili*). This letter provides a basis on which the Kecamatan (Sub-District Office) will issue an Indonesian ID card (*Kartu Tanda Penduduk*, KTP) on behalf of the municipality; a KTP, in turn, is the basis for accessing various benefits, such as scholarships and subsidized health care. Such official letters were thus a key to access rights as citizens. In elections to the RT, residents on railway land would vote and could get elected, like any other citizen. Indeed, some of the RTs had found space for sentry boxes for the neighborhood watch, as well as for small RT offices that used the railway tracks as a foundation.

Amenities

Most people who settled on the railway company's land had some degree of access to electricity, water, and sanitation. However, such services were not all acquired "by the book." Most houses had electricity. In principle, the electricity company had to insist on a letter from the legal landholder allowing the inhabitants to have electricity installed. None of the inhabitants we interviewed had actually had to produce such a letter from the railway company, however. Instead, people had simply paid the staff of the power company to "arrange everything" without such a permit. People then had a normal meter installed, in their own name, which was read regularly like those of other customers. There were cases where the occupants, for different reasons, could not obtain a proper connection. They generally made arrangements with the nearest neighbor to connect to their supply, and then shared the cost. Some tapped electricity directly from the nearest electricity wire without paying, but this seemed to be an exception, and was usually a temporary measure.

The municipal water company considered the settlement to be informal. The residents, therefore, in principle had not been able to apply for a proper water connection. However, in reality, some of the inhabitants had water connections with meters. The boundary between what is considered a regular settlement and what is informal squatting, in the eyes of the water company, moved over the years as houses appeared to be more and more permanent, and people had received ID cards making their addresses official in the 1990s. The owners of houses that were serviced like this sometimes extended pipes from their house to a neighbor's, and split the bill in various ways.

Generally, the neighborhoods along the railway land managed to provide themselves with sanitation services. Most of the houses had indoor toilets or bathrooms. Sometimes, neighbors would have shared facilities. Most people's houses were connected via the wastewater pipe to nearby streams and drainage systems. Some houses were equipped with individual septic tanks. They were generally put in when the owners improved the house. Finally, some had begun to connect the wastewater pipe to the nearby municipal main wastewater pipe. This was found in parts of the settlement that had benefited from public infrastructure projects.

Spaces lacking a clear legal status cannot benefit from government projects to improve infrastructure—in principle, that is. However, with the fall of Suharto in 1998, the onset of the financial crisis in the same year, and the decentralization reform a year later, opportunities for new practices opened up as the national government launched various social safety net programs along with job-creation and participation-related projects.[15] In

2012, a national program for urban community empowerment (*Program Nasional Pemberdayaan Masyarakat-Mandiri Perkotaan*, PNPM-MP) began to operate in the neighborhood along the inoperative railway. The project was based on community participation and required people to form a Community Self-Support Unit (*Badan Keswadayaan Masyarakat*, BKM). The activities generally started by recording the wishes of the community and public discussion to establish ways in which they could contribute to the construction and maintenance of infrastructure. The projects implemented by PNPM over the five kilometers we studied were sewerage systems, public sanitation (toilets, bathrooms, water taps), and alley pavements. The management of the PNPM project was very well aware of the unclear legal status of the land. However, there are few areas in Bandung and other cities where agencies such as PNPM can operate without encountering somewhat unclear legal situations, and trying to stick rigidly to rules would virtually paralyze their activities. The management, therefore, had decided to venture forth. In the annual audit reports on the project, the auditors indeed noted that PNPM was technically at fault, but decided that the activities could not be considered "corruption" and were therefore pardonable.

Property Tax and Transactions

Different kinds of more or less regular payments have featured since the first occupation. In the early phase, the inhabitants paid former staff of the train company for allowing them to stay on railway land. This payment also ensured that the plot was not transferred to others. Although eviction from this land never happened, it was and remained a concern of the residents.

Over time, some of the residents had begun to pay tax to the government of Indonesia. The residents on the railway land became registered taxpayers when *kelurahan* staff came to their neighborhood and measured their plots and the size of their buildings.[16] People were served a tax statement (*Surat Pemberitahuan Pajak Terutang Pajak Bumi dan Bangunan*, SPPT-PBB) stating the amount of property tax due. While the letter was not legal proof of ownership, many of the residents believed that this particular paper secured their tenure.[17] The train company seemed not to consider this a problem. According to the company managers, since people were squatting on state land, it was only appropriate that they should pay rent to the state. And rent payment would not turn people into owners according to law. In practice, however, the difference between access and formal legal ownership was diminishing, as I argue below.

Many of the houses changed hands on the railway land. Through inheritance and sales, property rights have effectively been transacted. Generally, people explained, they knew full well that they did not own the land, and *land* was not what was actually sold. *Houses,* on the other hand, were what people sold and rented. This was a convenient distinction in everyday situations. There may be a formal legal distinction between owning land and paying land tax for it, but living on the land in a house you owned bedimmed this distinction in the everyday semantics. People usually documented property transactions themselves. Buyers received a *kwitansi* (quittance, or receipt), and while the documentation by the tax authorities simply meant that the residents had changed, it still acknowledged the former and future resident; it endowed their presence with an air of legality.

Property and Citizenship on the Tracks

Before the occupation, the train company was the legal owner and later the legal tenant of the land. It was not challenged by any party, and the train company had rights to use and develop the land along the tracks. However, the gradual settlement on the railway land by ordinary people had institutional implications.

Although the initial occupation was not condoned by the railway company, neither was it actively opposed. In fact, the settlers managed to access the land by paying railway company personnel. Another way to maintain access to the land was by using the land in what was seen as a proper way. The settlers were therefore careful not to destroy railway property. They let the tracks and other train company assets remain on the land and cultivated the land along the track at the same time. This strategy meant that settlers were both visible and invisible at the same time, while accessing the land. The settlers demonstrated civic etiquette and compliance in their transgression. This allowed them to entrench and deepen their effective control over the space. An important element in this compliance was to establish an agreement or understanding with the company through its representatives.

The settlers would address the railway company for permission to use the land, even if they knew that the company would not be able, in any legally recognized way, to allow them to use it. Furthermore, it was unthinkable for the settlers to address the company as such. When we discussed this in interviews, it was clear that people did not know how to contact the company in a formal way, or which company official to address. Instead, adjusting to the situation, the obvious path was to address the railway company personnel on location. The track controller and the nearest train stationmaster seemed the way to go. To the settlers, they represented the train company.

Why would the railway company personnel go far beyond their authority and give their consent to the occupation of the land? The most obvious explanation would seem to be that the train company staff received something in exchange from the settlers (for rent-seeking and infrastructure, see Davidson 2015). For stationmasters and track controllers, such extra income would be quite welcome. However, our interviews suggest that something else was equally afoot. First of all, the payment of the officials was not untoward or underhanded. On the contrary, it was open, public, and ceremonial. In fact, among the ground-level personnel of the company, a set of practical norms seemed to develop. In situations with limited resources to conduct their formal tasks, ways of coping, while still delivering some service or performing some functions, tended to emerge.[18] On the railway line in Bandung, the task of the stationmaster and the track controller changed as the traffic on the tracks ceased. The priorities changed, from ensuring the safety of the passing train to securing the company assets from pilfering. Without any explicit instructions from above, company personnel improvised agreements with settlers regarding the use of the land.

In essence, what we see here is an exchange of recognition between settlers and train company staff. The former recognized the authority and capacity of the staff to allocate land, while the latter recognized the settlers' right to access the land and draw benefits from it. In fact, the settlers *invested* the company staff with this authority, and in turn, they *created* rights for the settlers to become recognized residents. This agreement, or social contract, was not static, however. Once investment in the authority of the train company staff had proved effective, the settlers continued to push to extend and consolidate their rights.

Another strategy employed by settlers was the construction of public infrastructure, such as mosques, neighborhood security posts, schools, kindergartens, neighborhood association offices, and other functional buildings — even badminton courts. It is hard to say whether this was a deliberate strategy from the outset, but the presence of such public goods on railway company land signified a community presence on the land. And, at the same time, those public infrastructures also functioned as cover and distraction from the settlers' efforts to improve the condition of their private houses. Public infrastructure allowed them to control the land relatively unnoticed by the statutory authorities. But gradual and incremental construction allowed them to test the train company's awareness. Some of the infrastructure was even introduced by government agencies. Just as the settlers needed development of the physical environment of the neighborhood, the PNPM project needed clients to justify its existence. The project staff turned a blind eye to the uncertain legal status of the settlement and, by doing so, actually helped to consolidate it. The visibility of the settlers as citizens made it possible to obtain indirect recognition from a government agency of their claim to residence.

A long period of settlement on the land, of social acceptance from the neighboring community, and construction of residential houses equipped with public infrastructure allowed the settlers to take the next step and register as property tax payers (*Pajak Bumi dan Bangunan*, land and building tax). People had their plot and building measured by *kelurahan* officers to determine the amount of municipal tax due.[19] Although property tax payment is not legal proof of ownership, it testifies to the residents' good intentions of becoming regular citizens.

While the settlers' rent payment to the railway company personnel entitled them only to cultivate land, it did, in fact, enable them to transfer the land to third parties by sale. The buyer could continue the practice of the earlier resident. He or she would have bought the *rights* of the former owner with whatever imperfection, uncertainty, indirect recognition, and threats of random arrogation it entailed. Company staff witnessed these transactions in the early days. After the track was fully closed down, the settlers continued the practice without the presence of railway company personnel. The previously visible marking of train company land began to disappear. Fences went completely, while signboards were few and far between. And the tracks were mostly buried under houses and buildings or encrusted in roads and pavement blocks. Most settlers had become affiliated to a neighborhood unit, registered as citizens and taxpayers, and received the annual property tax bill and payment slip. The settlers acquired the capacity to divide and allocate land, to sell and rent out rights to it. The settlers were able to use the land for purposes other than cultivation; they built infrastructures, and so on. As a result, while still verbally recognizing the train company as the legitimate land-right holder, the settlers managed to reduce the lease-ownership of the train company to a paper-thin right.

Having succeeded in occupying the land and received recognition from the train company personnel, the settlers seized the opportunity to lay another claim to various citizenship rights. Once they had occupied the place, they socialized with neighbors and affiliated to the nearest RT, or formed a new one. This affiliation opened up an access to multiple rights. The head of the RT could issue a letter of residence (a certificate of domicile) for the address the settlers had acquired. With this letter, they could apply to the *kelurahan* for ID cards, allowing them to participate in political events and government-initiated projects (poverty alleviation, infrastructure improvements, and so on), they could access subsidies, and apply for infrastructure services (water, electricity, sewerage). In short, settlers emerged as full national citizens.

Conclusion

Landholding is hard work. And citizenship, too, is acquired rather than granted. The two often go together, as the story of spontaneous privatization of the railway line in Bandung demonstrates. The most significant element

of the settlement process is, I believe, its gradual, multi-relational, and indirect character. When people first encroached on the railway company
land, they acquired very modest rights to farm and conduct a little trade,
which could easily be undone. Over time, people consolidated their residence by replacing temporary dwellings with more permanent ones and by
seeking recognition of the right to stay. People obtained recognition from
the community through compliance with community norms of mutual
help, and recognition from the local authorities (the RT and RW), from the
electricity company, and from the government program PNPM by acting
according to what was considered proper behavior. The first thing to notice
is that people who settled on the tracks did not have any single or privileged
social relation that enabled them to stay. Rather, they actively established a
web of interconnected relations of recognition. Visibility as a resident with
a numbered house and proper address, as a paying electricity customer, as a
property taxpayer, or as a well-respected neighbor made it easier to establish
social, political, and legal visibility in other capacities. The compliance in
the act of transgression worked to normalize the presence of the settler.

It makes sense to view people's access to the space on the tracks in terms
of rights—they were recognized claims. Obviously, these claims were not
always recognized by the appropriate *legal* entity in the statutory institutional fabric; the rival claimant to that same space, the railway company,
had competing rights legally recognized. Moreover, while the law, strictly
speaking, does not reward adverse possession with rights in Indonesia, some
actors and institutions acted *ultra vires* when they in practice recognized
claims. It was not easy to say at the time of people's initial settlement which
of the rights would eventually prevail. However, we may want to look at the
question of authority as something more dynamic than a formal government organizational chart. If authority is not merely established by law and
legislation, but also at times by its invocation—by those who seek authorization of a claim—then even a mere track controller can be invested with
authority to turn a claim into a right. He legalized the claim by mobilizing
the paraphernalia of state authority and by referring to his position as underpinned by law. He may not have had the capacity to protect the right if
heavily contested, but in the case of the railroad land in Bandung, that was

not necessary. This does not mean that there are no hierarchies between institutional powers, but it means that this is contingent. Formal attribution of authority is only a part of the picture—sometimes the smaller part.

Having said this, it is worth reflecting on the substance of the rights that were produced in this web of relationships. Residents unanimously told us that they did not own the land—the land belonged to the railway company and the Indonesian state. This is a politically convenient conflation of property and the "thing"—the land. By protesting their "propertylessness," residents refused to see the different rights to the space in property terms, and thus steered clear of a confrontation with government authorities. However, the right to reside, to construct, to rent out rooms, and the right to transact these rights (that is, sell them, though probably not mortgage them or translate them into financial instruments) were all connected to that specific space in Bandung, and were all elements of property rights. In theory, none of the rights would qualify as perfectly exclusive private property. In practice, however, the combinations of elements of rights enabled people to have rather secure and exclusive use of their property. The remarkable element is not that their rights were not fully exclusive—few rights are. In the conceptual universe of writers such as de Soto (2000), people's rights were weak and incomplete—well, hardly rights at all. What *is* remarkable, though, is that, over time, the imperfect and partial rights people enjoyed allowed them to find residence, exclude others, and improve and transact what they held on the tracks in Bandung with some significant measure of certainty. The nine-tenths of possession were complemented by a patchwork of hints of legalization. However, the fact that people's rights were not held as one single, discrete right of exclusive ownership in relation to one single institution might even have had its advantages. While a title deed embodying private property rights from a single government institution is coveted, it also involves risk. All rights could have been expunged simply if this single title was annulled; or, if the institution to which people were beholden for it was weakened or dissolved, the rights derived from this relationship would evaporate. With Indonesia's modern history in mind, multiple, partial, indirect, and interconnected rights seem more complicated to undo, and hence, possibly, more *certain* in all their incompleteness.

The residents' property rights did not represent any single relationship of recognition between the resident and a particular institution of public authority that guaranteed the entire bundle. On the contrary, the various property rights were linked to different citizenship rights in mutually constitutive ways. Recognized residence (addresses) led to eligibility to participate in local government (RT/RW). Presence in the eyes of local government made citizens eligible for improvement of public infrastructure (PNPM). Construction of mosques testified to the propriety and civic virtues of the residents, and it would have taken serious determination on the part of the railway company or the municipality to knock them down. Moreover, the construction of mosques gave the neighborhood an appearance of respectability and constituted a physical protection against possible operations of demolition. Payment of property tax entitled residents to have expectations of public services (sanitation and schools). Better public facilities increased the value of people's houses, and so on.

The rights to property and citizenship in this case were produced through continuous recursive construction of indirect rights. Claims to property and citizenship were interconnected and constituted a relatively robust security of tenure for the settlers. It is difficult to think of one single original right from which all other rights elements have derived. They connect in a web structure rather than in descending, linear ways. It would appear that we are dealing with rights as recognized claims, that this recognition flows from more than government institutions, and that while the multiple "small" claims may be concrete and specific, they amount to more general rights to citizenship. Obviously, this does not mean that these rights could not one day be eliminated. The history of land control in Indonesia is replete with examples of marginal groups who suffer momentary or enduring loss of rights through government enclosure, and expropriation. One reason for the local people's relative success is, no doubt, the odd shape of the land in question. The narrow cut of the railway land made it an unlikely candidate for a housing complex, a shopping mall, or a hotel. This peculiarity, however, allows us to see that at the brink of urban planning, at the margins of the predominant dynamics of dispossession in the city, countercurrents also flow, driven by common people's everyday situational adjustment and desire for legalization of their many claims. So far, thirty years of incremental, indirect recognition, and admittedly incomplete legalization, on the one hand, and the ostentatious display of civic virtues in acts of transgression, on the other, have secured them a livelihood on the tracks.

The participation of the common people in urban development is not confined to oddly shaped stretches of land. When former plantations become prime real estate, actors of all stripes flock to benefit. The next chapter offers a taste of this.

CHAPTER SEVEN

Another Fine Mess

Urban Property in Medan

In the purlieus of Medan, in Simalinka behind the municipal zoo, there is a ghost town. Some 300 terraced houses in regular lines lie empty. Their builder, one of Medan's important entrepreneurs and power brokers, acquired the land and built the complex, Golden Land, in anticipation of the nearby construction of a new university campus. However, not only was his acquisition of the former government plantation land incomplete or illegal, depending on one's point of view; the construction of the campus had not yet happened, either. Houses with uncertain legal status cannot fetch the full price, and the entrepreneur had decided not to sell them yet. The houses were not all empty, however. Around 50 houses were inhabited by people who were essentially house-sitting. They were strong enough to dissuade other squatters until the situation improved and weak enough to be turned out when it did. Moreover, two of the city's notorious gangs, *Pemuda Pancasila* and IPK, had checkpoints and sentry boxes in Golden Land. It was quite unusual for these gangs to share turf, but the entrepreneur was ambidextrous.

Medan is notorious. Even in Medan itself. In 2008, the mayor, Mr. Abdillah, was arrested and charged with corruption; in 2010, the provincial governor of North Sumatra, Syamsul Arifin, was arrested and charged with corruption. In 2014, the new mayor of Medan, Rahudman Harahap, was arrested and charged with corruption, and in 2015 the former governor of North Sumatra, Gatot Pujo Nugroho, was arrested and charged with corruption. In 2015, the speaker of the provincial parliament, Mr. Agiptia, was arrested and charged with corruption, and in the same year the chief judge of the state administrative court in Medan, Tripeni Irianto Putro, and two other judges were arrested and charged with corruption.[1] The executive, the legislative, and the judiciary; Montesquieu would have had an aneurysm.

All the same, this is the context in which a *legalization* of land claims is the great preoccupation. It may seem like a paradox, but corruption shows one thing above all others: Government officials hold a resource worth paying for. The fact that land rights (to farm smallholdings or plantations, to build, to develop, to transform the landscape, and so on) ultimately depend on a variety of state-granted leases, permits, and authorizations puts politicians and high-level civil servants alike at the center. They can launder theft. They can turn possession into property.[2]

Politics in Medan and much of Indonesia is characterized by predation, patronage, and *premanism*.[3] The connections between politicians, youth gangs, and land control, consolidated during the New Order, continued after that period, and in North Sumatra the emerging group of politicians were particularly concerned to ensure control over legal and illegal revenue from the plantation sector (Hadiz 2003: 123). While this is a familiar pattern throughout Indonesia, some of the most infamous and flamboyant gangs, like *Pemuda Pancasila* and IPK (*Ikatan Pemuda Karya*, Association of Workers' Youth), originated and first operated in Medan.[4] They developed very close relations with politicians and civil servants, and controlled prostitution, gambling, and other seamy aspects of life. They effectively controlled large areas of the city as their turf, where they would extort rent from legal and illicit businesses alike. Hence, the leader of IPK, *Bang* Olo ("uncle" Olo), was often referred to as the "night-time mayor" of Medan.

The city's expansion has largely taken place on land that was once under plantation leases. People and developers have not always waited for the land to be legally released for other purposes, and when leases finally lapsed, new urban neighborhoods or industry, rather than plantation crops, would already stand on it. This produced a legal conundrum. When a plantation lease expired, land would revert to the state of Indonesia. The state would then have several options: renewal of the lease or a change in land use and the issuing of other new leases. Renewal of a plantation lease for a densely built neighborhood spelled trouble, but so did issuing new leases for other land uses. In reality, a third, messier, option was often preferred: inaction, referral, kicking the can down the road, *post festum* approval, and leaving it to land-hungry people, movements, gangs, companies, soldiers, and government agencies to rough it out.

Roughing Out the Categories

As virtually all land in Indonesia is state land, government decides what is appropriate land use, and who should hold the lease. Large cities like Medan, therefore, presented particularly profitable prospects during the New Order—and no less after. Its two million inhabitants, sprawling peri-urban formations of industry, and less-than-planned housing stock have created an acute demand for land and a chronic demand for securing possessions, once gained.

No city played a more important role in shaping the landscape and economy of the plantation belt in North Sumatra than Medan, and it would be impossible to understand its growth and development without considering its relationship to the region around it. The city and the plantations have been co-constitutive. Medan grew, and while the Sultan of Deli moved to Medan and had a big mosque built next to his new palace—*Istana Maimoon*—colonial landmarks such as the post office, and the London-Sumatra plantation company's headquarters, also bedecked the city center. By the end of the First World War, Medan had some 44,000 inhabitants, of whom 400 were European. The city's growth picked up pace during the twentieth century with the construction of the railway line and train station, and with the development of manufacturing industry. The population of Medan hit the one-million mark in 1998 and reached two million in 2010

(Medan City 2016). Throughout the last century, Medan pushed outward, gnawing at the perimeter of the closest plantations, and areas such as Polonia and Helvetia owe their names to a European-owned past. These plantations, once outside of the city, became engulfed by it and transformed into urban neighborhoods. The city center now boasts government and office buildings, hotels and malls, together with the fading plumage of a few colonial buildings. Throughout the city, the main streets are lined with a perplexing variation of architecture (though the Dutch-inspired theme recurs: narrow but deep gabled houses with business on the ground floor). Each is decorated to suit the taste and purse of its individual owner. The main streets are also decorated with huge banners, commercial and political—from a memorable cigarette advertisement, "Never Quit," to the declarations of undying loyalty to youth gangs, assorted politicians, and military personalities. There are neighborhoods of comfortable-to-sumptuous houses for the well-to-do, and many more of modest character, where narrow lanes—just wide enough for a motorcycle—form the lattice-work of communication. These parts of Medan have maintained a somewhat rural aspect, with fields and one-story houses on land once producing rice, tobacco, sugar, rubber, cocoa, coconut, cloves, and cinnamon.

Urban development requires infrastructure: roads, water supply, sewage, electricity, and so on. This, in turn, requires planning. However, it is naive to assume that planning always comes first. Planning seems just as often to be chasing changes on the ground. Indeed, planning may be just as much a result of change, as change is a result of planning. Especially in open moments such as rapid urbanization and land use change, institutional entrepreneurs may exploit opportunities of the yet unsettled and thereby create new rules, rights, and riches. A simple and elegant, yet crucial observation is made by Navaro-Yashin in her work on make-believe spaces (2012). Space is materially crafted and constructed, *and* it is imagined and believed. *And*, not *or*. Turning space, once made up of plantations, into something new— as a city, as a popular, chic, or gated neighborhood, or even into an industrial estate, into high-rise buildings, or infrastructure—takes caloric effort. Leveling, draining, landscaping, founding, and construction represent huge investments of time and money, as well as the forfeiture of its alternative, of something instead. If it is a popular neighborhood, it cannot also be an

Field at the urban perimeter, Medan, North Sumatra (Photo: Fachrizal Sinaga)

industrial estate, a gated community, or an amusement park. And this is why the imagination or belief in the space is equally important. To fully realize the make-believe space, the *idea* of what it is must also be cultivated. But whereas physical space is finite, ideas about what it could be tend to tilt toward infinity.

Urbanization around Medan is a frontier process—that is, with changing land use, the suspension of previous resource control on spaces. The usurpation of space usually dissolves existing property systems, and challenges existing social contracts. Urbanization is, in effect, also territorialization, where competing interests attempt to re-territorialize space (Rasmussen and Lund 2018). When people justify their desires and ideas for what space should be, they draw on popular and professional imagination, on bureaucratic culture, and on law. They justify with reference to peasant livelihood, to middle-class aspirations, to modernity, or to growth, and they vindicate their claims by ostentatious deference to bureaucratic procedure. Finally, they contend that the law is on their side.

However, there is no guarantee that the ideas are coherent, that procedures are actually followed, or that struggles over legality are conducted by legal means alone. Rather, physical presence, construction, and possibly violence intertwine with bureaucratic processes that ultimately legalize the claim. Lease contracts, tax receipts, residence permits, construction permits, and receipts for payment of public utilities, together with court rulings, political announcements, road names and signs, and inaugurations attended by public officials—all these suggest rights, whether they are authentic or not. They may not prove land rights directly, but they serve as *indirect* recognition of the claim. One of the MPs of the North Sumatra Parliament put it this way: "This is gambling. If you can stay on the land, you win. If you are evicted, you lose *everything*."[5]

From the 1980s, land pressure grew in Medan. Spontaneous occupations by individuals, movements, gangs, and developers began to occur on the plantation lands bordering the city center. Many of the areas were already inhabited as plantation workers' quarters, and even people who had not actually worked there began to settle and build. When plantation leases expire, the legal status of the land is in limbo until the Ministry of Finance and the Ministry of State Assets (*Badan Usaha Milik Negara*) have reassigned it. With little exception, developers have tried to get hold of this expired plantation land. An often-used procedure in Medan has been for developers to apply for private land rights (*hak milik*) on behalf of local residents, yet unbeknownst to them.[6] Then, once the bureaucratic process was under way, the developers would engage one of the city's youth gangs and have them harass the inhabitants to surrender their land for a nominal sum. The gangs would offer the resident money to demolish his own house—half up front, and when the house owner could produce a Polaroid picture of the fully demolished house he would, with any luck, receive the rest of the compensation. These offers were difficult to refuse because the alternative was likely to be demolition without any compensation whatsoever.[7] The developer would then build while going about the paperwork of changing the status of the land once again. The Ministry of State Assets was notorious for not reacting with any promptitude, so lawyers, and ex-plantation company officials, academics, and people retired from or affiliated with the National

Land Agency, had carved out a lucrative niche as advisers to people who needed such legalizing paperwork done. As one retired academic with a substantial amount of public service under his belt explained: "There *is* indeed a master-plan for Medan. But most of the city is built in illegality."[8]

Gangs, on their own account, would also occupy chunks of land from the plantations. Sometimes this would succeed and businessmen managed to "develop" houses and warehouses. Just as often, however, the plantation company could buy back the land for a ransom from the gangs. And sometimes, the national plantation company, PTPN, would enter into a protection arrangement with one of the gangs to avoid occupations altogether. In some cases, management staff of PTPN have been known to sell off land to developers, if they considered that it would be taken over anyway. The plantation company management would reclassify land from "productive" to "unproductive" and transfer it to a developer for a sum.[9] Ex-workers would, from time to time, have secured certificates of residence by the village mayor, but in confrontation with youth gangs like IPK or *Pemuda Pancasila*, such paper documents were simply what they were, paper.

Once, and once only, in recent years did land from expired plantation leases become subject to land reform in Medan.[10] In the confusion of *reformasi*, a rumor had begun to circulate that all plantation leases had expired, and again land occupations multiplied around Medan. To stem the tide of occupations and the resulting violence between plantation security and the many people trying their luck, the governor of North Sumatra established a special team in 2003 to identify land that could be released for land reform. This was no easy task. The administrative overview of the land held by private and state-owned plantations was incomplete and sometimes rather approximate. After two years of investigation, however, the special team had identified 5,873 hectares which could be released for land reform. This would seem to be an opportunity for the government and the different peasant movements to finally deliver on their many promises. However, the 5,873 hectares identified consisted entirely of land already "lost" to different types of non-plantation occupation; it was not "extra" or "unused" land to be freely distributed, but land already in use. Nonetheless, a large number of "peasant movements" appeared out of the blue, all intent on becoming beneficiaries of this gesture of land reform. Many of these "movements," it turned out, were an assortment of fictitious associations puppeteered by developers, different youth organizations, political cronies, and their strawmen, who acquired land to sell, consolidate, and develop into commercial activities by co-manipulation with the National Land Agency.[11] "Becoming beneficiaries" is actually to stretch the term. The bureaucratic misadventure was never completed.

However, while the official paperwork of release of land from state assets ran aground, the popular legalization of land acquisitions picked up speed. Developers and youth gangs, as well as different movements, simply acquired or manufactured "formal" documentation *in the name of* the 5,873 hectare land-release, to legalize land *already otherwise illegally acquired elsewhere* in Medan. Shopping malls, business centers, housing estates, and industrial and trading estates seem to have been legalized in this process. Yet no one is able to say with any certainty exactly what land was legalized in the name of the 5,873 hectares—but only that it was many times more than that.[12] The 5,873 hectares exist. They are there, somewhere. But they have acquired a parallel, make-believe quality and elastic existence. The 5,873 hectares have been invoked to legalize innumerable other established facts of possession.

This context of rapid urbanization has been intense since *reformasi*. Transformation of a plantation landscape and economy, government control over spatial and property categories (at least in name), a political rupture of democratization and decentralization, and the struggle to own a place in the city all came together. Violence, political power, and paperwork of legalization intermeshed in various ways. The brief histories of three locations below—starting at the center of Medan and gradually moving to its periphery—demonstrate that while possession may be nine-tenths of the law, the last tenth of legalization still receives a lot of attention. The first case shows an enduring conflict between the Indonesian Air Force and the population of a popular neighborhood in Medan. Physical presence, construction, and violence are central, but so are efforts at legalization through records of public administration and legal decisions. The second case, from Marindal, shows how entrepreneurs with youth gang connections and a nous for politics operate. They turned a contested former Dutch plantation into a "respectable middle-class neighborhood" where property was secured by cumulated "insurances" in the wait for opportunities for legal documentation. The third case is more open-ended. Construction had only just begun to materialize, and the ideas about what this area might become were still many. Former workers, peasant groups, youth gangs, businessmen, and the plantation company all had designs on the land and competed over the future wealth. More than anything, however, all cases show how people, by producing the representations of rights, conjure up the thing they represent: property.

Creating Urban Property

Polonia

On August 17, when red and white flags mark the independence of Indonesia, no *Merah-Putih* waves in the wind in Sari Rejo in Polonia. While official buildings, schools, and many shops and private homes are aflutter with the Indonesian flag on this day, that is not the case in this particular neighborhood in Medan. Here, people have bones to pick with government, and refuse to celebrate.

In the center of Medan, 526 hectares make up the neighborhood of Polonia. The airport, Indonesian Air Force barracks, and the administrative buildings cover 270 hectares, whereas the rest—256 hectares—is a popular neighborhood, Sari Rejo. This part of Polonia is home to some 40,000 inhabitants. It is multicultural and multi-religious, with mosques, churches, and a Sikh *gurdwara*. There are shops, a post office, private medical clinics, pharmacies, and schools and kindergartens, with memorable names such as *Perjuangan* (Struggle), and *Karismatik*. *Ankots* and *ojeks*—minibuses and motorcycle taxis—have official stops, and there is piped water and electricity. But Polonia is also home to a long and bitter conflict over land.

Polonia owes its exotic name to the Polish Count Michalsky who obtained 700 hectares on a 75-year concession from the Sultan of Deli in 1869. He later sold the concession rights and his tobacco plantation to a larger company, Deli Maatschappij, in 1890, and in 1919, the land was transferred to the municipality of Medan. The intention was to construct a European housing estate in the area (E. Damanik 2016: 223–28, Ikhsan nd b, 2015, Ryter 2002: 170).[13] By 1949, however, after the Japanese occupation and the turbulent time of Dutch reoccupation and social revolution, the European community left Sumatra definitively, the entire area of Polonia was settled by local people, and an urban neighborhood materialized.[14] One sub-neighborhood was Sari Rejo. The new occupants did not have any official documentation of their presence, initially. Only by the 1970s did the inhabitants begin to pay a land tax and receive official recognition of their residence.[15] These documents did not amount to outright ownership, but they did represent an official recognition of presence in the area. Moreover, they were used as proof in land transactions when plots were bought and sold. Obviously, they could not prove exclusive ownership, but they documented who was the officially recognized resident. Strictly speaking, it can be argued that what was transacted was not the land itself but the right to reside there. Indeed, that is true for all land transactions; what changes hands is a set of rights, as they are: precarious or solid, tentative or established. However, this particular right of residence would be inviolable in the local understanding as well as in law. Only "state interests" could override such rights. From the 1970s ID cards also became common, and by, 2017, some 27,000 inhabitants noted Sari Rejo/Polonia as their place of residence, with an additional 10,000–12,000 residents registered with a different—often rural—location as their official home.

In 1928, the tobacco and rubber planters' associations (*Deli Planters Vereeniging* and *Algemeene Vereeniging van Rubberplanters ter Oostkust van Sumatra*) had sponsored the construction of the airstrip that was to become Polonia Airport. In 1957—a moment holding great perceived threats to the new Indonesian state—the Ministry of Defense gave emergency powers to the Medan air force base commander of the Polonia Airport. The decree further established a security zone within a three-mile radius of the airport.[16] In 1970, this decree was revised by the interior minister, who extended the air force's control for "as long as it was needed for security reasons" (Ryter 2002: 171).[17] These decrees concerned the space in (and around) Polonia for security purposes, and not the property rights.[18] However, as virtually all land in Indonesia is ultimately state land according to the constitution, it is easy to confuse "state land" with "government assets," and a "security zone" with air force "property." The area within the three-mile radius was inhabited and showed no visible signs of being different from the rest of the popular neighborhood.

By 1974, the regional air force commander informed the mayor of Medan that security was no longer an overhanging issue and that the air force would surrender the land for private development. This meant that, rather than handing over land to the city or the government, high-ranking officers began to sell land to private developers for their personal gain (Ryter 2002: 172). The actual method was to assist developers to obtain private ownership (*hak milik* rights) and permits to develop with the National Land Agency in Medan and effectively release the land to the developer.[19] In 1982, the interior minister issued a decree giving use rights (*hak pakai*) to the air force commander over the airfield, providing it was not already used by a third party.[20]

The sale of plots by air force officers to developers increased. Developers acquired plots, had the legalizing paperwork done, and then faced the task of evicting people. One such area, acquired by an important developer, was designated for a high-end housing complex to be named "Malibu." It covered no less than 20 hectares, already inhabited by ordinary people since the early 1950s. However, their houses were razed to the ground overnight.[21] Similar violent evictions became more frequent. In 1989, eighty-seven residents of Sari Rejo took the air force and the Indonesian government to court for unlawful eviction and transfer of their land to the developers. The High Court (*Pengadilan Tinggi*) of Medan ruled the evictions illegal and issued an injunction to stop the development. Important evidentiary elements supporting the case of the plaintiffs were their receipts for land tax (*surat keterangan tanah*, SKT), use right certificates (*hak pakai*), and certificates of residence (*surat ketarangan hak tanggal*).[22] In spite of the court ruling, however, demolition continued, and chunks of Polonia changed from a popular neighborhood with narrow lanes between modest houses, and street life, to high-end houses in gated compounds. The air force took over some land

and secured permits to construct barracks for its personnel, for example—
but instead, an upper-middle-class housing estate shot up. The houses were
sold, and another round of paperwork legalized the new land use.[23]

The situation grew conflictual and violent from 1991 when a company,
PT Anugrah Dirgantara Perkasa, obtained a permit from the provincial governor to develop 100 hectares in Polonia as luxury housing.[24] It is unknown
how much the company paid the air force to release the land, but its permit
stipulated compensation to the inhabitants who had to give up their houses.
However, while the inhabitants claimed 2 million Rupiah per square meter,
the company offered less than one percent of that amount. Negotiations
about compensation were brief, and instead the company subcontracted
several youth gangs. In Polonia, three youth gangs—FKPPI, the IPK, and
Pemuda Pancasila—engaged in the eviction business and began to fight
each other. These gangs already ran protection rackets and controlled gambling and prostitution; eviction would add another profitable string to their
bow. They were to intimidate residents into giving up their houses and to
make way for development. "Any youth group," according to Ryter, that
"succeeded in convincing a resident to sell, and carried out the demolition
of the surrendered property was promised a 750,000 Rupiah fee" by the
company (Ryter 2002: 174). This entailed massive intimidation of the residents with bullying, arson, and random ransacking of houses. In addition
to the intimidation by the gangs, air force soldiers would do their morning
exercise run through the popular neighborhood chanting obscene and violent songs, and the air force also began to use an unbuilt sliver of land in
Sari Rejo as a firing range.[25] Finally, the air force began to claim a production rent from the residents in Sari Rejo. Apparently, this was made to look
like a portion of an agricultural yield, which was quite odd considering that
the neighborhood was almost entirely urbanized. Besides, considering that
people already paid land tax, it was seen as sheer extortion. In any case, it
could hardly be called protection money, because it bought no protection.
Jealous fights over the eviction market had heightened the tension between
the gangs, and while different efforts at mediation from local officials would
cool off the violence for a while, the mediations were not to bring evictions to a halt; rather, they were to divide and organize the market between
the contenders.

On the eve of the New Order, different organizations began to emerge throughout Indonesia and also in Medan, Polonia, and Sari Rejo. Residents organized as the *Forum Masyarakat Sari Rejo* (Peoples Forum for the Residents of Sari Rejo, the "undeveloped" popular neighborhood of Polonia), or FORMAS.[26] The organization was led by Mr. Pintar, who was also involved in labor union work. This proved to be of value, as the ability to mobilize in numbers had hitherto been one of the weaknesses for the residents. It came to a number of stand-offs between the militant youth gang FKPPI (*Forum Komunikasi Putra-Putri Indonesia*, Indonesian Communication Forum for Sons and Daughters of Military Retirees) and the residents and union activists from Medan. In 2005, members of the Municipal Council of Medan met with representatives of the Ministry of Defense and the Jakarta branch of the National Land Agency. While the local councilors wanted the air force to relinquish its claim, and the land agency wanted to take steps to formalize the residents' rights, there was no agreement. The Ministry of Defense did not budge, and the National Land Agency was not inclined to formalize people's rights to their plots.[27]

Confrontations continued, and on several occasions Mr. Pintar was abducted from his house at night, brutalized, and spent days in the custody of the air force military police. Generally, the situation was very tense. In late 2007 and early 2008, FORMAS organized a demonstration in front of the National Land Agency's office in Medan and, later, demonstrations and sit-ins at the airport. These events drew headlines in Medan newspapers,[28] and the confrontations even reached the national press.[29] Following these incidents FORMAS negotiated with the mayor of Medan and argued that the High Court ruling of 1989 had not been respected. The air force had unsuccessfully appealed the injunction ruling twice.[30] The agricultural office of the municipality of Medan was subsequently tasked to adjudicate the land rights in Polonia. In the office's report, the competing claims were clarified, to the advantage of the residents.[31] The report emphasized the established nature of the neighborhood and its infrastructure, and the consistent payment of land tax dating back to the 1970s. However, the report also specified the basis for the air force claims, namely that parts of Polonia were indeed government assets, but that the neighborhood of Sari Rejo, the area of contention, was no one's asset as such. Later, in 2008, the chairman of the Municipal Council in Medan wrote to the minister of finance, the minister of defense, and the national director of the National Land Agency asking to have the boundaries of the government asset (no. 50506001) rectified and physically marked up, and that steps be taken to issue land rights to the residents on land outside the "state asset."[32]

Confrontations persisted, however. The residents blocked the airport on no fewer than eight occasions,[33] and marched in large numbers from Polonia to the town hall.[34] The air force, on the other hand, tried on several occasions to make the providers of public utilities (water and electricity) shut down Sari Rejo. The air force and FKPPI continued regular raids on the neighborhood and vandalized people's houses. In August 2016, the confrontations were especially violent. President Jokowi was due to visit Medan, and on the night of 14 August soldiers put up signs all over Sari Rejo declaring that it was air force land. Residents pulled down the signs and mounted a protest that led to violent clashes, with more than 50 seriously injured. The soldiers' vandalism against a mosque was caught on CCTV and went viral. This made imams and politicians from far and wide side with the local inhabitants, forcing an air force general to apologize in the local paper and the Human Rights Commission to begin an investigation.[35]

By 2017, the situation in Polonia remained unsettled.[36] The people of Sari Rejo continued to reside there, backed by some supporters on the municipal council, yet with land tax receipts as the most solid paper documentation of land rights. While the air force could produce a certificate asserting that the land was a government asset, it appeared to cover only some parts of Polonia, and land sales ceased. As a modest form of protest against government and the continued non-recognition of their property claims, the residents of Polonia continued to refuse to hoist the *Merah Putih*.

Marindal

Two signs compete for attention in Marindal, an area straddling Medan and the neighboring district of Deli Serdang. One sign proudly declares that this land is under the control of FOKRAT (*Forum Keadilan Masyarakat Tani*, the Forum for Peasant Justice). This testifies to accomplished land

reform. The other sign advertises the new real estate development, offering two classes of family houses, *Paradise* and *Elite*, that can be acquired
as middle-class family homes in the area. Marindal was not always under
peasant control, let alone an emerging suburb. It had been the name of a
1,600-hectare tobacco plantation established in 1862 and later taken over by
the Deli Maatschappij. Now, in 2017, 600 hectares of Marindal had become
quite urbanized, whereas the rest of the old plantation area was in the throes
of transformation.

During the Japanese occupation of Sumatra from 1942, Marindal was,
just like many other plantations, transformed into food crop production on
a smallholder basis. The Japanese army simply encouraged plantation workers and people around to take over the land. After independence in 1945,
the new smallholders stayed on the land. National legislation declared all
land to be state land, but the governor of Sumatra issued a decree acknowledging the settlers' rights in 1951.[37] In 1953, land was granted to the residents
on a more formal basis as part of a land reform program where landholders
received a land registration card and began to pay tax.[38]

In 1968, three years into Suharto's New Order, these smallholder rights
were overridden, however. The governor of Sumatra issued a decree turning over the land to the government-owned plantation company, PTPN.[39]
The transfer concerned the part of the old plantation which was in the
district of Deli Serdang, whereas the part that fell under the jurisdiction of
Medan municipality was allowed to urbanize. The smallholders were violently evicted throughout the 1970s by the plantation company in collaboration with the army. Hence, land was gradually included and operated as a
plantation with a variety of crops. Over the years, the plantation lease was
also modified to cover a larger area. At the turn of the millennium, several
events changed the situation. The original plantation lease from 1969 was
about to expire. This would mean that land would return to the state, which
in turn could do one of several things. The lease could be renewed, the land
could be released for land reform, or land could be returned to those who
had been evicted since 1968. However, before any of these choices were
made, the national political crisis heralding the fall of the New Order created an entirely new situation.

There was a rush of people onto the plantation land of Marindal. In a matter of weeks, the cacao and other plantation crops had gone, and people divided the land into smallholdings for food production. The new settlers, not especially well organized by a Mr. Duaribu, were soon confronted by descendants of the people who had been evicted in 1968. Mr. Limapuluh, leading the residents of the 1950s, failed to convince Mr. Duaribu and the new squatters that the lapse of the plantation lease did not open the land to all and sundry, but only to those who had lost it earlier. Mr. Limapuluh decided to take the new settlers to court, though such an operation would be risky, possibly termless, and no doubt costly.

This is where Mr. Nurman made his entry. Mr. Nurman had many talents and a past that made him conversant with the shadier sides of life.[40] He offered to back Mr. Limapuluh financially in return for 40 percent of the land should they win in court. He also wanted all the land certificates from the 1953 land grant, known as KTPPT cards, from Mr. Limapuluh and his associates.[41] Mr. Nurman received the cards, laminated them, and kept them in his safe in his office.[42] On these terms, Mr. Limapuluh went to court on behalf of himself and the other beneficiaries of the land reform of 1953, to recover the 454 hectares from Mr. Duaribu and his group. In 2001, they won.[43] Following this legal victory, the 454 hectares were divided up.[44] Mr. Nurman took possession of his newly acquired 183 hectares. However, he now faced a set of challenges. First, how to make sure that his land was not occupied again by other entrepreneurs, land-hungry farmers, or people in need of a place to live? And, second, how to turn land designated for farming into profitable real estate?

First, Mr. Nurman had violence on tap. Since he was a middle-level operative in *Pemuda Pancasila*, he could draw on this organization, and soon detachments of "youth" ostentatiously patrolled his land in their orange and black fatigues, discouraging any serious attempts to throw him off it. The second challenge was more institutional. In principle, his newly acquired land was now (re)designated for land reform and the beneficiaries should, in theory, be peasants organized in a movement. The transfer of 40 percent of the land in case of a win in court was a private arrangement between Mr. Nurman and Mr. Limapuluh, and it is doubtful whether it was actually legal, since Mr. Limapuluh and his friends were to hold the land under the terms of the land reform, according to the court ruling. Nonetheless, Mr. Limapuluh and his associates ceded 40 percent of the land to Mr. Nurman as agreed. Together with his key associate, Tangankanan, Mr. Nurman now created a movement, Forum for Peasant Justice (FOKRAT). In contrast to Mr. Nurman, Tangankanan was university-educated and had a past as a student activist and organizer. He had also worked actively for a local politician in an election campaign to become district mayor and, although they had lost, he had gained useful experience. Tangankanan managed the paperwork and had the peasant movement officialized and cleared with the local village mayor of Marindal, Mr. Blantik, himself a *Pemuda Pancasila* veteran, whose election campaign had been funded by Mr. Nurman. This made FOKRAT an official part of the local fabric of civil society. The movement had no real members, however, and the headquarters was Mr. Nurman's office. But it had enough of a legal existence (especially with the KTPPT-cards in the safe) to be the beneficiary of Mr. Nurman's 183 hectares through land reform.

The court ruling that land was no longer under a plantation lease to a state-owned enterprise, PTPN, did not mean, however, that the Ministry of State Assets automatically released it and made way for a legal land-use change and individual private land rights (*hak milik*) to housing plots.[45] This required a separate process, and, according to Mr. Nurman, it could drag on forever and cost a fortune in bribes and other lubrication to have the land formally released from governments assets. He therefore decided simply to go ahead with the house construction in the hope that planning and legalization would, eventually, catch up.

Construction began in 2014. Mr. Nurman and Tangankanan had a glossy prospectus made and also put it up as a large poster next to the FOKRAT sign. In the absence of completed paperwork from the Ministry of State Assets, and from the National Land Agency, prices were somewhat depressed. Houses would go for 200 million Rupiah on average but, as the pair of entrepreneurs assured me, they would be selling for 350 million each when all the paperwork was in order. "These are quality houses for good middle-class people!"

Not all guarantees of property need to be in paper form, however. Tangankanan contacted the local leaders of the four national alumni associations in Medan.[46] Each association was offered a house at a very favorable price for its local chapter by Mr. Nurman. University students generally join one of the four associations, and membership is important to people's future business and political networks at all levels. They used to be the recruiting ground for the future apparatchiks and political operators of the New Order regime and have remained important for political parties and government agencies (Hadiz 2010: 94). Tangankanan's logic was simple. Any governor, mayor, or police commander would think twice before demolishing the office of the local chapter of any of the alumni associations, incurring the risk of setting off an unpredictable reaction from levels of society that could bear upon his future career. In addition, Mr. Nurman and Tangankanan sold a plot to one of the managers of the plantation company, PTPN, whose colorful three-story house had already been erected there by 2016.[47]

In 2017, a new neighborhood was well under way. Houses were being built and sold. Streets were being named—the main street, Fokrat Boulevard, appearing on Google Maps—and there was no longer much daylight between legal and illegal. Mr. Blantik, the mayor of Marindal, had brokered a deal with the electricity company to supply the area, even if it was officially still agricultural. Lampposts and other infrastructure were adorned in *Pemuda Pancasila*'s orange and black colors, and the era of tobacco and cocoa production seemed irretrievably over. Moreover, a grant from the central government had allowed the village mayor to initiate roadbuilding linking the new settlement to the rest of Marindal and improving the connection to the main road. This followed the conventional pattern of public works in Medan. Mr. Blantik invited the three local youth gangs, AMPI, IPK, and *Pemuda Pancasila*, each to "protect and oversee a part of the project on behalf of the public" for a cut of the budget. The agreement was marked with a ceremony where the three gangs were presented as the social movements of civil society. Mr. Blantik expected "the reality of the many houses and the new road to be put into the official plan for the area in the nearest future."[48]

Thus the different new structures of Marindal headed toward legalization. The road to this point, though, had been traveled by an assortment of vehicles; some above board, some more illicit, but all displaying purpose and imagination. The legalizing paperwork may remain incomplete, but the efforts of all concerned suggest no dismissive attitude vis-à-vis documentation. However, while waiting for proper statutory recognition to emerge one day, improvisation—and a fine sense of what alternative documents would convince whom of what—underpinned the persuasion that this would become a fine example of middle-class property.

Saentis

Molotov cocktails are a rare sight in Medan. But in 2016, in April, a fracas between IPK, smallholders who refused to pay them protection money, and former workers on the plantation in Saentis spilled over violently. Kerosene-filled bottles were hurled between the groups. Several people were badly burned and ended up in hospital. While more violent than usual, it was only the latest incident in the struggle over land in Saentis.

Midway between Medan center and the city's new airport in Kuala Namu, some 60 kilometers apart, is Saentis. It was a 1,600-hectare Dutch-owned tobacco plantation until the 1950s and became part of the state-owned PTPN complex in the 1960s. The ruins of the redundant tobacco factory tell us that in 1926 investments and fortunes were made here. Long shacks for curing the tobacco can still be found, even if in the interim other crops like sugar cane became more important. The plantation lease lapsed around 2000, and in 2001, a large group of people moved onto the land and occupied some 650 hectares. Some of them were organized in BPRPI (*Badan Perjuangan Rakyat Penungu Indonesia*, Movement for the *Rakyat Penungu* People's Struggle, Indonesia), but most of the new occupants simply followed the flow.[49] People did not settle here to live, at first, but only staked out plots for farming. By the end of 2001, BPRPI members controlled some 80 hectares while more than 500 hectares were occupied in a much more individual fashion. Initially, settlers were not from Saentis itself but from farther afield. Most of the people who worked on the plantation lived in refurbished, yet crammed, plantation workers' quarters, *pondoks*. They worried that if they, too, would occupy land, the plantation company would turn them out of their houses, or worse.

The first violent conflicts in the area arose within BPRPI. The leadership insisted that the land was collectively owned and under the stewardship of the movement. Hence, members would receive a certificate of customary land rights and would have to pay a fee, or rent, to the movement for the use of its land. This meant that farmers and their families did not have any individual documentation of their residence or the exact location of the land to which they were entitled. Many, therefore, felt like tenants of the movement rather than members. Moreover, there were constant rumors about the movement leadership selling land to developers. As a result, members began to peel off and form their own small peasant groups.

As the peasant groups proliferated within and beyond BPRPI's 80 hectares, the movement's hold on the land grew tenuous. Dozens of smaller groups of 100–1,000 members with anything between 9 and 200 hectares divided up the land and put up signboards and banners. On several occasions, BPRPI mobilized members from Saentis and elsewhere—sometimes even members of the youth gangs—to push the renegades and opportunists off the land, but, each time, the independent peasant groups flowed back to their areas once the BPRPI members from farther afield had left. In between these scuffles, BPRPI tried to negotiate with the splinter groups, but no agreements were forthcoming. Even if the many peasant groups saw BPRPI as their common adversary, they also had to settle conflicts among themselves. Ground left undefended would be ground lost, and soon a system of night guards developed, with ramshackle huts and control points dotting the landscape.

Initially, PTPN was passive vis-à-vis the occupations. However, as they were hemorrhaging land, the plantation company had to come up with a counter-measure. So, in 2000, PTPN sublet 36 hectares of land to *Pemuda Pancasila* and other stretches of land to IPK in order to deter further land occupations by smallholders.[50] In principle, a plantation company with a valid lease could create a cooperative for its workers and sublet land to them (*Kooperasi Sarba Usaha*, Multipurpose Cooperative). Such cooperatives were completely under the control of the company, and transfers of land could be seen as a transaction internal to the company for all intents and purposes. To lease land to youth gangs under such terms obviously required a stretch of legal imagination—especially since the company's plantation lease had already expired. The strategy was not an unalloyed success. While the youth gangs successfully prevented smallholders from entering the land in question, they were less than trustworthy stewards of the land in their trust. On several occasions, they sold off land to developers who saw it as an opportunity and expected Medan to grow and reach Saentis soon. The new airport in Kuala Namu seemed to confirm this forecast of the direction of urban expansion.

In 2003, the governor of Deli Serdang regency issued a letter banning the widespread occupation of the land in Saentis.[51] It resembled the "stand-fasts" issued by the government in the 1950s (described in Chapter 2), both in its determined content and its modest effects. Hence, by 2005, most of the peasant groups had teamed up with various gangs, and most of Medan's gangs were represented in the area: *Pemuda Pancasila*, IPK, AMPI, and FKPPI. Now, each occupied area was marked by the presence of the gangs, and peasant groups incorporated elements of the gangs' names in their own, such as *Pancasila* [five principles], *Karya* [labor], and so on. The banners of the groups swayed from improvised flagpoles, while the walls of the small huts told the onlooker that "This is IPK turf," or something similar. However, for several of the peasant groups, this was a problematic relationship. Increasingly, the gangs began to take land from them. The process was simple: The gangsters contacted the individual farmer with an "offer"—a ridiculously low price for the land—and the farmer was made to understand that this was not negotiable. If the offer was refused, bad things would happen to him, his family, and his possessions. In most cases, therefore, people conceded the land to the gang. In some cases, land was sold off to investors from Medan.[52] In other cases, people were allowed to stay, paying rent to the gangsters if these "youths" had no other immediate design for the land. PTPN would then—quite mendaciously—be informed that the land was "cleared" and again under its control. The residents were thereby reduced to precarious tenants of the gang. Despite these unfavorable terms, the plantation workers also began to take part in this phase of the land rush, staking out claims to plots and fields.

This raises the question, as in the other cases above, of what was actually sold. Can someone—an individual, a gang, or a company—sell something they do not own? And what does "own" then mean? In essence, *Pemuda*

Pancasila, IPK, and the others ceded the land to developers for money and promised not to retake it, while leaving the paperwork of legalization to the new landholders. What was bought and sold was not land, or even land rights, but the *land right opportunity* to legalize this new possession as property.

The area in Saentis kept attracting new smallholders and "squatters of fortune," people who would take a piece of land in the hope of being bought off by the company, the movements, or possibly the gangs. Some were bought off, others simply chased off. Some managed to acquire a land certificate (*Surat Keterangan Tanah*, SKT) from the local village mayor, who saw an opportunity to make a killing by issuing fistfuls of land and residence papers. Frequent clashes between different groups, of new settlers, plantation workers who also wanted land, and gangs who defended their rent machine, were the order of the day. One of the settlers put it this way: "We don't know if we can keep this land. We experiment."[53] In 2016, a group of smallholders refused to pay rent or protection money to *Pemuda Pancasila* and IPK. It first resulted in a brawl with mutual threats, and finally a physical fight with sticks, stones, and Molotov cocktails. The gangsters reported the smallholders to the police, who coerced the farmers back into compliance.

In sum, PTPN's lease had lapsed but the company refused to give up the land. Equally, its sublease had lapsed, but although PTPN made several attempts to retrieve the land it had sublet to *Pemuda Pancasila* and IPK, this equally failed.[54] PTPN's instrument of protection of its plantation land had turned out to be corrosive. In the meantime, the gangs were selling land to businessmen from Medan, while smallholders were skipping from area to area on borrowed time. The interdigitating of legality and illegality was mesmerizing. The initial occupation was hardly lawful, and the plantation company's continued operations after the expiration of its lease also would appear to violate the law. Moreover, the violent entry of the gangs, and their extortion of the rent for the smallholders' irregular access to land, would discomfort any legal mind. On the other hand, the notions of a formal rental contract, and the creation of a cooperative (albeit for the irregular transfer of control to a gang), testify to an ambition of legalization, through the employment of the accessories of law. The steady purchase of land by businessmen and developers who would "see to the legalizing paperwork themselves" kept fueling the process. Topping off these examples by citing the gangsters' recourse to the police for the recovery of their rent from small-holders would suggest that these operators felt more than confident that the transition from illegal to legal was well under way.

Conclusion

Violence has been an integral part of urban development in Medan. Through land occupations, and systematic intimidation of smallholders and other ordinary people in popular neighborhoods, violence encompassed forceful eviction and destruction of houses and belongings to make space for new facts on the ground. Yet, the many actors who have had designs for the land in and around the city were concerned with locking in achievements as rights and property. The make-believe spaces of Medan have been claimed by both physical appropriation and legal beliefs. Construction, walls, roads, houses, and so on make up the physical facts on the ground, but it seems that such facts have almost always been accompanied by efforts to legalize possessions with reference to law. Certificates, maps, and tax receipts, as well as policy declarations, administrative announcements, and public speeches, are all representations of recognition by officialdom and the state. They were mobilized to convince the relevant public audience that "This is mine, and the state says so, too!" Even when power to assert possession has been overwhelming, the drive to legitimate it as a right through legalization has been evident.

For government institutions that can rely on the concept of state land, possessions were legalized *ex ante*, but for most ordinary people, businessmen, entrepreneurs, youth gangs, and other citizens of Indonesia, possession precipitated legalization. While the representations of legality suggest that they represent something already legal, they *are* the act of legalization. The signboard, the fence, the house number, the taxi stand, and even a kindergarten called *karismatik* all suggest an official existence. Therefore, it should be no surprise that people have tried to make their possessions look lawful. All actors have invested. They have invested labor and money in the physical structures, and they have invested in legalization with all the resourcefulness their experience allowed. And while few are inducted into formal law, most have had an acute sense of its importance and its language. Moreover, the people in Medan collectively obliterate the lazy assumption that clear property rights are the sine qua non that must precede any investment of cash, energy, or conviction.

There is no single formula for establishing the make-believe landscape; the facts on the ground; and the legal persuasion. Nonetheless, the public administration played an important part as the authority all actors wished to solicit in one way or another. As the source of policy pronouncements, and as a source of law, government institutions offered all actors the possibility of turning possession into property. Public administration can provide possession with the last tenth of legalization. The 2001 announcement that land was to be released for distribution was particularly effective. It opened a cat-flap the size of a barn door for legalization of unlawfully appropriated land, and the imaginary 5,873 hectares continued to provide this opportunity for legalization for years.

Law and legality are structures through which to decide what shall be property and what shall be crime, and the competition over future urban land impelled legalization in all its variety. Indeed, as the cases show, struggles over legality are not conducted by legal means alone. So, to call the panoply of illegal acts that we have witnessed "extra-juridical" may be to miss an important point. Classifying illegal acts as "extra-juridical" in the hope of preserving "juridical" for the orderly, the rule-bound, and the fair seems to deny the fact that the disruptive, erratic, and violently unfair use of law has been part and parcel of legalization of property in Medan—and, no doubt, many other places.

Medan *is* notorious. But maybe not exceptional. Even if, in 2017, the Ministry of the Interior named Medan *Kota terbaik tahun ini*: City of the Year.

CHAPTER EIGHT

The Last Tenth

If possession is nine-tenths of the law—of property—then legalization is the last tenth: the persuasion that the possession is legal. This persuasion depends on legal posturing to produce an air of legality to make claims pass as legal. Legalization is about meaning and social contract. Dismissing law and property as a hoax or a sham in order to focus on "actual," "factual" access, whether legalized or not, may effectively redact the production of meaning and social contracts in which people seem deeply engaged. It is tempting to argue that possession is a matter of fact, whereas property is a matter of right (Proudhon 1966: 43). However, since rights are produced in actual contexts, roughed out between competing claims, they are not theoretical fiction but as factual and real as possession. This should not lead to a law-centric approach to the analysis of land conflicts, however. First, an exclusive focus on positive law and statutory rules and institutions as the "facts" produces analyses that few people who feel the sharp end of justice will recognize. And, second, a law-centered approach takes for granted the existence of law and legal systems as something people approach rather than something that only exists because people create and enact them every day. I have tried in this book to work from the position that law and property are made up of both statutory procedures and very mundane details of legalization, all of which solicit and require recognition. Recognition affirms the aspiration to rights as well as the level-headed ambition to have others respect and enforce them. In the confluence of ideas about rights and the tenacity and reach of institutions, law and property represent ambitions as much as accomplishments, and persuasion as much as proof.

Indonesia's checkered history shows that law and property are no more settled facts than facts to settle. This is true for rural and urban settings alike. While asphalt, concrete, and heavy structures suggest irreversibility in urban areas, the exact land uses (different forms of use, such as housing, railway lines, and the like) are clearly not settled for good, even if it is unlikely that agriculture will return. The "making of rules and social and symbolic order," Moore reminds us, "is a human industry matched only by the manipulation, circumvention, remaking, replacing and unmaking of rules and symbols in which people seem almost equally involved" (1978: 1). This book is about how. First, the book shows that law is an institutionalized medium, a language, and a field of meaning coveted by all parties in Indonesia engaged in the struggle over land. Law pledges to consolidate achievements beyond the moment. It holds out the promise of taking claims safely through times of changing fortunes as recognized rights protected and enforced by the state. Second, however, access to this field is very unequal, if not entirely exclusive. People engage with determination and imagination, but also with disproportionate force and capacity. And there are structural reasons why.

Colonization established a deep structure of state ownership to land. For almost a century and a half, legal doctrine has insisted on state control over land in Indonesia. Whether this control was ownership, stewardship, craftsmanship, or sheer brinkmanship remains open to interpretation, but it has given government institutions an upper hand in the recognition of claims and rights. The nature of statutory law, asserting itself as the supreme form of legality, has combined very effectively with law's idea that government is the main representative of state rights to land. Violent enforcement of government land rights has dominated much of Indonesia's modern history. Even in the decades after *reformasi*, with its democratization and more open public sphere, government's delegation of land rights to plantation companies has prevailed in most instances. The book's cases from West Java, North Sumatra, and Aceh—Indonesia's classic frontiers of capitalism from the seventeenth, nineteenth, and twenty-first centuries—all show

how contemporary plantation interests have enjoyed the backing of political power.

Protests have challenged government's rights and government authority, all the same. Around the collapse of Suharto's reign, social movements emerged in an ebullient plethora of elaborate claims to land and its control. This was not without historical precedents. Earlier, especially during the 1950s and 1960s, peasant land occupations had also challenged government and plantation companies. Mainly organized and inspired by Communist leaders, peasant movements produced near-revolutionary change during those decades. Although this upsurge was cut short by the military coup in 1965, patterns of land occupation recurred from the late 1990s. One remarkable feature of this resurgence was legalization.

Peasants and the urban rank and file who have occupied land have used and emulated legal language. Old government and court documents, annotating the past like flies caught in amber, have been dug out from family chests, and policies that mention land reform have been loudly rehearsed. While social movements may have entertained ideas about radical change, all their projects seemed to rest on an ambition of achieving legality. No doubt, the fact that Indonesian statutory law offers a wide scope of interpretation has made this easier. When land was occupied, people and their movements produced representations of legal rights—their own deeds; they resolved conflicts, and even tried to pay taxes to Indonesian government authorities, in solicitation of public recognition of their claims as rights. Occupations may have been illegal, but not clandestine, and people have not tried to evade the state. The art of not being governed has seemed an unrealistic and unattractive proposition, and retreat, evasion, and autonomous sovereignty, so vividly described by Scott (2009), seemed not (or no longer) to be their preferred forms of resistance. Even when peasant movements experienced sovereign moments, these were spent in creating the rights and property that the movements believed Indonesian governments had pledged to uphold at independence and, later, in the Basic Agrarian Law.

Construction of claims to rights and legal subjectivity, and the search for social contracts, have been the chosen forms of engagement, and law their terrain. All the characters in this book have been law makers, even if they have not operated exclusively with legal means. So, when I suggest that law is the terrain, it is therefore as much in a prospective as a doctrinal sense. Statutory law is present, propped up by the redoubtable powers of enforcement of the state, but claims, rules, and forms of access that can be made to appear legal may possibly enjoy the same status and enforcement. These efforts to legalize are fueled by popular imaginations of the law and the desire that a claim should be seen as legal rather than be dismissed by the strictures of professional legal dogma. The field of legalization is therefore not the preserve of professionals. They may defend the boundaries of the field with knowledge, procedure, language, and enforcement, but people of all stripes tug at the hem. Legalization also takes place in settings unfamiliar to professionals. The forested slopes of West Java, the back alleys of Bandung, and the former plantation land in Medan are all sites of active legalization where ordinary people legalize and improvise to turn possession into property. The generalized legal posturing produces one of the great ironies: People refer to the law as if it was fixed and they were somewhat well versed in it, but by doing so they effectively make (up) the law, fragment by fragment, constructing what they believe to be already there.

Public representations of recognition are without number. From census stickers on the window, a functional address, and ostentatious tax payment to the inauguration of monuments and street names on Google Maps—all contribute to the visibility of the claim and facilitate its recognition. These efforts were all appeals to political authorities to see people as rights subjects and confer recognition on their claims. Whenever successful, this was the last tenth of property. Often, it has been difficult for ordinary people to obtain direct recognition of property claims. In fact, it is vanishingly rare that they achieve a clear legal and comprehensive right to land. Claims have been disconnected by default, because statutory law, or the way it has been interpreted by government, has left too little room. Instead, however, people have directed their energy and imagination toward forms of indirect recognition. Especially with *reformasi*, new civic rights have opened up new avenues of recognition. People have put forth demands as citizens in legitimate need of, say, a school, and they have complied with the statutory institutions' fields of intervention in selective and opportunistic fashion to pry open the law's emancipatory potential. Different expressions of citizenship

Foot bridge over a creek in West Java (Photo: Christian Lund)

legitimated residence and made eviction more difficult. This way, direct claims to citizenship had indirect territorial and property effects.

Popular expressions of what people believe to be "the law" are often improvised, crafted in context, and based on fragments of knowledge and memory from earlier encounters with the law. However, this is not reserved for the uninitiated. Powerful actors in Indonesia equally refer to the law inaccurately and opportunistically to make their claims stick without breaking stride. When district mayors let plantation companies prowl for land with a location permit as if it was a bona fide plantation permit, when soldiers organized photo shoots for compensation payment (only to snatch back the money once it had been documented), when local big men sold land plots cheaply to the prominent figures in society, when the National Land Agency registered all kinds of land claims in the name of the 5,873 hectares that no one could identify in Medan, and when a village mayor issued scores of residence papers for money to allow squatters to settle and get compensation in the event of eviction, these were not accidents. Legal posturing through state and law effigies produced the effect of legality.

This builds up to the fundamental paradox of law and power. Law, as language, institution, and socio-political instrument, and even as a construction site for all of this, is not the monopoly of government and the powerful in society. Every once in a while, law offers possibilities for smallholders and urban common folk to legalize claims and consolidate their access to land. Such occasional, often unprepossessing victories legitimate and thereby undergird the general belief in law as the solidifier of rights. This generalized belief, in turn, no doubt, enables stronger actors to use and manipulate the law to their advantage nine times out of ten. Thus the distinction between legal and illegal is not unimportant. On the contrary, the social, political, and legal *construction* of this distinction is pivotal for enduring dispossession.

Even though all were law makers, some have had the basic advantage of being part of government structures, such as government-owned plantation companies, armed forces, or ministries. As institutional incarnations of the state, they have benefited from the legal doctrine of state control over land. Ordinary people, on the other hand, have often been on the back foot, and only when they managed to organize as peasant or indigenous movements or neighborhood groups have they occasionally prevailed. Organization gave them the opportunity to express claims as rights, exercise them with some imagination as rights subjects, and, importantly, to do so over time. However, no fascination with common people's sustained success should cloud the fact of its relative exception.

The property rights enshrined in law and confirmed by successive governments from the colonial times through the Sukarno and Suharto years are not simply undone by an upset, a moment of *reformasi*, however promising. Just as legalization has the potential to encrust small gains of access, so is the deep structure of state-centered property inequality set hard by continuous institutional confirmation. This sedimented institutionalization has often been defended by force from army and police, as well as the violent gangs that operate in the twilight between lending government a hand, and crime. It is no small paradox that it is exactly the durability of legalized exclusion, and the fact that benefits of property rights are so firmly harnessed to the Indonesian state, that makes legalization with reference to the state through law such an attractive proposition for common people seeking to secure their possessions.

It is time to speak of justice, if only to end. It is hard to square the discrepancy between what rights law promises and the dispossession perpetrated in its name. Most of this book is about rights: how they come about, how they consolidate, and how they may dissipate or be quashed in more brutal ways. And while rights connect to justice, they are not the same. Rights are parts of social contracts, while justice is fairness. Rights are political and legal, whereas justice is philosophical. Yet, while the empirical sciences do not traffic in "original positions," ideas of justice may be a useful measure of injustice. Ideally and hypothetically, fairness could, Rawls (1999) suggests, be achieved if rules were made by people who did not know in advance which end of the stick they would hold in future. It is impossible to say what principles of justice would emerge if people in Indonesia had the possibility to step behind Rawls's veil of ignorance, but I feel quite confident that it is unlikely they would come up with the current situation. No one, Indonesian or otherwise, lingers in comfort behind any veil of ignorance, however. Injustice and marginalization are acutely felt, and any change to perpetual unfairness will depend on people's ingenuity, their ability to organize, and, ultimately, their desire for justice.

Chapter 1. Possession Is Nine-Tenths of the Law

1. For a particularly rich canon of the unjust use of law in colonial state formation, see Arendt (1973), Benton (2002), Cooper and Stoler (1997), Guha (1997), Mamdani (1996), Mattei and Nader (2008), Mitchell (2002), Nuijten (2003), Peluso (1992), Sundar (2009), and Tamanaha (2004). The problematic relationship between legality and legitimacy is by no means exclusively "colonial," however. See e.g. Agamben (2005), Cover (1986), Dworkin (1977), Habermas (1997), Rawls (1999), Schmitt (2004), and Weber (1968).

2. For important studies of how law is also available to the weak in society, even under authoritarian conditions, see Holston (2008), Moore (1998), O'Brien and Li (2006), Santos (1977), Scott (1985), Spector (2019), Thompson (1975), and Wolford (2010).

3. Law has proved vexingly difficult to define as a timeless phenomenon. As a structure of rules or a process of rule-making, definitions tend to be either over-restrictive and concern only laws passed through a proper legislature, or over-inclusive and look like social rules of society. In either case, different societies have different concepts of law and they change over time; see F. von Benda-Beckmann (1993), Bourdieu (1987), Comaroff and Comaroff (2016), Griffiths (2015), Guha (2016), Hart (1961), Latour (2010), Moore (1978), Raz (2005), and Tamanaha (2016).

4. For studies on the appearance of legality, see Campbell (2015), Das (2007), Lund (2008), Mattei and Nader (2008), Mitchell (1991, 2002), Moore (1986), Nader (2009), Rajkovic et al. (2016), and Rose (1994).

5. As Schmitt points out, "the legal holder of state power has the presumption of legality on his side. . . . The threefold general premium on legal possession of power is grounded in the ease of judgment, the supposition of legality, and the ability to achieve the immediate execution of one's dictates" (2004: 32–35). See also Bourdieu (2012: 94–100).

6. For studies on the artifactual importance of paper, see Campbell (2015), Correia (2013), Feldman (2008), Ferrier (2012), Graeber (2015), Hetherington (2011), Hull (2012), Latour (2010), Mathur (2016), and Sadiq (2009).

7. For some of the earlier legal regulations of trade, land use, and labor control, see Breman (1983, 2015), Djalins (2015), van Doorn and Hendrix (1983), Gaastra (2003), Gautama and Hornick (1974), Gordon (2010), Furnival (1939), Hoardley (1994), Leue (1992), Lev (2000), Onghokham (2003), Silaen and Smark (2006), Svensson (1991), Wolters (1998).

8. The exclusive and, to many outsiders, discombobulating language and procedure of law are captured in Latour (2010). For legal self-reference, see Luhmann (1988). The prize for fiction, however, must go to Dickens and *Bleak House:* "The lawyers have twisted it into such a state of bedevilment that the original merits of the case have long disappeared from the face of the earth. It's about a will and the trusts under a will—or it was once. It's about nothing but costs now. We are always appearing, and disappearing, and swearing, and interrogating, and filing, and cross-filing, and arguing, and sealing, and motioning, and referring, and reporting, and revolving about the Lord Chancellor and all his satellites, and equitably waltzing ourselves off to dusty death, about costs. That's the great question. All the rest, by some extraordinary means, has melted away" (1853: chapter 8).

9. There is a rich literature for Indonesia: Bakker (2009a+b, 2015, 2017), Butt and Lindley (2010), Dick and Mulholland (2010), Eilenberg (2012), Gilbert and Afrizal (2018), van Klinken (2009), Lindsey (2001), McLeod (2010), Mudhoffir (2017), I. Wilson (2015). Such government-corporate-gangster coalitions are by no means the preserve of Indonesia, however. Freedom of association and land claims are suppressed by such coalitions in many agrarian societies. See Borras and Franco (2005), Campbell (2015), Grajales (2011, 2016a+b), Sidel (2004), Walker et al. (2011), Woods (2011, 2018). See also Hansen (2005) and Volkov (2002).

10. It is an adaptation of the methods developed by Bierschenk and Olivier de Sardan (1997).

Chapter 2. Ground Work

1. North Sumatra Province was formed in 1950. It included the former residencies of East Sumatra, Tapanuli, and Aceh. The former residency of East Sumatra was the center of the "plantation belt" on the east coast. East Sumatra formed a separate republic supported by the Dutch in 1947. In 1950, East Sumatra was dissolved and became an integral part of North Sumatra and Indonesia. In 1956, Aceh split off to become a province on its own (Ricklefs 1993).

2. The data is from the National Land Agency in 2006 and 2008. While technically public, this data is not easily available, and 2006 and 2008 are the latest available figures. It is not clear from the National Land Agency data what qualifies as "1"

conflict. Nonetheless, in a context of 381 land concessions, 699 ongoing conflicts suggest that it is generalized.

3. This historical section draws especially on Breman (1989), E. Damanik (2016), Furnivall (1939, 1948), McTurnan Kahin (2003), Pelzer (1978, 1982), Reid (1979), Siagan et al. (2011), Silean and Smark (2006), and Stoler (1985a+b).

4. Tan Malaka, *Dari Pendjara ke Pendjara* [*From Jail to Jail*] (1970), here from Shiraishi (1997: 18).

5. Payment for leases varied from "nothing but earnings from export licences," over "a head tax on plantation workers," to "money for land in use" (Pelzer 1978: 67).

6. Working conditions in the plantations were generally unfree and unforgiving. "Slavery was legally abolished in the East Indies by the 1860s, but indenture was not" (Stoler 1985a: 28). Workers—invited, tricked, or forced from Java especially—were bound by indentured status, and housed and fed in estate barracks. Usually, workers were bound by three-year contracts, but most of them renewed their contracts indefinitely because of debt incurred during harvest carnivals organized by the company. Workers—contract coolies—were under company jurisdiction with its police, prosecutor, judges, and penal sanctions. The atrocious conditions of plantation workers were revealed to the Dutch public by a report from a local Dutch attorney in 1902. The indenture system was gradually abolished in the 1930s (Breman 1989, E. Damanik 2016, Pelzer 1978).

7. The Japanese government had promised independence for Indonesia in somewhat vague terms in 1944, and a Committee for the Preparation of Indonesian Independence was set up on August 7, 1945 (the day after the bombing of Hiroshima). The most prominent leaders of the committee were Sukarno and Mohammed Hatta, the later leaders of the *Partai Nasionalis Indonesia*, but different leaders of the *pemuda* were also included. Independence was declared on August 17, 1945 (Anderson 1972: 61–104). It is worth noting that the word "youth" should not be taken too literally. While many young people form part of the youth gangs, men of all ages find a place among their ranks.

8. In the West Coast Residency, the coalition of *pemuda* began to issue its own orders in defiance of the new nationalist government. They even "announced that the hundred-Rupiah bills of the Republic's paper currency were no longer valid and had begun recalling them, paying seven ten-Rupiah bills in return" (McTurnan Kahin 2003: 182). While this was most likely a way of duping people into subsidizing the *pemuda*, it bespeaks the uncertainty about authority at that moment.

9. In July 1947, the Dutch launched a full-scale military campaign to reclaim their colony and possessions. Forces were concentrated to Java and the plantation belt of East Sumatra. The campaign was successful, and by the end of 1947, the Dutch had sufficient territorial control to decree provisional recognition to the State of East Sumatra (*Negara Sumatera Timur*), independent of the new Republic of Indonesia. Although the new State of East Sumatra was the creation of the Dutch

intended for the protection of their plantation interests, a recovery of plantation land was not straightforward. Most plantations had been occupied, at least
partially, and many squatters even had some legal support of their claims. Japanese
ordinances from the war and an instruction issued by the republican government
immediately after the Japanese surrender supported smallholder rights to the
land. Moreover, with independence—Indonesian and East Sumatran alike—all
squatters now doubled as an electorate of citizens, forming a completely new social
actor. The new East Sumatra government therefore decided to tolerate the occupations that had occurred prior to June 1948, whereas any subsequent occupation
would face eviction. In some parts of the plantation belt, half of the area formerly
used as plantations was now farmed by smallholders (Pelzer 1982: 5–9). However,
when the Dutch no longer backed the new state militarily in 1950, it crumbled,
and East Sumatra returned to Indonesia.

10. See Djalins (2012), McVey (1965), Ricklefs (1993), Shiraishi (1990, 1997), Vickers
(2005), White (2016).

11. Of the different peasant organizations that had emerged in Java at independence
in 1945, the most significant ones had merged into the Peasant Front of Indonesia
(*Barisan Tani Indonesia*, BNI) by 1955. It was active nationwide, and its membership grew dramatically from around 800,000 people in 1954 to 8.5 million in 1965.
BNI was associated with the Communist Party, but all parties had their respective
affiliated labor and peasant organizations (Pelzer 1982: 45–58, see also White 2016).

12. The first court case in Medan District Court against farmers occupying plantation
land illustrates the situation: 126 peasant farmers were accused of occupying parts
of a plantation that the governor of Sumatra had decreed to be returned to the
company, Helvetia. However, the farmers argued, the land had once been given to
them during the Japanese occupation of Indonesia. Even if they had been evicted
once, after the departure of the Japanese army, their reoccupation of the land after
the demise of the State of East Sumatra was nothing more than taking back what
was rightfully theirs (Ikhsan nd a, 4–7). The planters, on the other hand, organized
in the General Association of Rubber-planters on Sumatra's East Coast (*Algemeene
Vereeniging van Rubberplanters der Oostkust van Sumatra*), argued that their rights
to plantation concessions had merely been suspended during the interregnum of
war and struggle for independence.

13. It came to incidents of massive confrontation between government and police, on
one hand, and the squatters and large masses of peasants from the movement on
the other. In one heated confrontation, four farmers were shot dead by the police.
Effectively, it put an end to the government's resettlement schemes, and fueled
new land occupations (Reid 1979).

14. Increasingly, the communists connected land occupations to international political
events. Thus, labor and youth organizations connected to the Communist Party

used the Congo rebellion as a cue to take over Belgian estates, the Malaysia issue to take over British estates, the American support to South Vietnam to take over Goodyear and other American estates. The occupations resonated with Indonesia's official position in international politics, and therefore made it difficult for the government to disavow these political actions at home (Pelzer 1982: 38).

15. A short-lived coup in North Sumatra had led to provincial martial law, which gave executive powers to the military (Pelzer 1982: 147).

16. From 1957 to 1962 the Constitution was suspended and martial law prevailed, under the euphemism "guided democracy." For analyses of Sukarno's reign from revolution, liberal parliamentarianism, through authoritarian, "guided" democracy with differentiated and curtailed citizenship rights to Indonesians of Chinese extraction, see Lev (2000: 3–12); McTurnan Kahin (2003); Rachman (2011); Ricklefs (1993); and Vickers (2005: 85–168).

17. While the Netherlands had recognized Indonesian sovereignty in 1949, this did not include West Irian (West Papua). The Netherlands had hoped for separate independence for this part of their Indies.

18. The military had already imposed illegal levies on businesses during the 1950s, but with the nationalizations from 1958, they took control of the lion's share of the former Dutch possessions and enterprises (Robison 1986: 260–70).

19. By Law of the Republic of Indonesia Number 1, 1958, on Liquidation of Private Lands (*Undang Undang Republik Indonesia Nomor 1, 1958 Tentang Penghapusan Tanah Tanah Partikelir*) and Law of the Republic of Indonesia Number 89, 1958, on Nationalization of Dutch Owned Companies (*Undang-Undang Republik Indonesia Nomor 89, 1958 Tentang Nasionalisasi Perusahaan-Perusahaan Milik Belanda*). According to Reerink (2011), the nationalization resulted in exodus of foreign workers and business owners, many of them Dutch. Some of them managed to sell up before they left, while some others simply abandoned their properties.

20. Moreover, government authority over land is split between competing ministries and departments, each interpreting what may constitute overriding state interests (Slaats et al. 2009).

21. This harked back to 1926 when the Communist Party was first banned by the Dutch (McVey 1965, Shiraishi 1997).

22. "An estimated half million people were killed and a million and a half were indefinitely detained as political prisoners. The families of such prisoners lived with the constant threat of harassment" (Farid 2005: 8, Huizer 1974). For an analysis of the shifts in policymaking and enforcement and the relations between armed forces and the leading political party, *Golkar*, during the New Order, see Slater (2010), and also Honna (2010) and Tajima (2014).

23. Land reform reentered the government vocabulary only in 2006 (Slaats et al. 2009, see also Lubis 2013).

24. The military and high-level bureaucrats established charitable foundations, *yayasan*, exempted from public audit. Such foundations held interests in companies and enabled the top brass and politico-administrative elite to acquire and control off-budget funds for discretionary use (Barber and Talbot 2003, Dick and Mulholland 2010, McCullough 2004, Robison 1986, Robison and Hadiz 2004; see also Baker and Milne 2015).

25. Plantation companies must go through a long process to obtain a lease. However, more often than not, the plantation companies did not have all documents and many of the ones they did have had expired, some had been acquired in the wrong order, and so on. Especially during the New Order, many companies were confident of having political backing, which made them somewhat cavalier about renewing their paperwork. Consequently, companies have often operated in illegality for some of the time. They have operated *as if* they had the right and all papers (see also Chapter 5).

26. The 1967 and 1999 Forestry Laws, the 1967 Mining Law, the 1967 Foreign Investment Law, and the 1972 Transmigration Law, as well as the 1974 and 1979 Regional and Village Government Laws were all tools government could use to legalize evictions from community lands.

27. A small note on terminology: Not all *ormas* or OKP are of the type mobilized for political violence. These categories are large and cover organizations from boy scouts and peasant movements to violent entrepreneurs engaged in protection rackets, enforcing the will of those who pay, and sometimes operating in somewhat autonomous fashion. In this book, I use the term "youth gangs" to describe groups of the latter character, whereas I specify the concrete nature of other organizations, such as boy scouts, peasant unions, alumni associations, and so on. See Aspinall and van Klinken (2010), Bakker (2009, 2015, 2017), Barker (2007), Karina (2008), van Klinken (2007), Onghokham (2003), Ryter (1998, 2002), I. Wilson (2010, 2015), and L. Wilson (2011).

28. In North Sumatra and Medan, the most significant ones include *Pemuda Pancasila* (Youth of the Five Principles of the Nation), IPK (*Ikatan Pemuda Karya*, Association of Workers' Youth), AMPI (*Angkatan Muda Pembaharuan Indonesia*, the Force for the Renewal of Indonesia's Youth), *Pam Swakarsa* (Swakarsa Public Security Force formed by the military in 1998), and FKPPI (*Forum Komunikasi Putra-Putri Indonesia*, Indonesian Communication Forum for Sons and Daughters of Military Retirees), mainly organizing children of police and army officers. Some groups refer to themselves as *laskar*, referring to the Shi'a tradition of the *al-askari* militia.

29. Although they collaborate with the political parties, none of the major youth gangs in North Sumatra have declared allegiance to a specific one. Rather, politicians can cultivate affiliations with any gang regardless of his party. This, in turn, has produced intense criss-crossing internal rivalry.

30. By 2011, LonSum was owned by a series of corporate investors, with some 60 percent of the shares owned by the Salim Ivomas group (itself a subsidiary of Indofood Agricultural Resources Ltd., listed on the stock market in Singapore). Other large shareholders included Credit Suisse Singapore, and Hong Kong and Shanghai Banking Corporation (HSBC) (Khairina 2013, ch. 4). Mr. Salim was part of President Suharto's circle of friends and business associates.

31. The most common certificates are the SKT (*Surat Keterangan Tanah*, Land Certificate), issued by the village head, and the KTPPT (*Kartu Tanda Pendaftaran Pemakai Tanah*, Land User Registration Certificate), sometimes also referred to as KRPT (*Kartu Registrasi Pemakaian Tanah*, Land Use Registration Card). The latter can be issued by the sub-village head, the *camat*. In practice, different local bureaucrats have been known to act *ultra vires* and issue all such certificates. Many smallholders were issued such land certificates but in no systematic way. The political climate, from villages to government circles, was marked by polarization between communist and anti-communist groupings, and one attempt at legalization of a land claim was canceled out by another. In addition to these land registration certificates, a variety of papers of a certificatory nature were issued in the 1970s in connection with land registration programs (Fitzpatrick 2006, Slaats et al. 2009: 511–17).

32. For the history of Harrison & Crossfield, see Cheng Hai (2015). See also Tate (1996).

33. Several village leaders were imprisoned, only to be released after 14 years in 1985. Others were detained and beaten by the police. Their release—half-naked and brutalized—instilled great fear in the community. Conversation between Wina Khairina, HARI, and the informants (2016).

34. See Ryter (1998, 2002, 2009). See also Anderson (2001), Bakker (2015, 2016, 2017), Barker (2007), Melvin (2018), Robinson (2018), and Wilson (2015).

35. They may have gotten the Emergency Law of 1954 wrong by a year, but the meaning was clear. And they could be forgiven considering that the country was under some form of emergency status for almost twenty years after independence (Kurniawan 2018: 49–63).

36. While all villagers were under attack, especially ethnic Chinese were targeted. Informants explained how it reminded them of the anti-communist, anti-Chinese pogroms in 1965. Interview in 2016.

37. BPM Image Map Special No. 148/04/IV/1997 (Feb. 28, 1997).

38. The Global Network of Public Interest Law (PIL-Net) registered some 12 mass arrests in Deli Serdang district between 2005 and 2007. Interview with PIL-Net and Bitra, Medan, 2015.

39. *Preman* is a most likely a deformation of the Dutch *vrijman*, a free man, a non-contract overseer, in the employ of a company though not bound to it (Ryter 1998: 48–51). In connection with land occupations and evictions, the popular use of *preman* refers to hired "muscle," which can be used for intimidation and violence.

40. Interviews with members of villagers' lawyers' team, 2017. Court case number: 275/pid.B/2005/PN/TTD.

41. Internal correspondence between the National Land Agency's national and district offices suggested that LonSum had actually acquired some 280 hectares more than what it was entitled to according to the lease. The tax office declared that some additional land was registered as fiscal objects of LonSum, although they were unsure of the actual acreage (Letter no. 570/961/VI/2001/July 17, 2001).

42. *Konsorsium Pembaruan Agraria* (KPA) was founded in 1995. The consortium consisted of scholars and activists ("organic intellectuals," in the words of Gramsci) from different organizations that in certain ways substituted for political parties during the New Order. KPA engaged in awareness-raising among politicians and the rural population. Books and pamphlets, but especially training and workshops for the latter groups, rekindled and organized the demands for land reform embedded in the Basic Agrarian Law. KPA also trained the new unschooled politicians who began to inhabit the new decentralized democratic institutions on what opportunities the new legislation provided to them. Also, a "study group" prepared material for the National Assembly to revive land reform through new legislation (Rachman 2011: 94).

Chapter 3. Indirect Recognition

This chapter builds on Lund and Rachman (2018). I am grateful to Noer Fauzi Rachman for letting me use and develop our joint work for the present book.

1. The area around Mount Halimun has been inhabited for centuries. Settlement can be traced back to as early as 1430 (Bolman 2006: 43).

2. Indonesia is divided into provinces. Provinces are made up of regencies and cities. Regencies and cities are divided into districts. Districts are divided into villages (*desa*) or urban communities (*kelurahan*). Villages and urban communities are sometimes made up of *kampungs* or sub-villages/hamlets.

3. Ministerial decree no. 40/1979.

4. For an analysis of rural migration to urban industry see Breman and Wiradi (2002).

5. Government control over land blurs the distinction between territory and property here. "State land" is under the control of government, and as long as it has not granted property rights of "state lands" to others, government would seem to govern it as territory *and* own it as property as well (see Wallace 2008).

6. Gazetting is a formal reservation of forests through permanent excision of an area from the category of state land (see Peluso and Vandergeest 2001: 781).

7. For the history of territorialization in the area, I draw significantly on Galudra et al. (2008) and on personal communication with Gamma Galudra in 2012 and 2013, for which I am grateful.

8. The Japanese encouraged food production and declared that the "Dutch forest conservation policy was no longer valid" (Harada 2003: 274). In 1949, "at least 400,000 hectares, or 14 per cent of Java's state forest areas, were allegedly occupied by peasants, or deforested by civilian and military wood thieves" (Galudra nd: 3).

9. In 1972, the State Forest Corporation (*Perum Perhutani*) was established as a state-owned timber company. The corporation was set to administer production and protected forests in Madura and East and Central Java. From 1978, production and protection forests in West Java and Banten were included under the corporation's jurisdiction (see Lounela 2009, 2012, Peluso 1992).

10. Bedner also notes, however, that when vital interests are at stake, Indonesian government institutions can be determined. "Within two years, the Ministry of Forestry had managed to gazette almost 60 per cent of the land that thus far had been only designated" (Bedner 2016a: 77).

11. During the early colonial period, the Dutch East India Company levied taxes on export goods and labor. The private company first established itself on Java in the late sixteenth century (Slaats et al. 2009: 494). Initially, the company focused on trade and did not intervene in the local land tenure arrangements. It did, however, with some success enforce compulsory cultivation of selected crops on one-fifth of farmers' land (Wallace 2008: 193). The Dutch East India Company bankrupted at the end of the eighteenth century. The company's debts and assets were taken over by the Dutch state. By this token, Indonesia became a colony (Peluso 1992: 45, Slaats et al. 2009: 495).

12. *Girik* is known since the Dutch colonial period as land tax on what was understood as indigenous farmland. It could be termed "customary freehold." As Leaf points out, this category is "fully legal, although unregistered" (Leaf 1993: 483). This form of property was not registered by the National Land Agency, but was considered to fall under *adat* law, and by this token to be, somehow, transitional. If such land were to be registered by the National Land Agency, it would entail "ownership rights" (*hak milik*).

13. Land tax was claimed through a notification of payable property tax SPPT-PBB: *Surat Pemberitahuan Pajak Terutang-Pajak Bumi dan Bangunan* (payable tax notification for land and buildings), and once paid, a receipt was issued: STTS-PBB, *Surat Tanda Terima Setoran-Pajak Bumi dan Bangunan* (building and land tax payment receipt).

14. After the fall of Suharto, villagers also tried to have their land registered with the village offices and with the National Land Agency. Their argument was that they had paid land taxes from long before the area was a national park.

15. Interview, Forest Watch (NGO), Bogor, October 15, 2012. Figures vary, though. Harada (2003: 272) cites figures from a JICA report from 1999 estimating a population

of 160,000 in 46 villages in and around the Mount Halimun area. Writers Team (2011: 7) refer to 141 (+/−) villages in the Halimun ecosystem area. Vitasari and Ramdhaniaty (2016) record that 44 villages were included by the extension of the national park in 2003. Differences in categories of villages and settlements and in the delineation of the area probably account for the variation in information. The key point remains: Many people lived in and around what became a national park.

16. The increasing political importance of indigeneity, autochthony, and belonging is not unique to Indonesia, but part of a much broader movement (Hilgers 2011).

17. For the New Order politics and *adat*, see also Afiff and Lowe (2007), Benda-Beckmann (1997), Benda-Beckmann and Benda-Beckmann (2011), Burns (2007), Henley and Davidson (2007a+b), Lev (1985), McCarthy (2006), McWilliam (2006).

18. In 2012, AMAN and two indigenous communities from Banten (near Mount Halimun, Java) and Riau (Sumatra) challenged the Forestry Law no. 41 of 1999 in Indonesia's Constitutional Court, referring to the rights of indigenous peoples enshrined in the constitution (Rachman and Siscawati 2016: 235).

19. RMI was established in 1992.

20. Since the early 1990s what is known as "counter-mapping" emerged in Indonesia as a strategy to create an alternative visibility of boundaries and land uses, of indigenous and other claims that would ordinarily be invisible in government cartography. Since the fall of the New Order, many NGOs adopted this, and thousands of villages have since been "counter-mapped" (Peluso 2005, Pramono et al. nd, Warren 2005). In fact, for many villages in Java, non-governmental counter-mapping was the first cartographic representation to include more than cultivated area—that is, rice fields (Peluso and Vandergeest 2001: 795).

21. Interview, anonymous, November, 2013.

22. *Deklarasi Kesepakatan Bersama Hutan Halimun Lestari Masyarakat Mandiri. Membangun Kawasan Konservasi Secara Kolaborasi Menuju Hutan Halimun Salak Lestari, Masyarakat Mandiri, Parigi, Bogor, 9 Februari 2010* (Agreement Toward Sustainable Forest Use in Halimun Salak with the Population of the Independent Community, Parigi, Bogor, February 9, 2010) (BTNGHS, no LCS/IU-T. 13/KH/2010). Document in private possession.

23. In 2013, the park authorities offered to pay a small sum for this "service." The payment was not given to individuals as day-laborers but to the village authorities, thus recognizing the community as a legitimate "service provider."

24. For a discussion of dilemmas of participatory and community mapping see Hodgeson and Schroeder (2000) and Warren (2005).

25. This was decreed by the provincial government of West Java (L.R. 12/D/VIII/54/1983).

26. The general opinion among our respondents was that the village leader had mortgaged the certificates for private gain, but no one knew for sure. Interview with *kampung* leader, November 2012.

27. Interview with a group of villagers, November 2012.
28. Copy of receipt in private possession.
29. RW and RT (*Rukun Tetangga*, RT, smaller neighborhood association) and *Rukun Warga*, RW, greater neighborhood association).
30. The actual work of setting the markers in the ground was carried out by officials from the National Land Agency. However, as they explained, they were "working on their own time" on weekends, meaning they did not do this in their official capacity but were hired privately to render service to the company. No doubt, the unofficial survey and boundary making borrowed both boundary stones and legitimacy from the agents' official jobs.
31. In the teachers' common room, for example, a trophy shelf boasted the primary and secondary schools' achievements in subdistrict competitions: Handicraft (third place), Environmental Drawing (third place), Relay Race (kindergarten, honorable mention).

Chapter 4. Occupied!

This chapter builds on Lund and Rachman (2016). I am grateful to Noer Fauzi Rachman for letting me use and develop our joint work for the present book.

1. Excerpt from Sundanese Peasant Union (*Serikat Petani Pasundan*, SPP) interviews with farmers who claimed back land in 2008. Farmers had to account for the history of the plot they claimed to receive a certificate from SPP. Document in private possession.
2. While the Basic Agrarian Law was intended to break with the colonial legal notion of *domain*, the law effectively operates with state land as a category. The colonial state was no longer the owner of domain; instead, according to the Basic Agrarian Law, the Indonesian state represented the largest community entrusted with the control of the national communal property. This legal hairsplitting meant that other communal rights to land could exist as long as they were not contradictory to the interests of the larger community, i.e. the state (Slaats et al., 2009: 500). As Wallace points out, by "using 'control' in contradistinction to 'ownership' to describe its power, the Indonesian state implied that the nature of its relationship with the people in regard to land was less intrusive or dominant than under the Dutch" (2008: 200). Notwithstanding the less intrusive wording, the concept of "control" provided a much wider latitude for government institutions to interpret, act, and influence decisions related to land than would generally befall an "owner."
3. The Basic Agrarian Law only explicitly defines rights, which are strictly individual. Similar to many other post-colonial legislations, the Basic Agrarian Law represents the recognition of the existence of customary forms of tenure, as well as the ambition that they will wane, become irrelevant, and be replaced by something new, uniform, and government regulated. So even if the Basic Agrarian Law recognizes

the *existence* of certain communal rights, it does not specify them, or their nature or extent. Reerink (2011: 61) points out, that the "state's right of control allows the state to grant individual land rights (*hak-hak perorangan*), to limit such rights, or to revoke them. If the state grants individual land rights, it still holds an indirect right of control over the land. Rights the state can grant comprise four primary rights: ownership right (*hak milik*), long-lease, or plantation rights (*hak guna usaha*), construction right (hak guna bangunan), and usage right (*hak pakai*). Someone holding an ownership right can grant a lease right (*hak sewa*), which forms a secondary right."

4. According to Swart's (1911) report on rubber companies in the Netherlands East Indies, the plantation was owned by Bandjarsarie (Java) Rubber Company, Limited. The tenure of the plantation was held on a Netherlands Indian Government lease (*erfpacht*) that would expire in 1975. For a map of the plantation, see van Diessen and Ormeling (2003: 255). The plantation was not included in the 1958 nationalization program of the Sukarno government, which established state-owned plantation companies.

5. In 1970, the system of Agrarian Courts was dissolved (see Benda-Beckmann and Benda-Beckmann, 2014: 112).

6. While thousands of alleged communists were killed throughout Indonesia by the army, by Islamist militias, and by youth gangs, an order made by the West Java army commander *not* to kill communists saved the lives of hundreds of villagers in Banjaranyar.

7. Van Klinken explains, "Before being freed [political prisoners] had to sign a declaration that they would not demand compensation. Despite a government order to return their possessions, in reality nobody has successfully reclaimed their books, land and homes. . . . Ex-Tapols were not permitted: 1) To work in any form of government service, nor in any state-owned corporation, strategic industry, political party, or news media. They were not permitted to become a minister in any religion, a teacher, village head, lawyer, or puppeteer (*dalang*); 2) To vote or be elected; 3) To obtain a passport and travel overseas, even for medical treatment (some allowance was made for those going to Mecca on pilgrimage); 4) To choose where to live or to move house freely; 5) To obtain credit from the bank, even when they fulfilled other requirements; 6) To receive the pensions to which they are entitled from their former employers when they were sacked in 1965" (van Klinken 1999: 17).

8. Delivery of the certificates to the 500 families took 31 days. The transcripts of each interview are between two and five typed pages long. Most of the histories trace alternating eviction and occupation for three generations (Material in private possession).

9. We did not hear of anyone who was refused land, but the procedure would have discouraged those with slim chances from making a claim.

10. This was not an idle threat. As for many of the plantation companies, the duration of the original lease was 35 years. This meant that many leases expired around 2000 and in the following years. Some companies had not taken care to renew them and were themselves technically squatting on the land.

11. In 2013, Ciamis district was divided into two: Ciamis and Pangandaran districts.

12. On historical aspects of the State Forest Corporation in relation to the government and village communities, see Lounela (2009), Peluso (1992), and Rachman (2011: 27–36). After including West Java forest land, "the territory controlled by the State Forest Corporation mirrored that controlled by the Dutch Forest Service in Java except for enclaves of forest land disputed by peasants placed there by the Japanese or occupying the land since the revolution" (Peluso 1992: 125).

13. The team was composed of officials from the District Military Office, West Java Police Office, West Java Civil Police Office, the National Land Agency's West Java Office, West Java Forest Office, and the State Forest Corporation. The team was assigned on the basis of a decision by the West Java Governor, No. 552.02/Kep.560-Binprod/2007 (*Surat Keputusan Gubernur Jawa Barat Nomor 552.02/Kep.560-Binprod/2007 tentang Tim Pengamanan dan Penanganan Gangguan Keamanan Hutan Negara dan Perkebunan Besar*).

14. Material in private possession.

15. Curiously, the Bandung-based NGO, Council for Forest Salvation, also participated. No doubt its presence represented "civil society."

16. It is not possible to establish whether villagers were indeed involved in logging trees planted by State Forest Corporation or whether, as villagers claim, this logging was part of an everyday routine of State Forest Corporation staff in collusion with police and local gangs. Villagers did cut trees, but claimed them to be "their own," and not planted by State Forest Corporation. The fact that some sawmills processing the illegally logged timber were owned and run by police officers did not make the picture any clearer.

17. SPP in Ciamis had organized training sessions in cartography and mapping for all activists, and a small group from Harumandala had participated.

18. The State Forest Corporation film crew also wanted to document the local smallholders destroying their own crops, but the smallholders refused.

19. All the local chapters of SPP we visited in October–November 2013 that had occupied State Forest Corporation land told similar stories of donations to village governments.

Chapter 5. Predatory Peace

I owe the title of this chapter to Edward Aspinall, who coined "predatory peace" in Aspinall (2014), and generously let me use it.

1. For details on Aceh's history, see Aspinall (2009a), Dijk (1981), Reid (2005, 2006), Schulze (2003, 2004).
2. Palm oil production took up some 175,000 hectares in 1996 and increased to almost 400,000 hectares and a production of 2 million metric tons of crude palm oil in 2013 (AICB 2015: 76; Eye on Aceh 2007: 8).
3. For agrarian issues in Aceh's rainforest frontier, see McCarthy (2006).
4. The basic legal framework in contemporary Aceh is provided by the Indonesian constitution and, secondarily, by the Aceh Governance Law. Elements of syariah law have been introduced through regional regulations passed by the provincial parliament. Syariah was not part and parcel of the GAM program, although its members were usually devout Muslims, like the majority of the general population of the province (Aspinall 2009a, Feener 2013, Kingsbury 2007).
5. GAM's control was quite uneven though. It was most firmly established on the northern coastal plains while it was "weaker and . . . remained a largely criminal organization lack[ing] the territorial control necessary for governance" in most of the rest of the Aceh province (Barter 2015: 231). Nonetheless, according to Schulze, by 2003, 99 out of 228 districts (*kecamatan*) and 4,759 out of 5,947 villages did not have functioning local government (2006: 231). "Human rights abuses committed by GAM include[ed] hostage-taking and the targeted killing of suspected informers, government officials and civil servants" (Amnesty International 2013: 5). See also Robinson (2001: 226).
6. But while such state functions of validation, recognition, and sanction were carried out, GAM only exceptionally managed to undertake any long-term infrastructural activities.
7. While GAM was fighting the Indonesian military as the representative of what it considered to be the Indonesian imperialist state, some collaboration between the two sides also took place. Sometimes, the same plantation paid both parties, and sometimes army and police would clash over who should "protect" a particular plantation. Sometimes, the GAM would sell "their" harvest though the police or army, and sometimes the army personnel would buy up harvest from smallholders through middlemen, who would then also act as informants (Eye on Aceh, 2007: 8–9). Between 1999 and 2009, active plantation areas increased only from 175,000 to 250,000 hectares in Aceh (Eye on Aceh, 2007: 8). It is difficult to assess the actual extent of collaboration, but there was enough to sustain elaborate conspiracy theories. Rumors circulated that the military delivered arms to GAM to justify its own role in fighting them. And sometimes the criminal activities of both sides aligned (Aspinall 2009a, Drexler 2008, Eye on Aceh 2007, McCulloch 2005a). Often the situation was simply that GAM controlled the interior while troops controlled the main roads. So, one needed to placate both sides to get the produce out. For small-scale traders and producers this was simple and expensive—one "simply" paid at checkpoints set up by the two sides in their respective areas of control. Plan-

tation owners had to make larger-scale deals or rely on brokers who could negotiate with both sides. But a lot of the plantations did become unproductive. As Aspinall (2009a: 152) states, "the guerrillas and their enemies were locked not only in mortal combat but also in an intimate embrace."

8. "Amnesty International and other bodies documented a range of violations committed by members of the security forces and their auxiliaries, including unlawful killings, enforced disappearances, torture, forcible displacement of civilians, arbitrary arrest and detention of those suspected of supporting GAM. . . . Amnesty International along with others has also highlighted the extent of violence against women during the conflict and stressed in its 2004 report *Indonesia: New military operations, old patterns of human rights abuses in Aceh* that there was a 'long-established pattern of rape and other sexual crimes against women' in the province" (Amnesty International 2013: 5). See also Amnesty International (1993).

9. The Peace Accord included the establishment of a Truth and Reconciliation Commission. In October 2016, the governor of Aceh, Zaini Abdullah, announced the appointment of the seven commissioners (AJAR and Kontras 2017: 16).

10. Actually, some key figures of GAM had been elected as top executives in the province and most districts in Aceh during the first postwar elections in 2006 (that is, before the establishment of *Partai Aceh*). The rank and file of GAM organized in the new *Komite Peralrihan Aceh* (Aceh Transition Committee), replicating the military and territorial structure of GAM's army. Despite some tensions between the old GAM elements, the Aceh Transition Committee became a mass organization and *Partai Aceh*'s street-level security arm, and a very effective political machine developed. *Partai Aceh* would fund the Aceh Transition Committee via direct budgetary transfers and more obscure accounting techniques. More recently, the old guard—the returning exiles—would appear to be losing influence to people whose authority is "derived from local resources and political institutions" (IPAC 2015a: 1).

11. In a well-publicized campaign, 11 illegal palm oil estates inside the Leuser National Park were destroyed, and it was estimated that another fifty may still operate inside the protected area. Gillian Murdoch, "Forests Fight Back as Indonesia Tackles Illegal Palm Oil," Reuters.com (accessed March 14, 2020).

12. It was to be implemented by the Aceh Re-integration Agency (*Badan Reintegrasi Aceh*) (Shohibuddin 2014: 14).

13. *Pembela Tanah Air* (PETA, Defenders of the Homeland) and *Forum Komunikasi Anak Bangsa* (FORKAB, Communication Forum for the Children of the Nation) were two such anti-separatist groups.

14. A rough estimate suggests that 50,000 persons—as potential beneficiaries (ex-fighters and victims) of 2 hectares per person, with space for infrastructure—would require some 125,000 hectares. No one ever identified exact locations for such an amount of land (Shohibuddin 2014: 21).

15. Compensation was not distributed evenly. More than a third of the category "victims" never received any compensation in cash or in kind (Shohibuddin 2014: 26). Generally, people acknowledge that the GAM ex-soldiers deserve some compensation for their war efforts, and that land would be an appropriate instrument. However, GAM veterans have often sold the land that government offered them. Shohibuddin (2014) documents, for Gayo District, that more than 40 percent of the allocated plots had been sold within a year of their allocation. Shohibuddin does not tell us who bought this land, but from the cases studied in this chapter, neighboring plantations would be a reasonable guess. After selling their allocated plots, ex-GAM fighters have been known to use their political capital from the war, and their standing with the present government, to intimidate others into giving them more land. Many villagers, nonetheless, still experience demands from already cash-compensated ex-fighters for land (or land rent) with reference to the Peace Accord MoU (Field notes, May 2015). This seems to be a postwar rent that government officials know about but dismiss as exceptional. The effect was that people often feared the veterans — whether the practice took place on a large scale or not. News traveled, and the potential for intimidation was there.

16. In some cases, ex-commanders from GAM did receive land. For example, in Linge District some former combatants received up to 850 hectares (Shohibuddin 2014: 32). See also Rutten et al. (2017).

17. Thus, palm oil was high on the agenda when the newly elected governor of Aceh, Irwandi, headed an Acehnese delegation to Malaysia in 2006 to discuss the potential for increased trade links. "Aceh's Golden Crop?" *Down to Earth* newsletter, no. 75, November 2007 (www.downtoearth-indonesia.org/story/acehs-golden-crop, accessed March 14, 2020).

18. The delivery of seedlings appears to have been little short of a disaster, with most of them damaged in some regions (Shohibuddin 2014: 31).

19. Confidential interview with two senior staff members of National Land Agency, Banda Aceh, in May 2015.

20. Confidential interview with two senior staff members of the National Land Agency, Banda Aceh, in May 2015.

21. This may now be changing with recent legislation, but it is too early to assess (Bedner 2016a: 81)

22. Ministry of Agriculture Decree No. 26/2007 on Permitting Guidelines for Plantation Business states that at least 20 percent of a company's total plantation area should be made up of smallholdings.

23. Interviews with villagers in three locations in Aceh in May 2015.

24. The current legal framework is Government Regulation no. 24, 1992.

25. These permits covered some 370,000 hectares (LBH 2015). The Legal Aid Foundation of Aceh registered 119 conflicts between planters and smallholders in the

period 2006–11. It is difficult to establish "what is a conflict," as social confrontations are rarely discrete events in time or space. But it seems reasonable to assume that the 119 conflicts registered by the Legal Aid Foundation (LBH 2015) represent a larger number of unreported skirmishes and a generalized tension between planters and smallholders.

26. It is worth recalling that the location permit (*izin lokasi*) would always cover a much larger area within which the smaller area for the actual lease would be carved out. Thus, operating *as if* the area for the location permit was indeed the area under lease would increase the area of operations quite significantly. See also Sirait (2009: 32–36).

27. We were consistently told how companies would spray farmers' fields with pesticides and herbicides to make work there unbearable. And often companies would simply move big equipment onto smallholder land, uproot plants, and dig canals for oil palm cultivation.

28. Confidential interview with informant in May 2015 in Banda Aceh.

29. Fieldwork is not a simple task in Aceh, and deserves particular mention. Even though the war is over, violence is never far off, and talking to ordinary people demands flexibility, discretion, and care. Sometimes interviews were cut short for security reasons because of the proximity of military, police, plantation security, or guerrillas. For example, one interview took place in a coffee bar. Some 20 persons attended, and while 3 or 4 of them engaged most directly in the interview, the rest came and went throughout. Halfway through our discussion a text message began to circulate that one of the old GAM guerrillas was nearby with his men. The guerrilla leader, Din Minimi, had refused to decommission his arms and still made sporadic attacks on government infrastructure and abducted people for ransom (IPAC 2015b). We broke off the meeting, and people scattered. Din Minimi had declared that he would only "arrest evil people." If that was meant to be reassuring, it did not work. The cases presented are selected from five cases studied in depth, and a dozen that were relayed to us in some detail. We interviewed farmers, civil servants, police, politicians, lawyers, academics, journalists, former GAM fighters, and intermediate staff of plantation companies. Fieldwork was conducted during three months in 2015. In the text, people, villages, and their organizations are anonymized and the exact dates of interviews are blurred.

30. Village names are anonymized. It was not possible to ascertain the age of all hamlets. People suggested that they dated back to around 1900.

31. After the fall of Suharto seven years later, villagers reported the incident to the district mayor and parliament. As of 2018, however, the deaths remained unsolved.

32. One of the villagers refused to sign the blank receipt and protested loudly. According to several informants, he "was disappeared," and his dead body was found a few weeks later.

33. In 2001, during the emergency, the Bumi Flora plantation became a notorious site of bloody violence as the military massacred some thirty people (Human Rights Watch 2002).

34. Government introduced PRONA in 1981. Its declared aim was to give effect to mass land titling (Löffler 1996, Slaats et al. 2009). PRONA's bureaucratic entitlement is as a land *administration* scheme rather than a land *distribution* scheme. On some occasions, however, the scheme and its budgets were used by the government to legalize what was dubbed "land reform from below"—in other words, land occupations by farmers' unions.

35. Anonymous villager from Bawang, November 2015.

36. While the first *Partai Aceh* governor of the district was somewhat sympathetic to the idea of a land reform after the peace treaty, it never materialized.

37. Separate interviews with two independent journalists and one civil servant, December 2015. Only corroborated information is used.

38. Interview with independent journalist, December 2015.

39. Anonymous villager, interview, May 2015. Property literature sometimes makes the point that "property is a right, not a thing" (Hohfeld 1913). This popular confusion is rooted in the fact that many property rights correspond to tangible "things" like a piece of land with its characteristics. The contract farming scheme in this case produced the perfect abstraction of property as the land to which the right once corresponded was physically dissolved into the plantation.

40. For a discussion of plantations and smallholdings in Southeast Asia, see Bisonnette and de Koninck (2017).

Chapter 6. On Track

This chapter builds on Nurman and Lund (2016). I am grateful to Ari Nurman for letting me use and rework our joint work for the present book (see also Nurman 2019).

1. See also Colombijn (2012: 232–33, 2013) and Jellinek (1991: 105).

2. When the Japanese left, the *tonarigumi* system survived and was adopted and adapted by the Indonesian government to become the present neighborhood association structure, the *Rukun Tetangga* (RT) and *Rukun Warga* (RW). The latest local legal regulation for these institutions in Bandung is the *Peraturan Daerah Kota Bandung* No. 2, 2013. An RT consists of 30–75 households (Article 6, number 1), whereas an RW consists of five to fifteen *Rukun Tetangga* (Article 7, number 1).

3. *Ordonantie "Onrechtmatige occupatie van gronden"* (Staatsblad [Government Gazette], no. 110, 1948).

4. In the 1980s, the government and the World Bank launched housing projects—*Kampung* Improvement Projects—for low-income populations (Moochtar 1980). The projects aimed to provide better infrastructure for *kampungs*, and to legalize

others through certification of tenure (Peters 2010: 572). Yet the gap between demand for urban housing and its supply remained, and urban *kampungs* continued
to grow (Benjamin and Arifin 1985, Sastrosasmita and Amin 1990, Tunas and
Peresthu 2010).

5. Stasiun Bandung, www.stasiunbandung.com, accessed February 2, 2013.
6. There is no valid information about the date. Some said it ceased to operate in
   1980, and other respondents said that they still witnessed a locomotive use the
   railway until 1984.
7. The takeover of the railway lines is commemorated annually as the Indonesia
   Train Day (*Hari Kereta Api Indonesia*).
8. At that time, the newly established republic had no state apparatus. Effective
   nationalization did not take place until 1949.
9. Tri Setiya, "The Brief History of Train in Indonesia," Factsofindonesia.com (accessed March 14, 2020).
10. Interviews with anonymous local lawyers, and a notary public. See also the com-
    pany's website (www.kereta-api.co.id/ under the header of "Tentang kami—>
    Sumber daya—>Asset Potensial," accessed April 15, 2015). Whether they pay rent
    has been impossible to establish.
11. The term *garapan* originally referred to farmland. In urban areas *garapan* land has
    developed to become residential areas. *Hak garapan* means right to farm, or reside,
    depending on the context (Leaf 1993, Winayanti and Lang 2004). When such a
    use-right is transacted for money, it looks quite close to freehold. The difference
    may be with what ease government can reacquire it for public purposes.
12. According to several informants, in the past all inhabitants along the track near to
    Cibangkong station paid "rent" to the stationmaster. Similarly, other informants
    confirmed that the inhabitants along the track near Buahbatu station paid "rent"
    to the stationmaster of that station. According to informants living along the track
    near Buah Batu Baru, Guntursari, and Turangga, people there paid the railway
    controller. The local residents referred to their land rights as *hak garap*, or right to
    cultivate, but gradually extended the land use to residence.
13. This tradition continued for years, even when the controllers no longer worked for
    the train company.
14. The administrative hierarchy is: Municipality, Sub-district (*Kecematan*), Sub-sub-
    district (*Kelurahan*), Greater neighborhood (*Rukun Warga*, or RW), and Smaller
    neighborhood (*Rukun Tetangga*, or RT). The RW usually consists of more than
    five RTs.
15. There are several projects that were funded by international finance organizations
    and implemented in the urban area in Bandung. Some of them are the Bandung
    Urban Development Project, BUDP I and II, *Program Pengembangan Kecamatan*,
    PPK (*kecamatan* improvement programs), which later became *Program Nasional
    Pemberdayaan Masyarakat-Perkotaan*, PNPM (national program for community

empowerment-urban), and *Program Nasional Pemberdayaan Masyarakat-Mandiri Perkotaan*, PNPM-MP (national program for community empowerment and urban self-sufficiency).

16. None of the respondents informed us when precisely they became registered as property tax payers. But if we refer to the law of property tax, law number 12/1985 (*Undang-undang* No. 12, 1985 *Tentang Pajak Bumi dan Bangunan*), which abolished compulsory contribution for local region (*Iuran Pendapatan Daerah*, IPEDA) and replaced it with the *Pajak Bumi dan Bangunan*, residents were, in all likelihood, registered as property tax payers after 1986 when the law was fully implemented.

17. The tax dates back to the colonial era and was a land rent. People generally paid according to the amount they cultivated, and the generalized understanding was that the tax payment receipt—connecting the name of the person and a specific area and its value—was proof of possession amounting to ownership. Indeed, these tax payment receipts were part of the essential documentation in case of land transfers (see Kano 2008: 311–44).

18. This dilemma of "street-level" or "front line" bureaucrats has been analyzed by Bierschenk and Olivier de Sardan (2014) and Lipsky (1969, 1971, 2010), among others. Due to inadequate resource support, threat and challenge to authority, and contradictory or ambiguous job expectation, the street-level bureaucrats develop practical norms. They use their discretion and interpret and make decisions based on personal experience through simplifications, prioritizations, compromises, self-adjustment, and so on.

19. In this case to *Kantor Pelayanan Pajak Bandung Satu*. For similar strategies of formalization legalization or certification of residence, see *inter alia* Benjaminsen et al. (2009), Reerink and van Gelder (2010), Sjaastad and Cousins (2009).

Chapter 7. Another Fine Mess

1. See *Jakarta Post*, July 10, 2015, and November 24, 2016, and A.T. Damanik 2016.
2. Obviously, arresting high-ranking officials for corruption could suggest that anti-corruption campaigns work. However, it is also possible to interpret the fact that the top echelon is investigated with the approval of the government in Jakarta as a message to the local elites that they "would not be allowed to run roughshod in spite of the expanded powers formally accorded by decentralization" (Hadiz 2010: 175).
3. *Preman* is most likely a deformation of the Dutch *vrijman*: a free man. It generally means gangster, or violent entrepreneur. See chapter 2.
4. In Medan, the largest and most influential youth groups, *Organisasi Kemasyara-katan Pemuda* (OKP), or, plainly, gangs, are *Pemuda Pancasila* (Youth of the Five Principles of the Nation), IPK (*Ikatan Pemuda Karya*, Association of Workers'

Youth), AMPI (*Angkatan Muda Pembaharuan Indonesia*, the Force for the Renewal of Indonesia's Youth), and FKPPI (*Forum Komunikasi Putra-Putri Indonesia*, Indonesian Communication Forum for Sons and Daughters of Military Retirees). Generally, for Indonesia, see *inter alia*, Aspinall (2005), Butt and Lindsey (2010), Cribb (2010), Dick and Mulholland (2010), Hadiz (2010), van Klinken and Aspinall (2010), McLeod (2010), Robison (1986), Simandjuntak (2009, 2012), Sulaiman and van Klinken (2007), and Wilson (2010, 2015).

5. Anonymous interview, November 2015.

6. It is worth noting that in 2016, the directors of the National Land Agency in the City of Medan and District of Deli Serdang were both arrested and charged with corruption for illegally turning land under plantation leases (*hak guna usaha*) into private land (*hak milik*). Interview with anonymous MP of the Parliament of North Sumatra, November 2016.

7. Interviews with several separate anonymous informants in Medan, November 2015, December 2016, November 2017.

8. Anonymous interview, November 2016.

9. Several anonymous interviews with staff of the National Land Agency, retired plantation company manager, retired board members, retired plantation security officer, lawyer for the plantation company, and independent scholars, 2015, 2016, and 2017.

10. There had been several policy declarations earlier on the intentions of releasing land, but there was never an administrative and operational follow-up. Interview with staff of Governor's Office, Medan in 2017, and academics in 2015 and 2016.

11. *Tim Independen Penelitian, 2005, Alternatif Penyelesaian Masalah Tanah ex HGU PTPN II di Sumatera Utara* (Independent Research Team, Alternative Solution of Land Problem in former Plantation land of PTPN II in North Sumatra), *Biro Pemerintahan Umum (Pemerintah Provinsi Sumatera Utara), 2016, Surat Keputusan Gunernur Sumatera Utara dan Surat Kepada Instansi Terkait Tentang Penyelesaian Permasalahan lahan eks HGU PTPN II, Sumatera Utara* (Bureau of Public Administration, Provincial Government of North Sumatra, 2016, Governor of North Sumatra Decree and Letter to the Related Institution About Settlement of former plantation land PTPN II, North Sumatra). Also interviews with anonymous informants (civil servants, academics, politicians, and activists), 2015, 2016, and 2017.

12. A wide range of sources ranging from movement activists and academics to bureaucrats, politicians, plantation companies, and members of different *pemuda* confirm this. Specialists working in the provincial government of North Sumatra estimated that more than ten times the area has been claimed under the "release" of 2001. As of 2016, the government was planning to reclaim at least some 23,000 hectares wrongfully legalized as part of the original 5,873 hectares (anonymous informant, November 2017).

13. In addition to European settlers, a community of Punjabi Sikhs from India were invited to settle by the Dutch. The purpose was for them to raise cattle and supply the European community in Medan with dairy products. In 1948, during the social revolution, the Deli Maatschappij formally transferred the grazing land to the Sikh community. The document was titled: *Izin pemiliharaan lembuh di sebalah selatan lapangan terbang di Medan. Tanah tersebut telah diserahkan Deli Maatschappij* [A cow breeding permit to the south of Medan's airfield. The land has been handed over by Deli Maatschappij]. Issued by *Plaat Selijk Bestuurambt Eenar di Medan* [The administrative office of Deli Maatschappij, Medan], November 23, 1948. Document in private possession.

14. While the Sikh community lost access to grazing land, they stayed on in Medan and remain one of Polonia's many communities. Interview with anonymous representative of the Sikh community, December 2016.

15. They received "letters of clarification" or land certificates [*Surat Keterangan Tanah*, SKT] and tax receipts [*Pajak Bumi dan Bangunan*, PBB] from the local *kapala desa* [village leader].

16. *Surat Keptusan Menderi Pertahanan* [Decree from Minister of Defence] MP/A/705/57, 1957. A 3-mile radius creates a circle of approximately 72 square kilometers, which is more than ten times the 526 hectares (or 5.3 square kilometers) of Polonia itself.

17. *Surat Keputusan Menteri Dalam Negeri* [Decree from Minister of Interior] no. 01/HPL/DA/70 on February 3, 1970, providing right to manage [*hak pengelolaan*] 137 hectares. From: *Kantor Pertanahan Kota Medan* [Agricultural Office of the City of Medan]: *Dukungan penyeleasian tuntutan masyarakat Sari Rejo atas seluas +/–260 ha di Kelurahan Sari Rejo, Kecamatan Polonia, Kota Medan, Provinsi Sumatera Utara* [Support for the demands of the community Sari Rejo for an area of +/–260 hectares in Sari Rejo Sub-district, District of Polonia, Medan City, North Sumatra Province]. Document in private possession.

18. The air force also received documentation from the Ministry of Defence that it possessed land registered as Government assets (*Inventarus Kekayaan Negara* [state assets registration] no. 50506001). However, only the parts occupied by army barracks and the actual airfield (some 300 hectares) had been certified as assets behalf of the Ministry of Defence, while the rest, some 290 hectares had not, and remained "state land." This comes from the air force commander himself: *Komando Operasi TNI Angkatan Udara, Pangkalan Ankatan Udara, Medan* [Air Force Base Commander, Medan], B732/II/2005, February 25, 2005. There is a slight difference in the area mentioned in this letter compared with other official documents, such as *Putusan* no. 310/Ptd.G/1989/PN-Mdn. Transcript of a court judgment (71 pages) in private possession.

19. Interview with three separate anonymous informants in Polonia, and anonymous employee at the Mayor's Office, November 2016.

20. Surat Keputusan menteri Dalam Negeri no. 150/DJA/1982, September 9, 1982. See *Kantor Pertanahan Kota Medan* [Agricultural Office of the City of Medan], *Dukungan penyeleasian tuntutan masyarakat Sari Rejo atas seluas +/–260 ha di Kelurahan Sari Rejo, Kecamatan Polonia, Kota Medan, Provinsi Sumatera Utara* [Support for the demands of the community Sari Rejo for an area of +/–260 hectares in Sari Rejo Sub-district, District of Polonia, Medan City, North Sumatra Province]. Document in private possession.

21. This area was listed as 1 of 34 (in Indonesia) that needed immediate consultation in 2004. *Dewan Perwakilan Rakyat, Republik Indonesia, no. 13B/DPR RI/2004–2005, Rekommendasi panititia khusis dewan perwakilan rakyat Republik Indonesia untuk mengadakan penyelidikan terhadap masalah pertanahan secara nasional* [House of Representatives: Recommendation from the special committee of the people's representative of the people of the Republic of Indonesia to conduct an investigation of the problems of land at national scale]. Document in private possession.

22. Putusan no. 310/Ptd.G/1989/PN-Mdn. Transcript of the court judgment (71 pages) in private possession.

23. Interview with anonymous notary in Medan, 2017.

24. In fact, the company could very well be owned by officers in the air force. Officers in Indonesia often name their private companies in honor of their military profession: Anugrah [grace], Dirgantara [sky or aerospace], and Perkasa [mighty].

25. Interview with several separate anonymous informants in Polonia, November 2016.

26. FORMAS only became an official registered organization in 2007.

27. *Kantor Pertanahan Kota Medan* [Agricultural Office of the City of Medan]: *Dukungan penyeleasian tuntutan masyarakat Sari Rejo atas seluas +/–260 ha di Kelurahan Sari Rejo, Kecamatan Polonia, Kota Medan, Provinsi Sumatera Utara* [Support for the demands of the community Sari Rejo for an area of +/–260 hectares in Sari Rejo Sub-district, District of Polonia, Medan City, North Sumatra Province]. Document in private possession.

28. *Medan Bisnis*, December 4, 2007. *Ribuan Warga Sari Rejo: Demo BPN Medan* [Thousands of residents from Sari Rejo demonstrate in front of Land Agency]. *Sindo News*, January 8, 2008, *Bandara Polonia Diblokade* [Polonia Airport Blocked]. Sumut Pos, January 8, 2008, *Desak BPN Keluarkan Sertificat* [(People) Urge Land Agency to issue Certificate].

29. *Kompas*, January 8, 2008. *Konflik Tanah. Diperkirakan Akan Meningkat.* [Land conflicts. Expected to increase].

30. *Putusan Pegadilan Tinggi Medan* [Ruling by Medan High Court] no. 294/PDT/1990/PT-MDN, September 26, 1990, and *Putusan Mahkamah Agung R.I.* [Ruling by Supreme Court] no. 229 K/Pdt 1991, May 18, 1995.

31. *Kantor Pertanahan Kota Medan* [Agricultural Office of the City of Medan], *Dukungan penyeleasian tuntutan masyarakat Sari Rejo atas seluas +/–260 ha di Kelurahan Sari Rejo, Kecamatan Polonia, Kota Medan, Provinsi Sumatera Utara*

[Support for the demands of the community Sari Rejo for an area of +/–260 hectares in Sari Rejo Sub-district, District of Polonia, Medan City, North Sumatra Province]. Document in private possession.

32. *Surat 28 May 20087 no. 16/SK/DPD Sumut/V/PP2008* [Letter from Provincial Council of North Sumatra] addressed to the Minister of Finance of the Minister of Defense and Chief of the National Land Agency.

33. From 2013, the new airport in Medan, Kuala Namu, took over commercial flights from Polonia Airport.

34. *Wasada*, 25 February 2016: *Warga Sari Rejo Demo* [Citizens of Sari Rejo demonstrate]; *Sumut Pos*, 25 February 2016: *Menhankam Diminta Keluarkan Lahan dari Dafter Aset* [Minister of Defence and Security is asked to write out land from Armed Forces' assets].

35. *Tribun*, August 19, 2016. "*Saya mohon maaf atas perbuatan yang kurang menyenankan dari prajurit saya. Saya suda membentuk tim investigasi. Serkarang tim dedang bekerja*" ["I apologize for the unfortunate acts of my soldiers. I have formed an investigation team, which is now working"], General Gatot Nurmantyo.

36. Most recently, in 2015, the descendants of the Sultan of Deli, who made the first formalized transfer of land by lease to Count Michalsky in 1869, began to stir. They had had a "legal opinion" made about the ownership of the land of Polonia in view of claiming it for the family (Ikhsan 2015). Thus, despite the social revolution from 1945 to 1949 and the annihilation of royalty and royal land as legal concepts, a significant claim may be on its way out of hibernation (see also van Klinken 2007).

37. There were, in fact, two decrees: first *Ketetapan Menteri Dalam Negeri No. 12/5/14 tanggal 28 Juni 1951*. And secondly, *Ketetapan Gubernur Sumatera Utara No. 36K/ AGR-Tanggal 28 September 1951 yang dikeluarkan Gubernur Kepala Daerah Provinsi Sumatera Utara u/b Residen/Kepala kantor penyelenggaraan tanah u/b Bupati Dp. Tanggal 20 Mei 1952* [Decree of the Minister of Home Affairs no. 12/5/14 dated June 28, 1951, and second a decree by the Governor of North Sumatra no. 36K/AGR-Date 28 September 1951 (issued jointly by the Governor of North Sumatra Province u/b Resident, Head of the land administration office for the Regent Dp. May 20, 1952)].

38. *Hak berdasarkan surat keterangan tentang pembagian dan penerimaan tanah sawah/lading. Patumbak/DS tanggal 27 April 1953 yang dikeluarkan oleh Gubernur Sumatera Utara dan Bupati, berkaitan dengan Kartu Tanda Pendaftaran Penduducan Tanah (KTPPT) No. 2330/I/V (Pt 05) Tanggal 21 November 1956* [Rights based on certificate of distribution and receipt of rice field/field Patumbak/DS dated April 27, 1953 issued by the Governor of North Sumatra and the Regent, in relation to Land Registration Card (KTPPT) No. 2330 / I / V (Pt 05) on November 21, 1956]. This letter was issued on behalf of the Head of East Sumatra Land Use Reorganization Office in relation to the permit to work on (Land) no. 05-PL dated

07 March 1967 issued by the Regional Land Reform committee of Deli Serdang regency.

39. *Surat Keterangan Gubsu* [Decree by the Governor of North Sumatra], July 16, 1969, no. 370/III/GSU/1968.

40. Mr. Nurman had a past as an auxiliary police officer but had left the force for reasons unknown. He had then been running a newspaper, *Prinsip Intelektuel*, made money in gambling and prostitution, and, in addition, owned a small medical clinic and hospital. After a fallout with *Bang* Olo, then the leader of one of the major gangs, IPK, who allegedly had the offices of *Prinsip Intelektuel* torched, Mr. Nurman shifted his allegiance to another gang, *Pemuda Pancasila*. All the lampposts outside his office were therefore now decorated in orange and black, imitating the colorful fatigues of this particular gang.

41. *Kartu Tanda Pendaftaran Pemakai Tanah*, KTPPT, Land User Registration Certificates.

42. Mr. Nurman even sent a trusted student to the colonial archives at the Van Vollenhoven Institute in Leiden, in the Netherlands, to make copies of documents pertaining to the area, such as the Sultan's lease documents, maps, and land registers. Such copies, Mr. Nurman assured me, "make buyers happy, even if they do not read Dutch or understand the exact legal implications."

43. *Putusan Pengadilan Negeri Lubik Pakam* No. 173/Pdt.G/2000/PN-LP [Decision from Lubik Pakam District Court]. Transcript, 95 pages, in private possession. The court case result spawned other court cases between PTPN and both Mr. Limapuluh and Mr. Duaribu. The result did not change the outcome of the first case, and I will leave the details aside for the present text.

44. Mr. Limapuluh and his side gave some 60 hectares to Mr. Duaribu and his followers for the sake of peace.

45. *Badan Usaha Milik Negara* (BUMN).

46. GMNI (*Gerakan Mahasiswa Nasional Indonesia*, National Student Movement of Indonesia), HMI (*Himpunan Mahasiswa Islam*, Islamic Students Association), GMKI (*Gerakan Mahasiswa Kristen Indonesia*, Protestant Students of Indonesia), and PMKRI (*Perhimpunan Mahasiswa Katolik Republik Indonesia*, Catholic Students of Indonesia).

47. Mr. Nurman also sold off a larger plot, some 10 hectares, to another investor in 2015, and according to Tangankanan, this investor managed to get 44 certificates of private land, *hak milik*, processed by the National Land Agency in Medan. "How?" was anyone's guess, according to Tangankanan.

48. Interview, 2017.

49. BPRPI was formed in 1953.

50. The figure of 36 hectares is not entirely certain. It was not possible to have it corroborated by the plantation company.

51. The letter was prompted by another letter to the governor from the local *camat* [sub-district mayor] from Perci Sei Tuan sub-district (no. 570/436) of August 15, 2013. Document in private possession (unfortunately it has not been possible to locate a copy of the governor's letter, and I only have the contents through interviews).

52. These businessmen were less difficult to trace than to meet. Allegedly, they had a cautious business strategy. They bought a small piece of land, and let it sit for a year to test if there were any problems, before they bought more and began to build.

53. Settler in Saentis, outskirts of Medan, 2016.

54. Letter from the *Koperasi Kapeda* PTP to five [anonymized individuals], asking them to vacate the land. July 31, 2015. Document in private possession.

REFERENCES

Abbott, K., R. Keohane, A. Moravcsik, A. Slaughter, and D. Snidal. 2000. "The concept of legalization." *International Organization* 54(3). Pp. 401–19.

Abeyasekere, S. 1989. *Jakarta: A History*. Singapore. Oxford University Press.

Aceh Investment Coordinating Board. 2015. *Aceh Investment Profile*. Banda Aceh. AICB.

Affandi, D.Y. 2016. "Negotiating *Adat.*" *Inside Indonesia* 123. Pp. 1–5.

Afiff, S., N. Fauzi, G. Hart, L. Ntsebeza, and N.L. Peluso. 2005. *Redefining Agrarian Power: Resurgent Agrarian Movements in West Java, Indonesia*. Berkeley. Center for Southeast Asia Studies, University of California Berkeley.

Afiff, S., and C. Lowe. 2007. "Claiming indigenous community: Political discourse and natural resource rights in Indonesia." *Alternatives: Global, Local, Political* 32(1). Pp. 73–97.

Afrizal. 2007. *The Nagari Community, Business and the State*. Bogor. Forest Peoples Programme and Sawit Watch.

Agamben, G. 2005. *State of Exception*. Chicago. University of Chicago Press.

Agrawal, A. 2005. *Environmentality: Technologies of Government and the Making of Subjects*. Durham. Duke University Press.

Agusta, I. 2013. "Slight progress: Wrong direction of agricultural development—Analysis of agricultural census, 2013." *Journal of Rural Indonesia* 1(1). Pp. 15–34.

AJAR and Kontras. 2017. *Transitional Justice: Indonesia Case Study*. Aceh. AJAR and Kontras.

Aji, G.B. 2005. *Tanah untuk Penggarap: Pengalaman Serikat Petani Pasundan Menggarap Lahan-lahan Perkebunan dan Kehutanan* [*Land to the Tiller: SPP's Experience in Occupying and Cultivating Plantation and Forest Land*]. Bogor. Pustaka Latin.

Ambarwati, A., R.A. Harahap, I. Sadoko, and B. White. 2016. "Land tenure and agrarian structure in regions of small-scale food production." In McCarthy, J.F., and

K. Robinson (eds). *Land and Development in Indonesia: Searching for the People's Sovereignty.* Singapore. ISEAS. Pp. 265–94.

Amnesty International. 1993. *Indonesia: "Shock Therapy"—Restoring Order in Aceh, 1989–1993.* London. Amnesty International.

Amnesty International. 2013. *Time to Face the Past: Justice for Past Abuses in Indonesia's Aceh Province.* London. Amnesty International.

Andéer, L., and K. Jelmin. 2004. *Peasants' Resistance in a Global Context: A Two-Case Study of Solidarity Within the Transnational Peasant Movement.* (B.Sc. thesis). Uppsala. Uppsala University Department of Government.

Anderson, B.R.O'G. 1972. *Java in a Time of Revolution: Occupation and Resistance, 1944–1946.* Ithaca. Cornell University Press.

Anderson, B.R.O'G. (ed.). 2001. *Violence and the State in Suharto's Indonesia.* Ithaca. Cornell University Press.

Anderson, P. 2014. "Business and politics in Indonesia's expanding palm oil sector." *Inside Indonesia* 117.

Ansori, M.H. 2011. *Between Self-Interested and Socio-Psychological Motivations: The Complexity and Dynamic of Ethnic Conflict Decision in Indonesia.* (Ph.D. Dissertation). Honolulu. University of Hawaii.

Ansori, M.H. 2012. "From insurgency to bureaucracy: Free Aceh Movement, Aceh Party, and the new face of conflict." *Stability* 1(1). Pp. 31–44.

Anugrah, I. 2015. "Peasant movements and state elites in post-New Order West Java: A case study of Sundanese Peasant Union." *Perspectives on Global Development and Technology* 14. Pp. 86–108.

Anugrah, I. 2018. *Elite-Peasant Relations in Post-Authoritarian Indonesia: Decentralization, Dispossession, and Countermovement.* (Ph.D. dissertation). DeKalb. Department of Political Science, Northern Illinois University.

Arendt, H. 1969. *On Violence.* New York. Harcourt.

Arendt, H. 1973 [1951]. *The Origins of Totalitarianism.* New York. Harcourt, Brace, Jovanovich.

Arizona, Y. 2010. *Antara Teks dan Konteks: Dinamika Pengakuan Hukum Teradap hak Masyarakat Adat atas Sumer daya Alam di Indonesia* [*Between the Text and Context: The Dynamics of Law Enforcement on Indigenous Peoples' Rights over Natural Resources in Indonesia*]. Jakarta. HuMa.

Arizona, Y., E. Cahyadi, M. Arman, and S. Karto. 2015. *Banyak perubahan tetapi belum banyak: Perkembangan hukum dan kebijakan paska putusan MK 35/PUU-X/2012* [*Many changes but not much has changed: Developments after law and policy decision MK 35/PUU-X/2012*]. Jakarta. Epistema.

Ascher, W. 1998. "From oil to timber: The political economy of off-budget development financing in Indonesia." *Indonesia* 65. Pp. 37–61.

Aspinall, E. 2005. *Opposing Suharto: Compromise, Resistance, and Regime Change in Indonesia.* Stanford. Stanford University Press.

Aspinall, E. 2006. "Violence and identity formation in Aceh under Indonesian rule." In Reid, A. (ed.). *Verandah of Violence: The Background to the Aceh Problem.* Singapore/Seattle. Singapore University Press/University of Washington Press. Pp. 149–76.

Aspinall, E. 2008. "Place and displacement in the Aceh conflict." In Hedman, E.-L. E. (ed.). *Conflict, Violence, and Displacement in Indonesia.* Ithaca. Cornell University Press. Pp. 119–46.

Aspinall, E. 2009a. *Islam and Nation: Separatist Rebellion in Aceh, Indonesia.* Stanford. Stanford University Press.

Aspinall, E. 2009b. "Combatants to contractors: The political economy of peace in Aceh." *Indonesia* 87, April. Pp. 1–34.

Aspinall, E. 2012. "Aceh: Democratization and politics of co-option." In Aspinall, E., R. Jeffrey, and A. Regan (eds). *Diminishing Conflicts in Asia and the Pacific: Why Some Subside and Others Don't.* London. Routledge.

Aspinall, E. 2014. "Special autonomy, predatory peace, and the resolution of the Aceh conflict." In Hill, H. (ed.). *Regional Dynamics in a Decentralized Indonesia.* Singapore. ISEAS. Pp. 460–81.

Aspinall, E., and G. van Klinken. 2010. "The state and illegality in Indonesia." In Aspinall, E., and G. van Klinken (eds). *The State and Illegality in Indonesia.* Leiden. KITLV Press. Pp.1–28.

Bachriadi, D. 2010. *Between Discourse and Action: Agrarian Reform and Rural Social Movements in Indonesia Post 1965.* (Ph.D. dissertation). The Flinders Asia Centre School of International Studies, Flinders University. Adelaide.

Bachriadi, D., A. Lucas, and C. Warren. 2013. "The agrarian movement and emerging political constellations." In A. Lucas and C. Warren (eds). *Land for the People: The State and Agrarian Conflict in Indonesia.* Columbus. Ohio University Press. Pp. 308–71.

Bachriadi, D., and G. Wiradi. 2011. *Six Decades of Inequality: Land Tenure Problems in Indonesia.* Bandung. Agrarian Resource Centre.

Baker, J. 2015. "Professionalism without reform: The security sector under Yudhoyono." In Aspinall, E., M. Mietzner, and D. Tomsa (eds). *The Yudhoyono Presidency: Indonesia's Decade of Stability and Stagnation.* Singapore. Institute of Southeast Asian Studies. Pp. 114–35.

Baker, J., and S. Milne. 2015. "Dirty money states: Illicit economies and the state in Southeast Asia." *Critical Asian Studies* 47(2). Pp. 151–76.

Bakker, L. 2009a. "Community, *adat* authority, and forest management in the hinterland of East Kalimantan." In Warren, C., and J. McCarthy (eds). *Community, Environment, and Local Governance in Indonesia.* London. Routledge. Pp. 121–43.

Bakker, L. 2009b. *Who Owns the Land? Looking for Law and Power in Reformasi East Kalimantan.* (Ph.D. dissertation). Nijmegen. University of Nijmegen.

Bakker, L. 2015. "Illegality for the general good? Vigilantism and social responsibility in contemporary Indonesia." *Critique of Anthropology* 35(1). Pp. 78–93.

Bakker, L. 2016. "Organized violence and the state." *Bijdragen to de Tal-, Land-en Volkenkunde* 172(2–3). Pp. 249–77.

Bakker, L. 2017. "Militias, security, and citizenship in Indonesia." In Berenschot, W., H. Schulte Nordholt, and L. Bakker (eds). *Citizenship and Democratization in Southeast Asia*. Leiden. Brill. Pp. 125–54.

Bakker, L., and S. Moniaga. 2010. "The space between: Land claims and the law in Indonesia." *Asian Journal of Social Science* 38. Pp. 187–201.

Bakker, L., and G. Reerink. 2015. "Indonesia's land acquisition law: Toward effective prevention of land grabbing?" In Carter, C., and A. Harding (eds). *Land Grabs in Asia: What Role for the Law?* London. Routledge. Pp. 83–99.

Barber, C.V., and K. Talbot. 2003. "The chainsaw and the gun: The role of the military in deforesting Indonesia." In Price, S.V. (ed.). *War and Tropical Forests: Conservation in Areas of Armed Conflict*. Philadelphia. Harworth Press. Pp. 131–60.

Barker, J. 2001. "State of fear: Controlling the criminal contagion in Suharto's New Order." In Anderson, B.R.O'G. (ed.). *Violence and the State in Suharto's Indonesia*. Ithaca. Cornell University Press. Pp. 20–53.

Barker, J. 2007. "Vigilantes and the state." In T. Day (ed.). *Identifying with Freedom: Indonesia After Suharto*. New York. Berghahn Books. Pp. 87–94.

Barter, S.J. 2015. "The rebel state in society: Governance and accommodation in Aceh, Indonesia." In Arjona, A., N. Kasfir and Z. Mampilly (eds). *Rebel Governance in Civil War*. Cambridge. Cambridge University Press. Pp. 226–45.

Becker, H. 2014. *What About Mozart? What About Murder? Reasoning from Cases*. Chicago. University of Chicago Press.

Becker, H. 2017. *Evidence*. Chicago. University of Chicago Press.

Bedner, A.W. 2000. *Administrative Courts in Indonesia: A Socio-Legal Study*. (Ph.D. dissertation). Leiden. University of Leiden.

Bedner, A.W. 2016a. "Indonesian land law: Integration at last? And for whom?" In *Land and Development in Indonesia: Searching for the People's Sovereignty*. J.F. McCarthy, and K. Robinson (eds). Singapore. ISEAS. Pp. 63–88.

Bedner, A.W. 2016b. "Autonomy of law in Indonesia." *Recht der Werkelijkheid* 37(3). Pp. 10–36.

Benda-Beckmann, F. von. 1993. "Le monopole d'État de la violence dans la perspective de l'anthropologie juridique." In Le Roy, É., and T. von Trotha (eds). *La violence et l'État: Formes et évolution d'un monopole*. Paris. l'Harmattan. Pp. 35–57.

Benda-Beckmann, F. von. 1997. "Citizens, strangers, and indigenous peoples. Conceptual politics and legal pluralism." *Law and Anthropology* 9. Pp. 1–42.

Benda-Beckmann, F. von, and K. von Benda-Beckmann. 2011. "Myths and stereotypes about adat law: A reassessment of Von Vollenhoven in the light of current struggles over *adat* law in Indonesia." *Bijdragen to de Tal-, Land-en Volkenkunde* 167(2/3). Pp. 167–95.

Benda-Beckmann, F. von, and K. von Benda-Beckmann. 2014. *Political and Legal Transformations of an Indonesian Polity: The Nagari from Colonialism to Decentralisation*. Cambridge. Cambridge University Press.

Benda-Beckmann, F. von, K. von Benda-Beckmann, and M. Wiber. 2006. "The properties of property." In Benda-Beckmann, von F., K. von Benda-Beckmann, and M. Wiber (eds). *Changing Properties of Property*, New York. Berghahn.

Benda-Beckmann, K. von. 1981. "Forum shopping and shopping forums: Dispute processing in a Minangkabau village in West Sumatra." *Journal of Legal Pluralism* 19. Pp. 117–62.

Benda-Beckmann, K. von. 1984. *The Broken Stairways to Consensus: Village Justice and State Courts in Minangkabau*. Dordrecht. University of Nijmegen.

Benjamin, S., and Arifin, M.A. 1985. "The housing costs of low-income kampung dwellers: A study of product and process in Indonesian cities." *Habitat International* 9(1). Pp. 91–110.

Benjamin, W. 2004 [1921]. "Critique of violence." In *Walter Benjamin: Selected Writings, Vol. 1, 1913–1926*. M. Bullock and M. W. Jennings (eds). Cambridge. Belknap Press and Harvard University Press. Pp. 236–52.

Benjaminsen, T.A., E. Sjaastad, S. Holden, and C. Lund. 2009. "Formalisation of land rights: Some empirical evidence from Mali, Niger, and South Africa." *Land Use Policy* 26(1). Pp. 28–35.

Benton, L. 2002. *Law and Colonial Cultures: Legal Regimes in World History, 1400–1900*. Cambridge. Cambridge University Press.

Benton, L. 2010. *A Search for Sovereignty: Law and Geography in European Empires, 1400–1900*. Cambridge/New York. Cambridge University Press.

Benton, L. 2012. "Historical perspectives on legal pluralism." In Tamanaha, B., C. Sage, and M. Woolcock (eds). *Legal Pluralism and Development: Scholars and Practitioners in Dialogue*. Cambridge. Cambridge University Press. Pp. 21–33.

Benton, L., and B. Straumann. 2010. "Acquiring empire by law: From Roman doctrine to early modern European practice." *Law and History Review* 28(1). Pp. 1–38.

Bettinger, K.A. 2015. "Political contestation, resource control, and conservation in an era of decentralisation at Indonesia's Kerinci Seblat National Park." *Asia Pacific Viewpoint* 56(2). Pp. 252–66.

Bhandar, B. 2018. *Colonial Lives of Property: Law, Land, and Racial Regimes of Ownership*. Durham. Duke University Press.

Bierschenk, T., and J.-P. Olivier de Sardan. 1997. "ECRIS: Rapid collective inquiry for the identification of conflicts and strategic groups." *Human Organization* 56(1). Pp. 35–43.

Bierschenk, T., and J.-P. Olivier de Sardan (eds). 2014. *States at Work, Dynamics of African Bureaucracies*. Leiden. Brill.

Bisonnette, J.-F., and R. de Koninck. 2017. "The return of the plantation? Historical and contemporary trends in the relation between plantations and smallholdings in Southeast Asia." *Journal of Peasant Studies* 44(4). Pp. 918–38.

Bolman, B.C. 2006. *Wet Rice Cultivation in Indonesia: A Comparative Research on Differences in Modernisation Trends.* (M.Sc. thesis). Wageningen. Wageningen University.

Borras, S. M., and J. C. Franco. 2005. "Struggles for land and livelihood." *Critical Asian Studies* 37(3). Pp. 331–61.

Bourdieu, P. 1985. "Social space and the genesis of groups." *Theory and Methods* 24(2). Pp. 195–220.

Bourdieu, P. 1987. "The force of law: Toward a sociology of the juridical field." *Hastings Law Journal* 38. Pp. 805–53.

Bourdieu, P. 1994. "Re-thinking the state: Genesis and structure of the bureaucratic field." *Sociological Theory* 12(1). Pp. 1–18.

Bourdieu, P. 2012. *Sur l'État: Cours au Collège de France 1989–1992.* Paris. Seuil.

Breman, J. 1983. *Control of Land and Labour in Colonial Java.* Leiden. Foris.

Breman, J. 1989. *Taming of the Coolie Beast: Plantation Society and the Colonial Order in Southeast Asia.* Oxford. Oxford University Press.

Breman, J. 2015. *Mobilizing Labour for the Global Coffee Market: Profits from an Unfree Work Regime in Colonial Java.* Amsterdam. Amsterdam University Press.

Breman, J., and G. Wiradi. 2002. *Good Times and Bad Times in Rural Java: Case Study of Socio-Economic Dynamics in Two Villages Towards the End of the Twentieth Century.* Singapore. Institute of Southeast Asian Studies.

Brown, D.W. 1999. *Addicted to Rent: Corporate and Spatial Distribution of Forest Resources in Indonesia; Implications for Forest Sustainability and Government Policy.* (Report no. PFM/EC/99/06). Jakarta. Indonesia UK Tropical Forestry Management Programme.

Burns, P. 2007. "Custom, that is before all law." In Davidson, J.S., and D. Henley (eds). *The Revival of Tradition in Indonesian Politics: The Deployment of Adat from Colonialism to Indigenism.* London. Routledge. Pp. 68–86.

Butler, J. 1990. *Gender Trouble: Feminism and the Subversion of Identity.* New York. Routledge.

Butt, S., and T. Lindsey. 2010. "Judicial mafia: The courts and state illegality in Indonesia." In Aspinall, E., and G. van Klinken (eds). *The State and Illegality in Indonesia.* Leiden. KITLV Press. Pp. 189–213.

Campbell, J. 2015. *Conjuring Property: Speculation and Environmental Futures in the Brazilian Amazon.* Seattle. University of Washington Press.

Centre for Village Studies (Gadjah Mada University). 1990. "Rural violence in Klaten and Banyuwangi." In Cribb, R. (ed.). *The Indonesian Killings 1965–1966.* Clayton, Monash University. Centre for Southeast Asian Studies. Pp. 120–57.

Chauveau, J.-P. 2017. "Le nexus État, foncier, migrations, conflits comme champ social." *Critiques Internationales* 75. Pp. 9–19.

Cheng Hai, T. 2015. "Malaysian corporations as strategic players in Southeast Asia's palm oil industry." In Pye, O., and J. Bhattacharya (eds). *The Palm Oil Controversy in Southeast Asia: A Transnational Perspective.* Singapore. Institute of Southeast Asian Studies. Pp. 19–47.

Colchester, M., and S. Chao. 2013. *Conflict or Consent? The Oil Palm Sector at a Crossroads.* Bogor. Forest Peoples Programme and Sawit Watch.

Colchester, M., N. Jiwan, Andiko, M. Sirait, A. Y. Firdaus, A. Surambo, and H. Pane. 2006. *Promised Land: Palm Oil and Land Acquisition in Indonesia—Implications for Local Communities and Indigenous Peoples.* Jakarta. Forest Peoples Programme, Perkumpulan Sawit Watch, HuMA and the World Agroforestry Centre.

Colchester, M., M. Sirait, and B. Wijardjo. 2003. *Obstacles and Possibilities: The Application of FSC Principles 2 & 3 in Indonesia.* Jakarta. Walhi/AMAN.

Colombijn, F. 2012. "Solid as a rock or a handful of dust? The security of land tenure in Indonesian cities from 1930–1960." In E. Bogaerts and R. Raben, eds. *Beyond Empire and Nation.* Leiden. KITLV Press.

Colombijn, F. 2013. *Under Construction: The Politics of Urban Space and Housing During the Decolonization of Indonesia, 1930–1960.* Leiden. KITLV Press.

Colombijn, F., and J. Coté (eds). 2015. *Cars, Conduits, and Kampongs: The Modernization of the Indonesian City, 1920–1960.* Leiden. Brill.

Comaroff, J., and J. Comaroff. 2006. "Law and disorder in the postcolony." In Comaroff, J., and J. Comaroff (eds). *Law and Disorder in the Postcolony.* Chicago. Chicago University Press. Pp. 1–56.

Cooper, F., and L.A. Stoler (eds). 1997. *Tensions of Empire: Colonial Cultures in a Bourgeois World.* Berkeley. University of California Press.

Correia, D. 2013. *Properties of Violence: Law and Land Grant Struggle in Northern New Mexico.* Athens. University of Georgia Press.

Cover, R. 1986. "Violence and the word." *Yale Law Journal* 95(8). Pp. 1601–30.

Cribb, R. 2010. "A system of exemptions: Historicizing state illegality in Indonesia." In Aspinall, E., and G. van Klinken (eds). *The State and Illegality in Indonesia.* Leiden. KITLV Press. Pp. 31–44.

Crouch, H. 1978. *The Army and Politics in Indonesia.* Ithaca. Cornell University Press.

Cybriwsky, R., and L.R. Ford. 2001. "City profile Jakarta." *Cities* 18(3). Pp. 199–210.

Damanik, A.T. 2016. "Medan, North Sumatra: Between ethnic politics and money politics." In Aspinall, E., and M. Sukmajati (eds). *Electoral Dynamics in Indonesia: Money Politics, Patronage, and Clientelism at the Grassroots.* Singapore. Singapore University Press. Pp. 70–85.

Damanik, E. 2016. *Deli: Historitas, Pluralitas dan Modernitas—Kota Medan Tahun 1870–1942.* [*Deli: History, Pluralism, and Modernity—The City of Medan, 1870–1943*]. Medan. Simetri Publisher.

Darusman, C. 2010. *Pelaksanaan Pemberian Hak Guna Usaha Kepada Pt: Bumi Flora di Kecamatan Banda Alam Kabupaten Aceh Timur [Implementation of the Granting of HGU to Pt: Bumi Alam Flora in East Aceh District]*. (M.Sc. thesis). Banda Aceh. Faculty of Law, Universitat Syiah Aceh.

Das, V. 2007. *Life and Words: Violence and the Descent into the Ordinary.* Berkeley. University of California Press.

Davidson, J.S. 2015. *Indonesia's Changing Political Economy: Governing the Roads.* Cambridge. Cambridge University Press.

De Groot Heupner, S. 2016 *The Palm Oil Plantation of North Sumatra: A System of Repression and Violence.* (M.Sc. Honours thesis). Perth, Murdoch University.

De Soto, H. 2000. *The Mystery of Capital: Why Capitalism Triumphs in the West and Fails Everywhere Else.* London. Basic Books.

Dick, H., and J. Mulholland. 2010. "The state as a marketplace: Slush funds and intra-elite rivalry." In E. Aspinall and G. van Klinken (eds). *The State and Illegality in Indonesia.* Leiden. KITLV Press. Pp. 65–85.

Dickens, C. 1853. *Bleak House.* London. Bradbury & Evans.

Dieleman, M. 2011. "New town development in Indonesia: Renegotiating, shaping, and replacing institutions." *Bijdragen tot de Taal-, Land-en Volkenkunde* 167(1). Pp. 60–85.

Diessen, J.R. van, and F.J. Ormeling. 2003. *Grote Atlas van Nederlands Oost-Indië [Atlas of the Dutch East Indies].* Utrecht. Koninklijk Nederlands Aardrijkskundig Genootschap/Royal Dutch Geographical Society Advisory Committee.

Dijk, C. van. 1981. *Rebellion Under the Banner of Islam: Darul Islam in Indonesia.* The Hague. Verhandlingen van het Koninklijk Instituut voor Taal-, Land-, en Volkenkunde.

Djalins, U. 2012. *Subjects, Lawmaking, and Land Rights: Agrarian Regime and State Formation in Late-Colonial Netherlands East Indies.* (Ph.D. dissertation). Ithaca. Cornell University.

Djalins, U. 2015. "Becoming Indonesian citizens: Subjects, citizens, and land ownership in the Netherlands Indies, 1930–37." *Journal of South East Asian Studies* 46(2). Pp. 227–25.

Doorn, J. van, and W.J. Hendrix. 1983. "The emergence of a dependent economy: Consequences of the opening up of West Priangan, Java, to the process of modernization." Rotterdam. CASP Paper no. 9. University of Rotterdam.

Drexler, E. 2008. *Aceh, Indonesia: Securing the Insecure State.* Philadelphia. University of Pennsylvania Press.

Dworkin, R. 1977. *Taking Rights Seriously.* Cambridge. Harvard University Press.

Eilenberg, M. 2012. *At the Edges of States: Dynamics of State Formation in the Indonesian Borderlands.* Leiden. KITLV Press.

Elson, R.E. 1994. *Village Java Under the Cultivation System, 1830–1870.* Sydney. Allen and Unwin.

Eye on Aceh. 2007. *The 'Golden' Crop? Palm Oil in Post-Tsunami Aceh.* http://www.aceh -eye.org (Accessed May 2014).

Fadillah, A. 2016. "The corruption of ex-GAM members: An irony of Aceh's development." Republika.co.id (www.republika.co.id/berita/en/speak-out/16/05/15/o77ipf 317-the-corruption-of-exgam-members-an irony-of-aches-development).

Faizal, A. 2010. *Human Rights Violation in the Palm Oil Plantation PT PP Lonsum Tbk-North Sumatra.* Jakarta. ELSAM.

Farid, H. 2005. "Indonesia's original sin: Mass killings and capitalist expansion, 1965– 66." *Inter-Asia Cultural Studies* 6(1). Pp. 3–16.

Fasseur, C. 2009. "Colonial dilemma: Van Vollenhoven and the struggle between *adat* law and Western law in Indonesia." In Davidson, J.S., and D. Henley (eds). *The Revival of Tradition in Indonesian Politics: The Deployment of Adat from Colonialism to Indigenism.* London. Routledge. Pp. 50–67.

Fauzi, N., and D. Bachriadi. 2006. "The resurgence of agrarian movements in Indonesia: Scholar-activists, popular education, and peasant mobilization." Paper presented at the conference *Land, Poverty, Social Justice and Development.* Institute of Social Studies. The Hague (9–14 January).

Fay, C., and H.-M. S. Denduangrudee. 2016. "Emerging options for the recognition and protection of indigenous community rights in Indonesia." In McCarthy, J.F., and K. Robinson (eds). *Land and Development in Indonesia: Searching for the People's Sovereignty.* Singapore. ISEAS. Pp. 91–112.

Feener, R.M. 2013. *Shari'a and Social Engineering: The Implementation of Islamic Law in Contemporary Aceh, Indonesia.* Oxford. Oxford University Press.

Feldman, I. 2008. *Governing Gaza: Bureaucracy, Authority, and the Work of Rule, 1917– 1967.* Durham. Duke University Press.

Ferrier, M. 2012. "Securing property in informal neighbourhoods in Damascus through tax payments." In Ababsa, M., B. Dupret, and E. Dennis (eds). *Popular Housing and Urban Land Tenure in the Middle East: Case Studies from Egypt, Syria, Jordan, Lebanon, and Turkey.* Cairo. American University in Cairo Press. Pp. 67–91.

Firawati, T. 2014. "Reconciliation through cooperation: The case of Aceh." In Satha-Anand, C., and O. Urbain (eds). *The Promise of Reconciliation.* New Brunswick. Transaction Publishers. Pp. 45–60.

Fitzpatrick, D. 1997. "Disputes and pluralism in modern Indonesian land law." *Yale Journal of International Law* 22. Pp. 171–212.

Fitzpatrick, D. 2006. "Private law and public power: Tangled threads in Indonesian land regulation." In Schulte Nordholt, H., and I. Hoogenboom (eds). *Indonesian Transitions.* Yogyakarta. Pustaka Pelajar. Pp. 75–113.

Fitzpatrick, D. 2008. "Beyond dualism: Land acquisition and law in Indonesia." In Lindsey, T. (ed.). *Indonesia: Law and Society.* Annandale NSW. The Federation Press. Pp. 224–46.

Ford, M. 2009. *Workers and Intellectuals: NGOs, Trade Unions, and the Indonesian Labour Movement.* Honolulu. University of Hawaii Press.

Fortmann, L. 1990. "Locality and custom: Non-aboriginal claims to customary usufructuary rights as a source of rural protest." *Journal of Rural Studies* 6(2). Pp. 195–208.

Foucault, M. 1978. *The History of Sexuality, Vol. I: An Introduction.* London. Penguin.

Furnivall, S. 1939. *Netherlands India: A Study of Plural Economy.* Cambridge. Cambridge University Press.

Furnivall, S. 1948. *Colonial Policy and Practice: A Comparative Study of Burma and Netherlands India.* Cambridge. Cambridge University Press.

Gaastra, F. 2003. *The Dutch East India Company: Expansion and Decline.* Zutphen. Walburg Press.

Galudra, G. [no date.] *Land Tenure Conflict in Halimun Area: What Are the Alternative Resolutions for Land Tenure Conflicts.* Mimeo.

Galudra, G., R. Nurhawan, A. Aprianto, Y. Sunarya, and Enkrus. 2008. *The Last Remnants of Mega Biodiversity in West Java and Banten: An In-Depth Exploration of Rapid Land Tenure Assessment in Mount Halimun-Salak National Park, Indonesia.* Bogor. World Agroforestry Centre.

Galudra, G., and M. Sirait. 2009. "A discourse on Dutch colonial forest policy and science in Indonesia at the beginning of the 20th century." *International Forestry Review* 11(4). Pp. 524–33.

Galudra, G., M. Sirait, N. Ramdhaniaty, F. Soenarto, and B. Nurzaman. 2005. "History of land-use policies and designation of Mount Halimun-Salak National Park." *Jurnal Manahjemen Hutan Tropika* 11(1). Pp. 1–13.

Gautama, S., and R. Hornick. 1974. *An Introduction to Indonesian Law: Unity in Diversity.* Bandung. Alumni Press.

Gellert, P. 2015. "Palm oil expansion in Indonesia: Land grabbing as accumulation by dispossession." *Current Perspectives in Social Theory* 34. Pp. 65–99.

Gellert, P., and Andiko. 2015. "The quest for legal certainty and the reorganisation of power: Struggles over forest law, permits, and rights in Indonesia." *Journal of Asian Studies* 74(3). Pp. 639–66.

Gilbert, D., and Afrizal. 2018. "The land exclusion dilemma and Sumatra's agrarian reactionaries." *Journal of Peasant Studies* 45(1) Pp. 1–22.

Gordon, A. 2010. "Netherlands East Indies: The large colonial surplus of Indonesia, 1878–1939." *Journal of Contemporary Asia* 40(3). Pp. 425–43.

Graeber, D. 2015. *The Utopia of Rules: On Technology, Stupidity, and the Secret Joys of Bureaucracy.* Brooklyn. Melville House.

Grajales, J. 2011. "The rifle and the title: Paramilitary violence, land grab, and land control in Colombia." *Journal of Peasant Studies* 38(4). Pp. 771–92.

Grajales, J. 2016a. *Gouverner dans la violence: Le paramilitarisme en Colombie.* Paris. Karthala.

Grajales, J. 2016b. "Violence entrepreneurs, law, and authority in Colombia." *Development and Change* 47(6). Pp. 1294–315.

Gramsci, A. 1971. *Selections from the Prison Notebooks*. London. Lawrence and Wishart.

Green, A. 2013a. *A Geography of Peace: An Investigation of Post-Conflict Property and Land Administration in Aceh*. (Ph.D. dissertation). Montréal. McGill University.

Green, A. 2013b. "Title wave: Land tenure and peacebuilding in Aceh." In Unruh, J., and R.C. Williams (eds). *Land and Postconflict Peacebuilding*. London. Earthscan. Pp. 293–319.

Griffiths, J. 2015. "Legal pluralism." *International Encyclopedia of the Social & Behavioral Sciences*. 2nd edition, Volume 13. Pp. 757–61.

Guha, R. 1996. *A Rule of Property for Bengal: An Essay on the Idea of Permanent Settlement*. Durham. Duke University Press.

Guha, R. 1997. *Dominance Without Hegemony: History and Power in Colonial India*. Cambridge. Harvard University Press.

Haasse, H.S. 2010. *The Tea Lords*. London. Portobello Books.

Habermas, J. 1997. *Between Facts and Norms: Contributions to a Discourse Theory of Law and Democracy*. Cambridge. Polity Press.

Hadiz, V.R. 2003. "Power and politics in North Sumatra: The uncompleted *Reformasi*." In Aspinall, E., and G. Fealy (eds). *Local Power and Politics in Indonesia: Decentralisation and Democratisation*. Singapore. Institute of Southeast Asian Studies. Pp. 119–31.

Hadiz, V.R. 2010. *Localising Power in Post-Authoritarian Indonesia: A Southeast Asia Perspective*. Stanford. Stanford University Press.

Hall, D., P. Hirsch, and T. Li. 2011. *Powers of Exclusion: Land Dilemmas in Southeast Asia*. Singapore. National University of Singapore Press.

Hansen, T.B. 2005. "Sovereigns beyond the state: On legality and authority in urban India." In Hansen, T.B., and F. Stepputat (eds). *Sovereign Bodies: Citizens, Migrants, and States in the Postcolonial World*. Princeton. Princeton University Press. Pp. 169–91.

Harada, K. 2003. "Attitudes of local people towards conservation and Gunung Halimun National Park in West Java, Indonesia." *Journal of Forestry Research* 8. Pp. 271–82.

Hart, H.L.A. 1961. *The Concept of Law*. Oxford. Clarendon Press.

Hefner, R.W. 1990. *The Political Economy of Mountain Java*. Berkeley. University of California Press.

Henley, D., and J.S. Davidson. 2007a. "In the name of *adat*: Regional perspectives on reform, tradition, and democracy in Indonesia." *Modern Asian Studies* 42(4). Pp. 815–52.

Henley, D., and J.S. Davidson. 2007b. "Radical conservatism: The protean politics of *adat*." In Davidson, J.S., and D. Henley (eds). *The Revival of Tradition in Indonesian Politics: The Deployment of Adat from Colonialism to Indigenism*. London. Routledge. Pp. 1–49.

Hetherington, K. 2011. *Guerrilla Auditors: The Politics of Transparency in Neoliberal Paraguay*. Durham. Duke University Press.

Hilgers, M. 2011. "Autochthony as capital in a global age." *Theory, Culture & Society* 28(1). Pp. 34–54.

Hoadley, M. 1994. *Selective Judicial Competence: The Cirebon-Priangan Legal Administration, 1680–1792*. Ithaca. Cornell Southeast Asia Program.

Hodgson, D. L., and R. A. Schroeder. 2002. "Dilemmas of counter-mapping community resources in Tanzania." *Development and Change* 33(1). Pp. 79–100.

Hohfeld, W. N. 1913. "Some fundamental legal conceptions as applied in judicial reasoning." *Yale Law Review* 23. Pp. 16–59.

Holston, J. 1991. "The misrule of law: Land and usurpation in Brazil." *Comparative Studies in Society and History* 33(4). Pp. 695–725.

Holston, J. 2008. *Insurgent Citizenship: Disjunctions of Democracy and Modernity in Brazil*. Princeton. Princeton University Press.

Honna, J. 2010. "The legacy of the New Order military in local politics: West, Central, and East Java." In Aspinall, E., and G. Fealy (eds). *Soeharto's New Order and Its Legacy*. Canberra. Australian National University.

Hudalah, D. 2010. *Peri-urban Planning in Indonesia Contexts, Approaches and Institutional Capacity*. (Ph.D. dissertation). Groningen. Rijksuniversiteit Groningen.

Hugenholtz, W.R. 1994. "The land rent question and its solution, 1850–1920." In Cribb, R. (ed.) *The Late Colonial State in Indonesia: Political and Economic Foundations of the Netherlands Indies, 1880–1942*. Leiden. KITLV Press. Pp. 139–72.

Huizer, G. 1974. "Peasant rebellion and land reform in Indonesia." *Review of Indonesian and Malayan Affairs* 8. Pp. 81–138.

Hull, M.S. 2012. *Government of Paper: The Materiality of Bureaucracy in Urban Pakistan*. Berkeley. University of California Press.

Human Rights Watch. 2002. "Indonesia: Accountability for human rights violations in Aceh." *Human Rights Watch* 14(1). Pp. 1–15.

Hussain, N. 2003. *The Jurisprudence of Emergency: Colonialism and the Rule of Law*. Ann Arbor. University of Michigan Press.

Ikhsan, E. 2015. *Konflik Tanah Ulayat dan Pluralisme Hukum: Hilangnya Ruang Hidup Orang Melayu Deli* [*Land Conflicts and Legal Pluralism: The Deli Malay's Loss of Land*]. Jakarta. Yayasan Pustaka Obor Indonesia.

Ikhsan, E. [no date a.] *Okupasi Liar, Kaaphout in Landbouw Concessie dan Tanah Jaluran: Kriminalisasi Petani dalam Zaman Setelah Perang di Sumatera Timur (1947–1960)* [*Wild Occupations, Kaaphout Land Concession, and Jaluran Fallow Land: Criminalization of Farmers in the Age After the War in East Sumatra (1947–1960)*]. Mimeo.

Ikhsan, E. [no date b.] *Pendapat Hukum Status Hak Atas Tanah Eks Konsesi Polonia (Sekarang di bawah status kepemilikan Negara cq Angkatan Udara Republik Indo-*

nesia [*Legal Opinion on the Status of Rights to Land Concession in Ex Polonia (now under the ownership status of the State represented by the Indonesian Air Force)*]. Mimeo.

Ikhsan, E. [no date c.] *Nasionalisasi Perkebunan Belanda di Sumatera Utara: Diantara Inkonsistensi dan Stigmatisasi* [*The nationalization of the Dutch plantations in North Sumatra: Between consistency and stigma*]. Mimeo.

IPAC (Institute for Policy Analysis of Conflict). 2014. *Aceh's Surprising Election Results*. Jakarta. IFPC Report no. 10.

IPAC (Institute for Policy Analysis of Conflict). 2015a. *Political Power Struggles in Aceh*. Jakarta. IFPC Report no. 16.

IPAC (Institute for Policy Analysis of Conflict). 2015b. *Din Minimi: The Strange Story of an Armed Group in Aceh, Indonesia*. Jakarta. IFPC Report no. 23.

Jellinek, L. 1991. *The Wheel of Fortune: The History of a Poor Community in Jakarta*. London. Allen and Unwin.

JICA. 2006. *Rencana Pengelolaan Taman Nasional Gunung Halimun-Salak* [*National Park Management of Mount Halimun-Salak*]. Jakarta. JICA.

Julia and White, B. 2012. "Gendered experience of dispossession: Oil palm expansion in a Dayak Hibun community in West Kalimantan." *Journal of Peasant Studies* 39(3–4). Pp. 995–1016.

Juliawan, B.H. 2011. "Street-level politics: Labour protests in post-authoritarian Indonesia." *Journal of Contemporary Asia* 41(3). Pp. 349–70.

Kammen, D., and K. McGregor. 2012. "The contours of mass violence in Indonesia, 1965–68." In Kammen, D., and K. McGregor (eds). *The Contours of Mass Violence in Indonesia, 1965–68*. Singapore/Copenhagen. National University of Singapore/Nordic Institute of Asian Studies. Pp. 1–14.

Kano, H. 2008. *Indonesian Exports: Peasant Agriculture, and the World Economy, 1850–2000*. Athens. Ohio University Press.

Karina, N. 2008. *Dinamika Social Politik Organisasi Pemuda Pancasila Sumatra Utara* [*Socio-Political Dynamics of the Youth Organization Pemuda Pancasila, North Sumatra*] (M.Sc. thesis). Medan. Universitas Sumatera Utara.

Khairina, W. 2013. *Konflik Agraria Masyarakat Desa Pergulaan VS PT. PP London Sumatera Indonesia Tbk. Kab. Serdang Bedagai, Sumatera Utara* [*Agrarian Conflict Between the Village Community of Pergulaan and PT. PP London Sumatra Indonesia Tbk. Kab. Bedagai Serdang, North Sumatra*]. (M.Sc. thesis). Medan. Antropologi Sosial Sekolah Pascasarjana, Universitas Negeri Medan.

King, P. 2003. "Putting the (para)military back into politics." *Inside Indonesia* 73.

Kingsbury, D. 2007. "The Free Aceh Movement: Islam and democratisation." *Journal of Contemporary Asia* 37(2). Pp. 166–89.

Kingsbury, D., and McCulloch, L. 2006. "Military business in Aceh." In Reid, A. (ed.). *Verandah of Violence: The Background to the Aceh Problem*. Singapore/Seattle. Singapore University Press/Washington University Press. Pp. 199–224.

Klinken, G. van. 1999. "Coming Out." *Inside Indonesia* 58 (April–June). Pp. 16–17.

Klinken, G. van. 2007. "Return of the Sultans." In Davidson, J.S., and D. Henley (eds). *The Revival of Tradition in Indonesian Politics: The Deployment of Adat from Colonialism to Indigenism.* London. Routledge. Pp. 149–69.

Klinken, G. van. 2009. "Patronage democracy in provincial Indonesia." In Törnquist, O., N. Webster, and K. Stokke (eds). *Rethinking Popular Representation.* London. Palgrave/Macmillan. Pp. 141–59.

Klinken, G. van. 2018. "Citizenship and local practices of rule in Indonesia." *Citizenship Studies* 22(2). Pp. 112–28.

Klinken, G. van, and E. Aspinall. 2010. "Building relations: Corruption, competition, and cooperation in the construction industry." In Aspinall, E., and G. van Klinken (eds). *The State and Illegality in Indonesia.* Leiden. KITLV Press. Pp. 139–63.

Krier, J. 1994. *Displacing Distinction: Political Processes in the Minankabau Backcountry.* (Ph.D. dissertation). Cambridge. Harvard University.

Kubo, H., and B. Suprianto. 2010. "From fence-and-fine to participatory conservation: Mechanisms for transformation in conservation governance at the Gunung Halimun-Salak National Park, Indonesia." *Biodiversity Conservation* 19(6). Pp. 1785–1803.

Kunz, Y., J. Hein, R. Mardiana, H. Faust. 2016. "Mimicry of the legal: Translating *de jure* land formalization processes into de facto local action in Jambi province, Sumatra." *Austrian Journal of South-East Asian Studies* 9(1). Pp. 127–46.

Kurniawan, Y. 2018. *The Politics of Securitization in Democratic Indonesia.* Cham. Palgrave/Macmillan.

Lakhani, S. 2016. "Consolidating peace through Aceh Green, Governance." In Bruch, C., C. Muffett, and S. S. Nichols (eds). *Natural Resources, and Post-Conflict Peacebuilding.* London. Earthscan. Pp. 859–76.

Latour, B. 2010. *The Making of Law: An Ethnography of the Conseil d'Etat.* Cambridge. Polity.

LBH (Legal Aid Foundation, Aceh). 2015. *Potret Konflik Agraria di Aceh [Portrait of Agrarian Conflict in Aceh].* Banda Aceh. Indonesian Legal Aid Foundation.

Leaf, M. 1993. "Land rights for residential development in Jakarta, Indonesia: The colonial roots of contemporary urban dualism." *International Journal of Urban and Regional Research* 17(4). Pp. 477–91.

Leaf, M. 1994. "Legal authority in an extra-legal setting: The case of land rights in Jakarta, Indonesia." *Journal of Planning, Education, and Research* 14. Pp. 12–18.

Leue, H.-J. 1992. "Legal expansion in the age of the companies: Aspects of the administration of justice in the English and Dutch settlements of maritime Asia, c. 1600–1750." In Mommsen, W.J., and J.A. de Moor (eds). *European Expansion and Law.* Oxford/New York. Berg. Pp. 129–58.

Lev, D. 1985. "Colonial law and the genesis of the Indonesian state." *Indonesia* 40. Pp. 57–74.

Lev, D. 2000. *Legal Evolution and Political Authority in Indonesia: Selected Essays.* The Hague. Kluwer Law International (The London-Leiden Series on Law, Administration and Development).

Li, T.M. 2000. "Articulating indigenous identity in Indonesia: Resource politics and the tribal slot." *Comparative Studies in Society and History* 4(1). Pp. 149–79.

Li, T.M. 2001. "Masyarakat Adat, difference, and the limits of recognition in Indonesia's forest zone." *Modern Asian Studies* 35(3). Pp. 645–76.

Li, T.M. 2007. *The Will to Improve: Governmentality, Development, and the Practice of Politics.* Durham. Duke University Press.

Li, T.M. 2014. *Land's End: Capitalist Relations on an Indigenous Frontier.* Durham. Duke University Press.

Li, T.M. 2015. *Social Impact of Oil Palm in Indonesia: A Gendered Perspective from West Kalimantan.* Occasional Paper 120. Bogor. CIFOR.

Li, T.M. 2017. "After the land grab: Infrastructural violence and the 'mafia system' in Indonesia's oil palm plantation zones." *Geoforum* 96. Pp. 328–37.

Lindsey, T. 2001. "The criminal state: *Premanisme* and the new Indonesia." In Lloyd, G., and S. Smith (eds). *Indonesia Today: Challenges of History.* Singapore. ISEAS. Pp. 283–97.

Lipsky, M. 1969. *Towards a Theory of Street-Level Bureaucracy.* Madison. University of Wisconsin Press.

Lipsky, M. 1971. "Street-level bureaucracy and the analysis of urban reform." *Urban Affairs Review* 6(4). Pp. 391–409.

Lipsky, M. 2010. *Street-Level Bureaucracy: Dilemmas of the Individual in Public Services.* New York. Russell Sage Foundation.

Locke, J. 1994 [1689]. *Two Treatises of Government.* Cambridge. Cambridge University Press.

Löffler, U. 1996. *Land Tenure Developments in Indonesia.* Bonn. GTZ.

Lounela, A. 2009. *Contesting Forests and Power: Dispute, Violence, and Negotiations in Central Java.* Helsinki. University of Helsinki.

Lounela, A. 2012. "Contesting state forests in post-Suharto Indonesia: Authority formation, state forest land dispute, and power in upland Central Java, Indonesia." *ASEAS—Austrian Journal of South-East Asian Studies* 5(2). Pp. 208–28.

Lubis, I. 2013. "Testimony: Occupying land is not outmoded or based on old theory or practice." *Journal of Peasant Studies* 40(4). Pp. 755–61.

Lucas, A., and C. Warren. 2003. "The state, the people, and their mediators: The struggle over agrarian law reform in post–New Order Indonesia." *Indonesia* 76. Pp. 87–126.

Lucas, A., and C. Warren (eds). 2013. *Land for the People: The State and Agrarian Conflict in Indonesia.* Columbus. Ohio University Press.

Luhmann, N. 1988. "The unity of the legal system." In Teubner, G. (ed.) *Autopoietic Law: A New Approach to Law and Society.* Berlin. Walter de Gruyter. Pp. 12–35.

Lund, C. 1998. *Law, Power, and Politics in Niger: Land Struggles and the Rural Code*. Hamburg. Lit Verlag.

Lund, C. 2008. *Local Politics and the Dynamics of Property in Africa*. Cambridge. Cambridge University Press.

Lund, C. 2013. "The past and space: On arguments in African land control." *Africa* 83(1). Pp. 14–35.

Lund, C. 2014. "Of what is this a case? Analytical movements in qualitative social science research." *Human Organization* 73(3). Pp. 224–34.

Lund, C. 2016. "Rule and rupture: State formation through the production of property and citizenship." *Development and Change* 47(6). Pp. 1199–1228.

Lund, C., and N.F. Rachman. 2016. "'Occupied!' Property, citizenship, and land in rural Java." *Development and Change* 47(6). Pp. 1316–37.

Lund, C., and N.F. Rachman. 2018. "Indirect recognition: Frontiers and territorialization around Mount Halimun-Salak National Park, Indonesia." *World Development* 101. Pp. 417–28.

MacPherson, C.B. 1978. *Property: Mainstream and Critical Positions*. Oxford. Basil Blackwell.

Marx, K. 1978 [1867]. *Capital. Vol. I*. Moscow. Progress Publishers.

Mathur, N. 2016. *Paper Tiger: Law, Bureaucracy, and the Developmental State in Himalayan India*. Cambridge. Cambridge University Press.

Mattei, U., and L. Nader. 2008. *Plunder: When the Rule of Law Is Illegal*. London. Blackwell.

McCarthy, J. 2005. "Between *adat* and state: Institutional arrangements on Sumatra's forest frontier." *Human Ecology* 33(1). Pp. 57–82.

McCarthy, J. 2006. *The Fourth Circle: A Political Ecology of Sumatra's Rainforest Frontier*. Stanford. Stanford University Press.

McCarthy, J. 2010. "Processes of inclusion and adverse incorporation: Oil palm and agrarian change in Sumatra, Indonesia." *Journal of Peasant Studies* 37(4). Pp. 821–50.

McCarthy, J., and R. Cramb. 2009. "Policy narratives, landholder engagement, and oil palm expansion on the Malaysian and Indonesian frontiers." *The Geographical Journal* 175(2). Pp. 112–23.

McCarthy, J., and C. Warren. 2009. "Communities, environments, and local governance in reform-era Indonesia." In Warren, C., and J. McCarthy (eds). *Community, Environment, and Local Governance in Indonesia*. London. Routledge. Pp. 1–25.

McCawley, P. 2014. "Aceh's economy: Prospects for revival after disaster and war." In Hill, H. (ed.). *Regional Dynamics in a Decentralized Indonesia*. Singapore. ISEAS. Pp. 482–507.

McCulloch, L. 2004. "*Trifungsi*: The role of the Indonesian military in business." In Brommelhorster, J., and W.-C. Paes (eds). *Military as an Economic Actor: Soldiers in Business*. Gordonsville. Palgrave-Macmillan. Pp. 94–123.

McCulloch, L. 2005a. *Aceh: Then and Now*. London. Minority Rights Group International.

McCulloch, L. 2005b. "Greed: The silent force of conflict in Aceh." In Kingsbury, D. (ed.). *Violence in Between: Conflict and Security in Archipelagic Southeast Asia*. Clayton/Singapore. Monash Asia Institute/Institute of Southeast Asian Studies. Pp. 203–30.

McLeod, R.H. 2010. "Institutionalized public-sector corruption: A legacy of the Suharto franchise." In Aspinall, E., and G. van Klinken (eds). *The State and Illegality in Indonesia*. Leiden. KITLV Press. Pp. 45–63.

McTurnan Kahin, G. 2003 [1953]. *Nationalism and Revolution in Indonesia*. Ithaca. Cornell Southeast Asia Program.

McVey, R. 1965. *The Rise of Indonesian Communism*. Ithaca. Cornell University Press.

McWilliam, A. 2006. "Historical reflections on customary land rights in Indonesia." *Asia Pacific Journal of Anthropology* 7(1). Pp. 45–64.

Medan City. 2016. *Kota Medan Dalam Angka 2016: Medan City in Figures, 2016*. Medan. Medan City (Badan Pusat Statistik Kota Medan).

Melvin, J. 2018. *The Army and the Indonesian Genocide: Mechanisms of Mass Murder*. London. Routledge.

Miller, M.A. 2009. *Rebellion and Reform in Indonesia: Jakarta's Security and Autonomy Policies in Aceh*. London. Routledge.

Mitchell, T. 1991. "The limits of the state: Beyond statist approaches and their critics." *American Political Science Review* 85(1). Pp. 77–96.

Mitchell, T. 2002. *Rule of Experts: Egypt, Techno-Politics, Modernity*. Berkeley. University of California Press.

Moeliono, T.P. 2011. *Spatial Management in Indonesia: From Planning to Implementation—Cases from West Java and Bandung. A Socio-Legal Study*. (Ph.D. dissertation). Leiden. Leiden University.

Moniaga, S. 2007. "From *bumiputera* to *masyarakat adat*: A long and confusing journey." In Davidson, J.S., and D. Henley (eds). *The Revival of Tradition in Indonesian Politics: The Deployment of Adat from Colonialism to Indigenism*. London. Routledge. Pp. 1–49.

Moochtar, R. 1980. "Urban housing in Indonesia." *Habitat International* 4(3). Pp. 325–38.

Moore, S.F. 1978. *Law as Process*. London. Routledge & Kegan Paul.

Moore, S.F. 1986. *Social Facts and Fabrications: 'Customary' Law on Kilimanjaro, 1880–1980*. Cambridge. Cambridge University Press.

Moore, S.F. 1987. "Explaining the present: Theoretical dilemmas in processual ethnography." *American Ethnologist* 14(4). Pp. 727–36.

Moore, S.F. 1998. "Systematic judicial and extra-judicial injustice: Preparations for future accountability." In Werbner, R. (ed.). *Memory and the Postcolony: African Anthropology and the Critique of Power*. London. Zed Books. Pp. 126–51.

Moore, S.F. 2005. "Comparisons: Possible and impossible." *Annual Review of Anthropology* (34). Pp. 1–11.

Mudhoffir, A.M. 2017. "Islamic militias and capitalist development in post-authoritarian Indonesia." *Journal of Contemporary Asia* 47(4). Pp. 495–514.

Multatuli. 1987 [1860]. *Max Havelaar*. London. Penguin.

Nader, L. 2009. "Law and the frontiers of illegalities." In von Benda-Beckmann, F., K. von Benda-Beckmann, and A. Griffiths (eds). *The Power of Law in a Transnational World*. New York. Berghan Books. Pp. 54–73.

Navaro-Yashin, Y. 2012. *The Make-Believe Space: Affective Geography in a Postwar Polity*. Durham. Duke University Press.

Neilson, J. 2016. "Agrarian transformations and land reform in Indonesia." In McCarthy, J.F., and K. Robinson (eds). *Land and Development in Indonesia: Searching for the People's Sovereignty*. Singapore. ISEAS. Pp. 246–64.

Nuijten, M. 2003. *Power, Community, and the State: The Political Anthropology of Organisation in Mexico*. London. Pluto Press.

Nurman, A. 2019. *Dynamics of Control of Urban Public Land in Bandung-Indonesia*. (Ph.D. dissertation). Copenhagen. University of Copenhagen.

Nurman, A., and C. Lund. 2016. "On track: Spontaneous privatization of public urban land in Bandung, Indonesia." *South East Asia Research* 24(1). Pp. 41–60.

O'Brien, K., and L. Li. 2006. *Rightful Resistance in Rural China*. Cambridge. Cambridge University Press.

Onghokham. 2003. *The Thugs, the Curtain Thief, and the Sugar Lord: Power, Politics, and Culture in Colonial Java*. Jakarta. Metaphor Publishing.

Peluso, N. 1991. "The history of state forest management in colonial Java." *Forest & Conservation History* 35(2). Pp. 65–75.

Peluso, N. 1992. *Rich Forests, Poor People: Resource Control and Resistance in Java*. Berkeley. University of California Press.

Peluso, N. 2005. "Seeing property in land use: Local territorializations in West Kalimantan, Indonesia." *Danish Journal of Geography* 105(1). Pp. 1–15.

Peluso, N., S. Afiff, and N. Fauzi Rachman. 2008. "Claiming the grounds for reform: Agrarian and environmental movements in Indonesia." *Journal of Agrarian Change* 8(2–3). Pp. 377–407.

Peluso, N., and C. Lund. 2011. "New frontiers of land control." *Journal of Peasant Studies* 38(4). Pp. 667–81.

Peluso, N., and P. Vandergeest. 2001. "Genealogies of the political forest and customary rights in Indonesia, Malaysia, and Thailand." *Journal of Asian Studies* 60(3). Pp. 761–812.

Pelzer, K. 1978. *Planter and Peasant: Agrarian Struggle and the Colonial Policy in East Sumatra, 1863–1947*. 'S-Gravenhage. Verhandlingen van het Koninklijk Instituut voor Taal-, Land-, en Volkenkunde.

Pelzer, K. 1982. *Planters Against Peasants: The Agrarian Struggle in East Sumatra, 1947–1957.* 'S-Gravenhage. Verhandlingen van het Koninklijk Instituut voor Taal-, Land-, en Volkenkunde.

Peñalver, E.M., and S.K. Katyal. 2010. *Property Outlaws: How Squatters, Pirates, and Protesters Improve the Law of Ownership.* New Haven. Yale University Press.

Peters, R. 2010. "The wheels of misfortune: The street and cycles of displacement in Surabaya, Indonesia." *Journal of Contemporary Asia* 40(4). Pp. 568–88.

Phelps, A. A., T. Bunnell, and M.A. Miller. 2011. "Post-disaster economic development in Aceh: Neoliberalization and other economic-geographic imaginaries." *Geoforum* 42. Pp. 418–26.

Pichler, M. 2015. "Legal dispossession: State strategies and selectivities in the expansion of Indonesian oil palm and agro-fuel production." *Development and Change* 46(3). Pp. 508–33.

Potter, L. 2016. "How can the people's sovereignty be achieved in the oil palm sector? Is the plantation model shifting in favour of smallholders?" In McCarthy, J.F., and K. Robinson (eds). *Land and Development in Indonesia: Searching for the People's Sovereignty.* Singapore. ISEAS. Pp. 315–42.

Pramono, A.H., I. Natalia, and Y. Janting. [no date.] *Ten Years After: Counter-Mapping and the Dayak Lands in West Kalimantan, Indonesia.* Mimeo.

Proudhon, P.J. 1966 [1840]. *What Is Property? An Enquiry into the Principle of Right and of Government.* New York. Howard Fertig.

Purba, R. 2016. *Petani, Perjuangan Lahan, dan Pemanfatannya (Studi Etnografi di Dusun Anggrek Baru Desa Perkebunan Ramunia Kecamatan Pantai Labu Kabupaten Deli Serdang) [Farmers and Land Struggle: Ethnographic Studies in Dusun Baru Anggrek Desa Plantations Ramunia District of Pantai Labu Deli Serdang].* (B.Sc. thesis). Medan. Antropologi Sosial, Universitas Sumatera Utara.

Rachman, N.F. 2011. *The Resurgence of Land Reform Policy and Agrarian Movements in Indonesia.* (Ph.D. dissertation). Berkeley. University of California.

Rachman, N.F. 2013. *Undoing Categorical Inequality: Masyarakat Adat, Agrarian Conflicts, and Struggle for Inclusive Citizenship in Indonesia.* Bogor. Sajogyo Institute.

Rachman, N.F. 2016. *Land Reform dan Gerakan Agraria Indonesia [The Resurgence of Land Reform Policy and Agrarian Movements in Indonesia].* Yogyakarta. Insist Press.

Rachman, N.F., and M. Siscawati. 2016. "Forestry Law, Masyarakat Adat, and struggle for inclusive citizenship in Indonesia." In Antons, C. (ed.). *Routledge Handbook of Asian Law.* London. Routledge. Pp. 224–49.

Rajkovic, N.M., T. Aalberts, and T. Gammeltoft-Hansen. 2016. "Introduction: Legality, interdisciplinarity, and the study of practices." In Rajkovic, N.M., T. Aalberts, and T. Gammeltoft-Hansen (eds). *The Power of Legality: Practices of International Law and Their Politics.* Cambridge. Cambridge University Press. Pp. 1–25.

Rasmussen, M.B., and C. Lund. 2018. "Reconfiguring frontier spaces: The territorialization of resource control." *World Development* 101. Pp. 388–99.

Rawls, J. 1999 [1971]. *A Theory of Justice*. Cambridge. Harvard University Press.

Raz, J. 2015. "Can there be a theory of law?" In Golding, M.P., and W.A. Edmunson (eds). *The Blackwell Guide to Philosophy of Law and Legal Theory*. Oxford. Blackwell. Pp. 324–42.

Reerink, G. 2011. *Tenure Security for Indonesia's Urban Poor: A Socio-Legal Study on Land, Decentralisation, and the Rule of Law in Bandung*. Leiden. Leiden University Press.

Reerink, G., and J.-L. van Gelder. 2010. "Land titling, perceived tenure security, and housing consolidation in the kampongs of Bandung, Indonesia." *Habitat International* 34(1). Pp. 78–85.

Reid, A. 1979. *The Blood of the People: Revolution and the End of Traditional Rule in Northern Sumatra*. Kuala Lumpur. Oxford University Press.

Reid, A. 2005. *An Indonesian Frontier: Acehnese and Other Histories of Sumatra*. Singapore. National University of Singapore.

Reid, A. (ed.). 2006. *Verandah of Violence: The Background to the Aceh Problem*. Singapore/Seattle. Singapore University Press/University of Washington Press.

Ribot, J., and N. Peluso. 2003. "A theory of access." *Rural Sociology* 68(2). Pp. 153–81.

Ricklefs, M.C. 1993. *A History of Modern Indonesia Since c. 1300*. Stanford. Stanford University Press.

Robinson, G. 2001. "*Rawan* is as *Rawan* does: The origins of disorder in New Order Aceh." In Anderson, B.R.O'G. (ed.). *Violence and the State in Suharto's Indonesia*. Ithaca. Cornell University Press. Pp. 213–42.

Robinson, G. 2018. *The Killing Season: A History of the Indonesian Massacres, 1965–66*. Princeton. Princeton University Press.

Robison, R. 1986. *Indonesia: The Rise of Capital*. Sydney. Allen and Unwin.

Robison, R., and V.R. Hadiz. 2004. *Reorganizing Power in Indonesia: The Politics of Oligarchy in an Age of Markets*. London. Routledge.

Rose, C. 1994. *Property and Persuasion: Essays on the History, Theory, and Rhetoric of Ownership*. Boulder. Westview Press.

Ross, M. 2005. "Resource and rebellion in Aceh, Indonesia." In Collier, P., and N. Sambaing (eds). *Understanding Civil War—Evidence and Analysis*. Washington, D.C. World Bank. Pp. 35–58.

Rousseau, J.-J. 1977 [1762]. *Du contrat social*. Paris. Éditions du Seuil.

Rutten, R., L. Bakker, M.-L. Alano, T. Salerno, L.A. Savitri, and M. Shohibuddin. 2017. "Smallholder bargaining power in large-scale land deals: A relational perspective." *Journal of Peasant Studies* 44(4). Pp. 891–917.

Ryter, L. 1998. "Pemuda Pancasila: The last loyalist free men of Suharto's Order." *Indonesia* 66. Pp. 43–73.

Ryter, L. 2002. *Youth Gangs and the State in Indonesia*. (Ph.D. dissertation). Seattle. University of Washington.

Ryter, L. 2009. "Their moment in the sun: The new Indonesian parliamentarians from the old OKP." In van Klinken, G., and J. Barker (eds). *State of Authority: State and Society in Indonesia*. Ithaca. Cornell University Press. Pp. 181–218.

Sadiq, K. 2009. *Paper Citizens: How Illegal Immigrants Acquire Citizenship in Developing Countries*. Oxford. Oxford Universsity Press.

Safitri, M. 2010. *Forest Tenure in Indonesia: The Socio-Legal Challenges of Securing Communities' Rights*. Leiden. Leiden University Press.

Sahide, M.A.K., and L. Giessen. 2015. "The fragmented land use administration in Indonesia: Analysing bureaucratic responsibilities influencing tropical rainforest transformation systems." *Land Use Policy* 43. Pp. 96–110.

Santos, B. de S. 1977. "The law of the oppressed: The construction and reproduction of legality in Pasargada." *Law and Society Review* 12(1). Pp. 5–126.

Sastrosasmita, S., and A.T.M.N. Amin. 1990. "Housing needs of informal sector workers." *Habitat International* 14(4). Pp. 75–88.

Sato, S. 1994. *War, Nationalism, and Peasants: Java Under the Japanese Occupation, 1942–1945*. Sydney. Allen and Unwin.

Schmitt, C. 2004 [1932]. *Legality and Legitimacy*. Durham. Duke University Press.

Schulte Nordholt, H., and G. van Klinken (eds). 2007. *Renegotiating Boundaries: Local Politics in Post-Soeharto Indonesia*. Leiden. KITLV Press.

Schulze, K.E. 2003. "The struggle for an independent Aceh: The ideology, capacity, and strategy of GAM." *Studies in Conflict and Terrorism* 26(4). Pp. 241–71.

Schulze, K.E. 2004. *The Free Aceh Movement (GAM): Anatomy of a Separatist Organization*. Washington D.C. East-West Center (Policy Studies 2).

Schulze, K.E. 2006. "Insurgency and counter-insurgency: Strategy and the Aceh conflict. October 1976–May 2004." In Reid, A. (ed.). *Verandah of Violence: The Background to the Aceh Problem*. Singapore/Seattle. Singapore University Press/University of Washington Press. Pp. 225–71.

Schulze, K.E. 2007a. "GAM—*Gerakan Aceh Merdeka* (Free Aceh Movement)." In Heiberg, M., B. O'Leary, and J. Tirman (eds). *Terror, Insurgency, and the State: Ending Protracted Conflicts*. Philadelphia. University of Pennsylvania Press. Pp. 83–120.

Schulze, K.E. 2007b. "The conflict in Aceh: Struggle over oil?" In Kaldor, M., T. Lynn Karl, and Y. Said (eds). *Oil Wars*. London. Pluto Press. Pp. 181–224.

Scott, J. 1985. *Weapons of the Weak: Everyday Forms of Peasant Resistance*. New Haven. Yale University Press.

Scott, J. 2009. *The Art of Not Being Governed: An Anarchist History of Upland Southeast Asia*. New Haven. Yale University Press.

Shiraishi, T. 1990. *An Age in Motion: Popular Radicalism in Java, 1912–1926*. Ithaca. Cornell University Press.

Shiraishi, T. 1997. "Policing the phantom underground." *Indonesia* 63. Pp. 1–46.

Shohibuddin, M. 2014. *Making Peace or Sustaining Conflict: Securitisation of Land Distribution Programme in Post-War Aceh, Indonesia.* Amsterdam. NOW-Working Paper.

Siagan, S., A. Siahaan, Buyung, and N. Khairani. 2011. *The Loss of Reason: Human Rights Violations in the Oil-Palm Plantations in Indonesia—A Report Based on the Case of Labuhan Batu.* Medan. Lentera Rakyat/Brot für die Welt.

Sidel, J. 2004. "Bossism and democracy in the Philippines, Thailand, and Indonesia: Towards an alternative framework for the study of 'local strongmen.'" In Harriss, J., K. Stokke, and O. Törnquist (eds). *Politicising Democracy: The New Local Politics of Democratisation.* London. Palgrave/Macmillan. Pp. 51–74.

Sikor, T., and C. Lund. 2009. "Access and property: A question of power and authority." *Development and Change* 40(1). 1. Pp. 1–22.

Silean, P., and C. J. Smark. 2006. "The 'Culture System' in Dutch Indonesia, 1830–1870: How Rawls's original position ethics were violated." *The Business Review* 6(1). Pp. 1–8.

Simandjuntak, D. 2009. "Milk coffee at 10 A.M.: Encountering the state through *pilkada* in North Sumatra." In van Klinken, G., and J. Barker (eds). *State of Authority: State and Society in Indonesia.* Ithaca. Cornell University Press. Pp. 73–94.

Simandjuntak, D. 2012. "Gifts and promises: Patronage democracy in a decentralized Indonesia." *European Journal of East Asian Studies* 11. Pp. 99–126.

Simarmata, R. 2012. *Indonesian Law and Reality in the Delta: A Socio-Legal Inquiry into Laws, Local Bureaucrats, and Natural Resource Management in the Mahakam Delta, East Kalimantan.* Leiden. Leiden University Press.

Sirait, M. 2009. *Indigenous Peoples and Oil Palm Plantation Expansion in West Kalimantan, Indonesia.* Amsterdam. Amsterdam University Law Faculty.

Sjaastad, E., and B. Cousins. 2009. "Formalisation of land rights in the South: An overview." *Land Use Policy* 26(1). Pp. 1–9.

Slaats, H., E. Rajagukguk, N. Elmiyah, and A. Safik. 2009. "Land law in Indonesia." In Ubink, J., A. Hoekema, and W. Assies (eds). *Legalising Land Rights: Local Practices, State Responses, and Tenure Security in Africa, Asia, and Latin America.* Leiden. Leiden University Press. Pp. 493–526.

Slater, D. 2010. "Altering authoritarianism: Institutional complexity and autocratic agency in Indonesia." In Mahoney, J., and K. Thelen (eds). *Explaining Institutional Change: Ambiguity, Agency, and Power.* Cambridge. Cambridge University Press. Pp. 132–67.

Somers, M. 2008. *Genealogies of Citizenship: Markets, Statelessness, and the Right to Have Rights.* Cambridge. Cambridge University Press.

Spector, R. 2019. "Property, lawfare, and the politics of hope in weak states." *Polity* 51(1). Pp. 3–34.

Steinebach, S. 2013. "'Today we occupy the plantation—tomorrow Jakarta': Indigeneity, land, and oilpalm plantations in Jambi." In Hauser-Schäublin, B. (ed.). *Adat and Indigeneity in Indonesia.* Göttingen. Universitätsverlag Göttingen. Pp. 63–79.

Stoler, A.L. 1985a. *Capitalism and Confrontation in Sumatra's Plantation Belt, 1870–1979.* New Haven. Yale University Press.

Stoler, A.L. 1985b. "Perceptions of protest: Defining the dangerous in colonial Sumatra." *American Ethnologist* 12(4). Pp. 642–58.

Stoler, A.L. 1988. "Working the revolution: Plantation laborers and the people's militia in North Sumatra." *The Journal of Asian Studies* 47(2). Pp. 227–47.

Strathern, M. 1999. *Property, Substance, and Effect: Anthropological Essays on Persons and Things.* London. Athlone Press.

Sulaiman, M.I., and G. van Klinken. 2007. "The rise and fall of Governor Puteh." In Schulte Nordholt, H., and G. van Klinken (eds). *Renegotiating Boundaries: Local Politics in a Post-Suharto Indonesia.* Leiden. KITLV Press. Pp. 225–52.

Sundar, N. 2009. "Framing the political imagination: Custom, democracy, and citizenship." In Sundar, N. (ed.). *Legal Grounds: Natural Resources, Identity, and the Law in Jharkhand.* New Delhi. Oxford University Press.

Sundar, N. 2016. *The Burning Forest: India's War in Bastar.* Delhi. Juggernaut.

Svensson, T. 1991. *State Bureaucracy and Capitalism in Rural West Java: Local Gentry Versus Peasant Entrepreneurs in Priangan in the 19th and 20th Century.* Copenhagen NIAS Report no. 1. Nordic Institute of Asian Studies.

Swart, A.G.N. 1911. "Rubber companies in the Netherland East Indies." Compiled for the Netherlands Commission for the International Rubber Exhibition in London. Amsterdam. J.H. De Bussy.

Tajima, Y. 2014. *The Institutional Origins of Communal Violence: Indonesia's Transition from Authoritarian Rule.* Cambridge. Cambridge University Press.

Tamanaha, B. 2004. *On the Rule of Law: History, Politics, Theory.* Cambridge. Cambridge University Press.

Tamanaha, B. 2016. *What Is Law?* St. Louis. Washington University in St. Louis Legal Studies Research Paper No. 15-01-01.

Tate, D.J.M. 1996. *The RGA History of the Plantation Industry in the Malay Peninsula.* Commissioned by the Rubber Growers' Association (Malaysia) BERHAD. Kuala Lumpur. Oxford University Press.

Taussig, M. 2005. *Law in a Lawless Land: Diary of a Limpieza in Colombia.* Chicago. University of Chicago Press.

Tempo. 2012. "Requiem for a massacre." 1–7 October.

Thompson, E.P. 1975. *Whigs and Hunters: The Origin of the Black Act.* New York. Pantheon.

Tilly, C. 1998. *Durable Inequality.* Berkeley. University of California Press.

Timmer, J. 2010. "Being seen like the state: Emulations of legal culture in customary labor and land tenure arrangements in East Kalimantan, Indonesia." *American Ethnologist* 37(4). Pp. 703–12.

Tiominar, B. 2011. *Plantations and Poverty: Notes from a Village Deep in Oil Palm Territory*. Colchester. Down-to-Earth.

Toer, P.A. 1982. *This Earth of Mankind [Bumi Manusia]*. London. Penguin.

Tsing, A. 2005. *Friction: An Ethnography of Global Connection*. Princeton. Princeton University Press.

Tunas, D., and A. Peresthu. 2010. "The self-help housing in Indonesia: The only option for the poor?" *Habitat International* 34(3). Pp. 315–22.

Ubink, J. 2009. "Legalising land rights in Africa, Asia, and Latin America." In Ubink, J., A. Hoekema, and W. Assies (eds). *Legalising Land Rights: Local Practices, State Responses, and Tenure Security in Africa, Asia, and Latin America*. Leiden. Leiden University Press. Pp. 7–31.

Urano, M. 2010. *The Limits of Tradition: Peasants and Land Conflicts in Indonesia*. Kyoto. Kyoto University Press.

Vickers, A. 2005. *A History of Modern Indonesia*. Cambridge. Cambridge University Press.

Vitasari, D.M., and N. Ramdhaniaty. 2015. *Jalan Panjang Pengakuan Hukum Lima Belas Tahun Pendampingan Masyarakat Kasepuhan [The Long Road: Legal Recognition of Fifteen Years of Community Assistance Among the Kasepuhan]*. Jakarta. Epistema.

Volkov, V. 2002. *Violent Entrepreneurs*. Ithaca. Cornell University Press.

Vu, T. 2009. "Indonesia's agrarian movement: Anti-capitalism at a crossroads." In Caouette, D., and S. Turner (eds). *Agrarian Angst and Rural Resistance in Contemporary Southeast Asia*. London. Routledge. Pp. 180–205.

Walker, R. T., C. S. Simmons, and S. P. Aldrich. 2011. "The Amazonian theater of cruelty." *Annals of the Association of American Geographers* 101. Pp. 1156–70.

Wallace, J. 2008. "Indonesian land law and administration." In Lindsey, T. (ed.). *Indonesia: Law and Society*. Sydney. Federation Press. Pp. 191–223.

Warren, C. 2005. "Mapping common futures: Customary communities, NGOs, and the state in Indonesia's reform era." *Development and Change* 36(1). Pp. 49–73.

Weber, M. 1958. *From Max Weber: Essays in Sociology*. Gerth, H., and C. Mills (eds). New York. Oxford University Press.

Wells, P., N. Franklin, P. Gunarso, G. Paoli, T. Mafira, D.R. Kusumo, and B. Clanchy. 2012. *Indonesian Constitutional Court Ruling Number 45/PUU-XI/2011 in Relation to Forest Lands*. Jakarta. Daemeter/Trobenbos/Makarin and Tiara S.

White, B. 2016. "Remembering the Indonesian Peasants' Front and Plantation Workers' Union (1945–66)." *Journal of Peasant Studies* 43(1). Pp. 1–16.

Wightman, A. 2011. *The Poor Had No Lawyers: Who Owns Scotland (and How They Got It)*. Edinburgh. Birlinn.

Wilson, I. 2010. "Reconfiguring rackets: Racket regimes, protection, and the state in Post-New Order Jakarta." In Aspinall, E., and G. van Klinken (eds). *The State and Illegality in Indonesia*. Leiden. KITLV Press. Pp. 239–60.

Wilson, I. 2015. *The Politics of Protection Rackets in Post-New Order Indonesia: Coercive Capital, Authority, and Street Politics.* London. Routledge.

Wilson, L. 2011. "Beyond the exemplary centre: Knowledge, power, and sovereign bodies in Java." *Journal of the Royal Anthropological Institute* 17(2). Pp. 301–17.

Winayanti, L. 2010. *Community Struggles for Land in Jakarta: A Case Study of Kampung Community Struggle to Obtain Security of Tenure.* Saarbrücken. Lambert Academic Publishing.

Winayanti, L., and H.C. Lang. 2004. "Provision of urban services in an informal settlement: A case study of Kampung Penas Tanggul, Jakarta." *Habitat International* 28(1). Pp. 41–65.

Wolford, W. 2010. *This Land Is Ours Now: Social Mobilization and the Meaning of Land in Brazil.* Durham. Duke University Press.

Wolters, W.G. 1998. "Land, property, and credit contracts in Priangan, West Java, 1870s through the 1920s: Legal framework and legal ordering." In Hunt, R., and A. Gilman (eds). *Property in Economic Context.* Lanham/New York/Oxford. University Press of America. Pp. 289–315.

Woods, K. 2011. "Ceasefire capitalism: Military-private partnerships, resource and military-state building in the Burma-China borderlands." *Journal of Peasant Studies* 38(4). Pp. 747–70.

Woods, K. 2018. "Rubber out of the ashes: Locating Chinese agribusiness investments in 'armed sovereignties' in the Myanmar-China borderlands." *Territory, Politics, Governance* 7(1). Pp. 79–95.

Writers Team. 2011. *Land Grabbing and Women Struggle from Oppression: Stories of Women Struggle Facing the Impact of Land Grab in Lowland and Upland Villages of Java.* Bogor. RMI.

Zanden, J.L. van. 2010. "Colonial state formation and patterns of economic development in Java, 1800–1913." *Economic History of Developing Regions* 25(2). Pp. 155–76.

Zanden, J.L. van, and D. Maas. 2012. *An Economic History of Indonesia, 1800–2010.* London. Routledge.

INDEX